EAT INK

RECIPES. STORIES. TATTOOS.

Birk O'Halloran & Daniel Luke Holton

Aadamsmedia
AVON, MASSACHUSETTS

Published by
Adams Media, a division of F+W Media, Inc.
57 Littlefield Street, Avon, MA 02322. U.S.A.
www.adamsmedia.com

ISBN 10: 1-4405-4346-1
ISBN 13: 978-1-4405-4346-3
eISBN 10: 1-4405-4344-5
eISBN 13: 978-1-4405-4344-9

Printed in the United States of America.

10 9 8 7 6 5 4 3 2 1

Library of Congress Cataloging-in-Publication Data

O'Halloran, Birk.
  Eat ink / Birk O'Halloran and Daniel Luke Holton.
    pages cm
  Includes bibliographical references and index.
  ISBN-13: 978-1-4405-4346-3 (paper over board : alk. paper)
  ISBN-10: 1-4405-4346-1 (paper over board : alk. paper)
  ISBN-13: 978-1-4405-4344-9 (eISBN)
  ISBN-10: 1-4405-4344-5 (eISBN)
1. Cooking, American. 2. Cooks--United States--Biography. 3. Tattooed people--
United States--Biography. I. Holton, Daniel Luke. II. Title.
  TX715.O374 2013
  641.5973--dc23

2013030933

Always follow safety and commonsense cooking protocol while using kitchen utensils,
operating ovens and stoves, and handling uncooked food. If children are assisting in the
preparation of any recipe, they should always be supervised by an adult.

Photos courtesy of Daniel Luke Holton with the exception of
the photo on page 160, which is provided by Rick Tramonto.
Illustrations © 123rf.com.

This book is available at quantity discounts for bulk purchases.
For information, please call 1-800-289-0963.

DEDICATION

Dedicated to those crazy souls who sacrifice
their blood, sweat, and flesh to keep us
full of fine food and art.

ACKNOWLEDGMENTS

Thank you to the chefs. This book would not exist without you. We are forever indebted to you for your generosity of food, tales, spirit, and skin.

Thank you Chelsea Lindman, our agent who believed in the project from the beginning. Thank you Brendan O'Neill and Katie Corcoran Lytle, who kept everything on track and pushed us forward.

Thank you to our industry friends: Alyson Careaga, Josh Greene, Chris Schmid, Andre Mack, Dan Petroski, and everyone we met along the way. This book would not exist without your extremely generous contributions of time, advice, and networks.

Finally, thank you to our loving friends and family who supported and helped us in creating *Eat Ink* in more ways than we could have ever imagined. Bethany, Delanie, Nichole, and Lisa, your love and support are incredible.

CONTENTS

Introduction 7

Measure Up 9

PART 1:
HOOFED 11

Andy Husbands: *Smoked Ham Hock Croquettes with Dijon Aioli* 15

Chris Barron: *Coppa and Egg* 19

Zak Walters: *Beer Braised Chili Pork over Grits* 23

Carla Pellegrino: *Vitello alla Milanese* 29

Christina Wilson: *Pan Roasted Fillet, Glazed Heirloom Carrots, and Gorgonzola Potato Purée, with Red Wine Bone Marrow Sauce* 34

Marc Forgione: *Veal Tenderloin, Boudin Noir, Fingerling Potatoes, Grilled Green Garlic, Pearl Onions, and Porcini Mushrooms, with a Mustard Reduction* 40

Tomas Curi: *Crispy Braised Mangalitsa Belly with Bitter Greens and Citrus* 47

Gabriel Rucker: *Beef Carpaccio, Broccoli, Oysters, and Wasabi Vinaigrette* 51

John Eisenhart: *Batsoa* 55

Ben de Vries: *Luella's Coca-Cola Braised Pork Shoulder* 60

Manny Arce: *Tamarind Braised Short Ribs with Sweet Potato Purée, Arugula, Golden Raisins, and Spiced Pumpkin Seeds* 65

Duskie Estes: *Brussels Sprouts, Gravenstein Apple, and Black Pig Bacon Salad* 69

John Stewart: *Black Pig Bacon and Duck Egg Carbonara* 73

Jonathan Power: *Bacon and Egg* 77

Michael Berardino: *Malloreddus* 81

Jason French: *Pastured Pork, Sauerkraut, and Whey Sauce* 86

Keith Fuller: *Pork Belly, Scallops, and Reindeer Lichen, with an Elderberry Gastrique* 92

Will Morris: *Crispy Pork Belly with Littleneck Clams and Trumpet Royale Mushrooms* 98

PART 2:
FINNED 101

Tony Marciante: *Pan-Seared Diver Scallops with Seasonal Vegetables and Crispy Sweet Potatoes* 106

Justin Warner: *Frog Legs with Spicy Dr. Pepper Glaze* 111

Kevin Adey: *Roasted Scallops with Sunchoke Purée, Wilted Spinach, and Walnut Salad* 115

Derek Simcik: *Sautéed Red Snapper with Purple Cauliflower Medley and Cauliflower Purée* 119

Michael Fiorelli: *Grilled Spanish Octopus with Salsa Verde, Fried Potatoes, Piquillo Peppers, Green Onion, Preserved Lemon, and Chorizo* 123

Ed McFarland: *Lobster Rolls* 129

Jesse Schenker: *Roasted Red Snapper, Corn Puree, Fresh Corn, Rock Shrimp, and Lobster Butter* **133**

Mike Isabella: *Kapnos Octopus* **138**

Ed Witt: *Duck Fat Poached Salmon, Forbidden Rice, Plum Wine BBQ Sauce, and Snap Peas* **143**

Andrew Markert: *Drew's Mama's Crab Cakes with Mustard Cider Reduction and Walnut Brown Butter* **147**

Francesco Palmieri: *Lobster Cobb Salad* **151**

PART 3:
WINGED 155

Rick Tramonto: *Gemelli con la Salsa dell Erba e Pollo (Gemelli with Chicken and Spring Herb Sauce)* **161**

Gregory Gourdet: *Curry Noodles, Slow Chicken, Pickled Mustard Greens, and Toasted Chili* **165**

Ian Marks: *Duck Frites* **169**

Anthony Paone: *Chef's Day-After Breakfast* **174**

Johnny Clark and Beverly Kim: *Nasi Goreng* **183**

Seamus Mullen: *Tosta Huevo Roto* **187**

Matt Selby: *Truffle Salt–Cured Foie Gras* **190**

PART 4:
ROOTED 193

Jill Barron: *Ma Po Tofu* **197**

Scott Malloy: *Nuka Pickle* **201**

Carolynn Spence: *Lightly Toasted Brioche Roll* **205**

Scott Anderson: *Tomato Soup with Ciabatta Toast and Grilled Cheese* **209**

Lish Steiling: *Autumn in a Bowl: Roasted Parsnip and Kale Salad* **213**

Matt McCallister: *Roasted Cauliflower Soup* **217**

Robin Leventhal: *Sunrise Lentil Cakes* **221**

Will Artley: *Sourdough Pizza Dough* **227**

Sean Hawes: *Beet Salad* **231**

Brandon Baltzley: *Butternut Squash with Goat's Yogurt, Spirulina, and Stevia* **236**

Brandon Biederman: *Tiger Wings with Som Tum* **241**

Chris Curren: *Panzanella with Roasted Acorn Squash* **245**

Mark DeNittis: *Warm Panzanella Salad with Porchetta di Testa, Pepperoni, Mustard Greens, Fennel, and Tomato* **251**

Aaron Bennett: *Hazel Dell Mushroom Bruschetta with Local Goat Cheese* **255**

Anthony Bucco: *Potato Gnocchi with Surry Farms Ham and Micro Arugula* **259**

PART 5:
SUGAR 261

Duff Goldman: *Pineapple Hummingbird Cake* **265**

Alina Eisenhauer: *Bread Pudding with Almond Brittle and Beer Jelly* **269**

Lisa Higgins: *Vanilla Cinnamon Coffee Cake* **273**

Douglas Richey: *Foieaffle with Peach Sauce and Farm Egg* **277**

Jake Godby: *Secret Breakfast Ice Cream* **280**

Andy Ricker: *Gin Rummy* **285**

Dominique Crenn: *Birth* **290**

Joshua Valentine: *Lemongrass Panna Cotta with Mint Meringue, Lemon Curd, and White Chocolate Brown Butter Ganache* **295**

Appendix: Metric Conversion Chart **296**

General Index **297**

Recipe Index **301**

INTRODUCTION

Michelin stars. TV show accolades. James Beard Awards.

The rewards of culinary success are great, but the path to the top is not for the faint of heart—or the thin-skinned. In a world where careers are won and lost with the changing palate of the public, the kitchen is no place for a person who lacks passion. As such, the bodies of chefs are marked with burns from hot pans, scars from the slip of a bone-sharp blade, and marks from any sort of kitchen accident you can imagine. Many chefs wear their scars with pride, as badges of honor of a job well done and a career set on its way to the top. But the chefs you'll find in this book— from Seamus Mullen to Dominique Crenn to Duff Goldman—are marked with more than these by-mistake memories of their time in the trenches. Instead, they've marked their successes and failures with needles and time in the chair and have had their passions permanently inked onto their bodies.

Eat Ink tells you the stories behind these tattoos and shows you the talent of the tattoo artists who excel at their craft the same way the chefs profiled throughout excel at theirs. And, in case you've forgotten how these talented chefs got to the top, you'll also find a recipe alongside each entry that highlights the chef's culinary point of view, a dish served in the chef's restaurant, or an ingredient that the chef can't cook without. With dishes like Gabriel Rucker's Beef Carpaccio, Broccoli, Oysters, and Wasabi Vinaigrette; Alina Eisenhauer's Bread Pudding with Almond Brittle and Beer Jelly; and Rick Tramonto's Gemelli with Chicken and Spring Herb Sauce, you can forget about ordering off the menu. With *Eat Ink*, you have unlimited access to the chef's table and beyond.

MEASURE UP

Different chefs create their dishes in different ways.

As you work your way through this book, you'll notice that some recipes call for ingredients to be measured out by weight while others call for ingredients to be measured out by volume. To make sure you have the correct supplies on hand to make any of the dishes throughout, be sure to have a set of measuring cups and spoons at the ready to measure out cups, teaspoons, and tablespoons, as well as a kitchen scale to get an accurate measurement in grams or ounces. If you need to convert any of the measurements to the metric system, see the conversion chart in the Appendix. Note that we have tried to format the recipes similarly for consistency, however just as each chef's ink is a form of self-expression, so are their recipes. We have tried to keep them as close to their original form as possible to give you the best understanding of their cooking style.

PART 1
HOOFED

EXECUTIVE CHEF/OWNER

TREMONT 647 AND SISTER SOREL, BOSTON, MA

ANDY HUSBANDS

"What I like about tattoos is it's a piece of me, it becomes part of me. I know where I was, I know who I was with . . . it's a mark of time, it's a passage of a place in your life."

—Andy Husbands

ANDY HUSBANDS is the author of three cookbooks and the chef/owner of two restaurants—Tremont 647 and Sister Sorel—in downtown Boston, yet his culinary career started when he was just fourteen working as a baker after school. Andy graduated from Johnson & Wales University with a degree in food service management in 1993 and says, "I loved it, every minute of it." Andy accepted his first sous-chef position in 1993 at the East Coast Grill, in Cambridge, MA. There, he worked under James Beard Award–winning chef Chris Schlesinger and, in 1994, was appointed executive chef. Later, he took his motorcycle and traveled cross-country to work on a farm in New Mexico and apprentice in a few restaurants in San Francisco. His time out west later influenced his cooking, and he chose to focus on seasonal menus and bold flavors when he returned to Boston. In 1996, along with high school friend Chris Hart, Andy opened Tremont 647. The bistro's new American cuisine centered around clean, classic grilling, but Andy pulled heavily from the spice rack as well and gained recognition for flavorful meals ranging from black bean soup to coconut jasmine rice. The combination of classic grilling with creative twists shows its longevity in Tremont 647's continued success sixteen years after its opening.

> **" Sometimes I'll think long-term about [getting tattooed], like the one on my shoulder is a very serious piece. But, sometimes I'm like, I'll just go get a tattoo. "**

In 2000, Andy opened Sister Sorel, a second restaurant next door to Tremont 647 that still featured Andy's signature bold and innovative style but was more casual in its concept. In September of 2004, after the success of his restaurants, Husbands released his first cookbook featuring his bold style, *The Fearless Chef*. In both 2008 and 2009, he was a semifinalist for the James Beard Awards' Best Chef. In 2009, he competed on Season Six of *Hell's Kitchen*, finishing eighth out of seventeen.

In between all of his successes, Andy started competing in BBQ competitions with his team iQue BBQ. He says, "We just started doing it, me and my buddies. It's a weekend of cards and drinking and goofing around, but at some point we started getting really serious about it." In fact, they got so serious that iQue BBQ took first place out of 510 teams in the brisket category at the Kansas City Royal in 2007, and in 2009 they won the Jack Daniel's Invitational World Championships in Tennessee. The experience inspired Andy and his coauthors to create his second cookbook, *Wicked Good Barbecue*, which came out in 2012. Today, Andy continues to compete with iQue BBQ at various competitions throughout the country.

As Andy was starting to get interested in cooking, he was also getting interested in tattoos. He got his first tattoo, the Led Zeppelin "Swan Song" logo, in 1987 and just

kept going. In the mid-'90s Andy started getting inked by Fat Ram of Pumpkin Tattoo, a well-known Boston tattoo artist who had one of the first legal tattoo licenses in the city. They worked together to come up with the piece that is now the medley of vegetables on his right shoulder, which is still in progress. However, not all of Andy's tattoos were as planned out. He says, "Sometimes I'll think long-term about [getting tattooed], like the one on my shoulder is a very serious piece. But, sometimes I'm like, I'll just go get a tattoo." The tattoos of the pig, the cow, and the rooster down his right arm fall into that category. All three were done in separate settings and were spur-of-the-moment decisions to "just get a tattoo." Today, Andy continues to enjoy the success of his restaurants, his desire for more tattoos, and his place among the best BBQ chefs in America.

Smoked Ham Hock Croquettes with Dijon Aioli

Adapted from *The Fearless Chef*, Andy Husbands's first cookbook, coauthored with Joe Yonan in 2004.

SERVES 2–4 AS AN APPETIZER

FOR CROQUETTES:
1 large baking potato
1 ounce Grafton Cheddar or sharp Cheddar cheese, grated
1 ounce smoked ham hock meat or any smoked pork (bacon bits work great), minced
1 tablespoon all-purpose flour
Salt and freshly ground black pepper, to taste
Vegetable oil, for frying

FOR DIJON AIOLI:
MAKES ABOUT 1¼ CUPS

1 large egg yolk
1 tablespoon fresh lemon juice
2 cloves garlic, peeled and roughly chopped
1 tablespoon plus 2 teaspoons Dijon mustard
1 cup canola oil or vegetable oil
Salt and freshly ground black pepper, to taste

TO COMPLETE:
Green onion, chopped, for garnish
Crumbled bacon (or bacon bits), for garnish

1 **For Croquettes:** Place the potato in a pot of cold salted water to cover. Bring to a boil over high heat. Cover, and reduce heat to medium. Boil for 25 to 30 minutes, or until the potato is just cooked through (it can be pierced with a fork without breaking apart). Drain well and let cool to room temperature.

2 Meanwhile, combine the cheese and the smoked ham hock in a small bowl. Peel and grate the cooled potato on the large holes of a box grater, and spread onto a large plate. Sprinkle with the flour and a generous amount of salt and pepper. Mix well, tasting to adjust seasoning, and divide the mixture into 8 mounds.

3 Form each mound into a flattened ball. Add about 1 to 2 teaspoons of the meat-cheese mixture in the center of each round and wrap the potato around the cheese to form a croquette (a.k.a. a tater-tot-shaped cylinder), making sure the cheese is fully enclosed.

4 In a saucepan, heat 3 inches of vegetable oil to 350°F. (Test the oil by dropping a piece of potato in; it should sizzle vigorously and immediately on the surface of the oil without sinking or burning.) Fry the croquettes until golden brown, about 2 minutes, working in batches if necessary to avoid crowding the pan. Drain on paper towels and season with salt and pepper.

5 **For Dijon Aioli:** Put the egg, lemon juice, garlic, and mustard in a food processor or blender; purée. Slowly drizzle the oil into the food processor until the mixture is smooth, thick, and shiny. Season with salt and pepper. Can be used immediately or refrigerated for up to 1 week, covered.

6 **To Complete:** Spread 2 tablespoons of Dijon Aioli onto plate. Place two Croquettes on top of Aioli. Garnish with chopped green onion and crumbled bacon (or bacon bits).

CHRIS BARRON

"The [tattoos] would just come to me, but some are just fun."

—Chris Barron

CHEF

FRANCESCA'S FORNO, CHICAGO, IL

CHRIS BARRON has worked in restaurants for more than twenty years. He started out as a bar back, stocking and cleaning, but decided that he felt more at home in the back of the house. His first kitchen job was making sandwiches, but he now works as a chef at Francesca's Forno in Chicago, Illinois, where he cooks rustic Italian comfort food. Chris has cooked all over the United States. He says, "I've had the privilege of working so many great places." He's cooked in St. Louis, Los Angeles, and has orchestrated a dinner at the James Beard House in New York City. He's even outlasted a few of the great restaurants he has worked at, including Chicago's famous Charlie Trotter's restaurant. Named the thirtieth-best restaurant in the world by *Restaurant* magazine, and fifth-best in the United States in 2007, Charlie Trotter's finally closed in 2012. Chris has also done time at Ritz Carlton, Beverly Hilton, Border Grill, and Park Hyatt, and today he's with Francesca's Restaurant Group. But no matter where he's cooking, Chris's passion for good food and great ingredients comes through. Despite cooking for a living, he still enjoys cooking at home. Both Chris and his wife, Jill Barron (see entry in Part 4), the owner and chef of MANA Food Bar in Chicago, love to raid their local Chinatown market for fresh seasonal ingredients. Chris says, "I have been very lucky and privileged to work in many low- to high-end places with exceptional people. Over the years, I have come around to the philosophy of less is more. Less manipulation to ingredients is more natural."

Chris has been getting tattoos almost as long as he has been cooking. As he has traveled, he has collected myriad tattoos, his skin becoming a scrapbook of his life. Most are tattoos of fun things or concepts that caught Chris's attention. For example, the flying eye across his right arm is taken from the Von Dutch hot rod logo, and he got the square watermelon on his left arm nearly fifteen years ago after reading an article about the Japanese growing watermelons in boxes to make them fit into their refrigerators better. He says, "The idea cracked me up." Chris's left shin has the word "BACON" written in Scrabble pieces. He says, "I love bacon, and my wife kind of found out I'm pretty good at Scrabble and it makes her nuts."

Chris's culinary bent has also inspired many of his tattoos. Surrounding the Scrabble tiles is a garden of many of Chris's favorite mushrooms to cook with. He got the snow peas on his right arm during a time when he was cooking a lot of pan Asian food and dealing with snow peas every day. And he actually got one of his favorite tattoos because of a severe allergy to shrimp and lobster. The tattoo, which stretches across his left forearm, shows a shrimp with a banner reading "My Nemesis." Chris does still taste the dishes he creates with shrimp, but he can't ingest the crustacean.

Though Chris admits that he isn't motivated to get more ink, he probably isn't done with getting tattoos. His back tattoo, a skeleton chef brandishing a T-bone steak and a knife, was started years before. However, he didn't get the rest of his tattoos until several years later by a different artist. He says, "I still don't know if it is done, but it works for now."

Coppa and Egg

**YIELDS APPROXIMATELY
4 (16-OUNCE) SERVINGS**

1 pound dry spaghetti
4 eggs
½ pound sliced coppa or capicola ham
2 tablespoons olive oil
½ pound unsalted butter, divided
Kosher salt, to taste
Freshly ground black pepper, to taste
½ cup ground pecorino cheese
4 teaspoons chopped Italian parsley

1 Cook pasta in salted boiling water, strain, and reserve 2 cups water for the pan sauce.

2 In a nonstick pan, cook the eggs sunny-side up and hold warm.

3 In a large sauté pan over high heat, sauté chopped ham in 2 tablespoons each olive oil and butter for 2 minutes. Add the pasta with the rest of the butter. At this point add about a ½ cup pasta water and season with salt and pepper. Cook for about 1 minute. Thicken with ground pecorino cheese. Cook 1 more minute, just until coated. Add more pasta water if needed. Add a generous amount of the ground black pepper. Taste for salt.

4 Twirl pasta into 4 bowls and top each serving with an egg. Garnish with chopped Italian parsley.

CO-OWNER/CHEF

SALT'S CURE, LOS ANGELES, CA

ZAK WALTERS

"May Your Name Spread Like Oil"

—Translation from the Latin inscription *Oleum Effusem Nomen Tuum* found on the entrance to an olive grove in Andalusia, Spain

IF YOU LIKE CLEAN, locally sourced cuisine, Zak Walters's restaurant, Salt's Cure, will be right up your alley. Opened in late summer of 2010, Salt's Cure—which Zak opened along with his fellow chef/business partner Chris Phelps—has had great success. Being named one of the 99 Essential Restaurants by *LA Weekly* in 2011, this small American eatery has been called the restaurant of the future more than once. However, Salt's Cure would look more at home in *Mad Max* than *Space Odyssey*. Their website is simply a logo and a grainy cell phone picture of a chalkboard where they write their daily menus, and the bright restaurant is also starkly minimal. The whole space only seats thirty-four, and the majority of the room is a bar that wraps around the open kitchen. "I like small restaurants, sixty seats max," Zak says. "When I got started as a chef in Oklahoma, I worked at a 300-seat restaurant that would do 900 for lunch. I tell you a hell of a lot more bad frittatas than good ones went out." But despite its small size, Salt's Cure seems to be on top of and ahead of every rising trend in food: friendly, informal service; minimal, clean restaurant design; a dedication to doing all their butchery in-house; a focus on fresh local ingredients; and a full snout-to-tail menu.

Zak expresses himself by the food he cooks—and by his tattoos. His right arm is wrapped in an olive branch, and is inscribed with the Latin phrase *Oleum Effusem Nomen Tuum*, which he found in Paula Wolfert's *Mediterranean Cooking*. In her book, she talks about traveling in Andalusia, in Spain, where she saw the phrase carved on the entrance to an olive grove. According to the proprietor, the words mean "May Your Name Spread

Like Oil" and date back to when the property was a church. The Catholic monks were making an analogy to the way oil covers everything, much like the word of God. Zak got the tattoo when he started to work in kitchens and found that he was burning himself a lot. He says, "I noticed how girls looked at the scars and thought, well, chicks like things on guys' arms so what the hell." After talking to several tattoo artists who passed on the idea because of the level of intricacy he wanted in the design, a friend of a friend who worked at a shop called the Electric Pen in North Hollywood did the whole piece for $100. "It's a funny thing to have; I haven't been to church since I was seven." Zak laughs explaining it. "But it relaxes me when I lose my temper, which seems to be happening a lot these days."

> **" I noticed how girls looked at the scars and thought, well, chicks like things on guys' arms so what the hell. "**

Beer Braised Chili Pork over Grits

SERVES 6–8

FOR CHILI RUB:
Dried ancho chili
Chile de árbol
Coriander
Black pepper
Mustard seed

FOR BRAISED PORK:
5 pounds pork butt, cut into 10 (8-ounce) pieces
10 ounces Chili Rub (1 ounce per piece of pork)
10 teaspoons salt (1 teaspoon per piece of pork)
24–32 ounces beer (I like IPA and porter)
1 bay leaf

FOR GRITS:
¼ cup diced yellow onion
2 cups water
1 cup ground dried corn or hominy
2 teaspoons salt
1 teaspoon black pepper
Butter, to taste

TO COMPLETE:
3 cups pork stock (chicken stock is an okay substitute)
Grilled red onions (if it is spring, use spring onions), or a heavy braising green such as black kale, for garnish

1 For Chili Rub: Grind all ingredients together. The parts are up to you and how you would like the braise to come out.

2 For Braised Pork: Marinate pork butt with rub and salt for 24 hours.

3 The next day, preheat oven to 200°F. Then sear pork butt in a deep braising pot over high heat until outside is crispy and golden. After meat is seared, deglaze pot with whatever beer you are drinking at the time. Add a bay leaf to the pot. Fill the pot with enough beer so the pork is submerged by half. Cover and cook in the oven for 6 hours or until tender and soft. Meanwhile . . .

4 For Grits: Put onion and water into a saucepan over high heat and bring to a simmer. Add the grits, salt, and pepper. Turn down the heat and simmer uncovered slowly for an hour. If grits start to thicken, add a bit more water. Butter is always a welcome addition . . . as much as you want is fine with me. Taste the grits to know when they are finished. They should not be al dente; they should be creamy and/or buttery. Once cooked, remove grits from heat and transfer to a container with lid or a sheet of foil.

5 To Complete: In a bowl, add the Grits, Braised Pork, and stock. Garnish with either grilled onions or a heavy braising green such as black kale.

NOTES FROM THE CHEF

The amounts of each ingredient in the rub are up to you. Just use what you like. You will need about 10 ounces of rub to cover each piece of pork, so keep that in mind as you mix.

CARLA PELLEGRINO

"I started to link cooking with love . . .
I'll say 'let me cook for you,' because that
is a way for me to tell you I like you."

—Carla Pellegrino

CHEF/OWNER

BRATALIAN AND MEATBALL SPOT, LAS VEGAS, NV

> **❝**I did it backwards. . . . Once you go to a culinary school, it would take usually between seven and ten years for you to become a chef. I actually became a chef before, and I had to go there to learn how to put my food out.**❞**

CARLA PELLEGRINO, once Carla Madeira, was born in Rio de Janeiro, Brazil, and fell in love with cooking at an early age. By age ten, she was helping run her mother's catering business, and when she was sixteen, she moved by herself to her aunt's house in Liguria, Italy. There, she opened a small fish store and strengthened her passion for Italian cooking by conducting daily cooking demonstrations. In 1997, Carla moved to New York City where she met Frank Pellegrino Jr., the son of restaurateur and actor Frank Pellegrino Sr., whose family owns the more than 100-year-old restaurant Rao's in East Harlem. The meeting was fortuitous.

Every weekend Carla would have ten to twenty people to her home to cook for them and entertain. Her friends started to encourage her to open a restaurant, and she began to explore the idea. "My fiancé at the time, who was very Italian, said no way, this is not a woman's job. You'll become fat and smell like garlic." She laughs. "It stuck with me. To this day I work out and take care to wash to never smell like [garlic]." In 1999, with the Pellegrino family backing her, Carla started to work on a plan to open a small café somewhere in downtown Manhattan. Carla says, "I never thought I would make money at [cooking]. That was Frank's vision. . . . He had that American way of thinking where you see money everywhere, which was a good thing." And Frank's vision

was especially helpful because by the time all was said and done, Carla's small café had turned into a 2-million-dollar restaurant with the capacity for 280 people in Midtown on 49th Street. Before the restaurant even opened, *The Wall Street Journal* and *The New York Times* ran articles about its much-anticipated opening. Carla says, "I had never run a restaurant before. I got so scared. I got cold feet." Carla tried to back out of the restaurant, but by then it was too late. The restaurant was being built, and many of their friends and family had invested money. Carla agreed to move forward with the project if Frank sent her to culinary school so she could learn to cook on a large scale in a professional kitchen. She attended the French Culinary Institute in NYC, and in 2000, the same year her Italian restaurant Baldoria opened, she graduated with honors. "I did it backwards. . . . Once you go to a culinary school, it would take usually between seven and ten years for you to become a chef. I actually became a chef before, and I had to go there to learn how to put my food out." Despite her initial reservations, Baldoria was a major success, and in 2006, both Carla and Frank Jr., who had married in 2002, moved to Las Vegas to open Rao's Las Vegas. Carla successfully led the culinary team at Rao's Las Vegas to host significant events, including cooking at the prestigious James Beard House in New York City in 2008 and 2009.

opening for friends and family, only her sister, her sous-chef, and she were working. In their hurry to turn out food for over 100 people, Carla badly burned her right arm. Once healed, Carla got a scrollwork tattoo with flowers and five names across it to cover the scars. The names—Clea, Carla, Marcelle, Alessandra, Clea—are the names of the women of her family: her mother, herself, her daughter, her sister, and her niece. The tattoo represents the strength and endurance of the women of her family.

Since the divorce, Carla has shown again and again how strong she is. She opened three restaurants: Bratalian, Bacio by Carla Pellegrino, and Meatball Spot. She closed Bacio by Carla Pellegrino in 2012 in order to open Meatball Spot and pursue her other culinary endeavors, and Bratalian is still going strong. Over the years, Carla has been featured on *The Today Show*, *CBS Morning Show*, *Fox News National*, *Throwdown with Bobby Flay* (which she won), *Food & Wine*, and *Bon Appétit*. In 2012, she competed on *Top Chef* but was eliminated in the third round.

Carla continues to run her two successful restaurants and has started to work on her first cookbook.

Carla got her first tattoo, a small unicorn on her upper back, in the early '90s, but decided to make a change after an elderly woman saw the tattoo while standing in line behind her and tried to wipe it off, thinking it was a bit of dirt. Carla says, "I thought, okay it is time for a cover-up. People don't even know it is a tattoo anymore." She decided to cover up the unicorn in 2010 with a tattoo of a storm that wraps around her right shoulder. At the time she and Frank were getting divorced, and the storm reflected the changes that were coming in her life. She says, "I knew I would leave Rao's, and I knew it would be hard and painful. I thought to do something big and thought if I could get through this, it was fifteen hours, and that if I could go through this pain, I could go through anything." In 2011, Carla teamed up with the Tropicana Las Vegas to open Bacio. The night of the

Vitello alla Milanese

SERVES 4

FOR VEAL CHOPS:
4 veal chops, bone-in
8 eggs
2 tablespoons vegetable oil
Parsley, to taste
2 tablespoons Parmesan cheese
Salt and pepper, to taste
8 cups bread crumbs
Clarified butter, enough to fill a 14" pan
    about ¼ full

FOR ARUGULA SALAD:
1 pound arugula lettuce
2 cups Roma tomatoes, cut in half
    lengthwise and then sliced
¼ of a medium red onion, sliced in half-
    moon shape
1½ tablespoons fresh lemon juice
3 tablespoons extra-virgin olive oil
Salt and ground white pepper, to taste

1 For Veal Chops: Leaving the bone in, pound the veal meat thin; then break eggs into a bowl and whisk. Add the vegetable oil, parsley, Parmesan cheese, salt, and pepper; whisk all together and set the mixture in a half-size hotel pan. Set the bread crumbs in a second half-size hotel pan.

2 Dip the pounded veal chops in the egg mixture; then transfer them to the pan with the bread crumbs. Cover each chop with bread crumbs, tapping the bread into the meat with your hands until the whole chop is equally breaded.

3 Put a 14" pan ¼ full with clarified butter over medium-high heat and heat butter to 375°F. Carefully add breaded chops one by one until all chops are in the pan and fry until golden. Remove chops from butter, place on a paper towel–lined plate to get rid of the excess butter, and sprinkle with salt.

4 For Arugula Salad: In a nonreactive bowl, mix the arugula, tomatoes, and red onions. Dress the salad with fresh lemon juice, extra-virgin olive oil, salt, and ground white pepper.

5 To Complete: Place each Veal Chop on an 11" oval plate and top with Arugula Salad. Serve immediately.

CHRISTINA WILSON

"My mom, growing up whenever we complained too much or got sad about something, she would always tell us, when you get up in the morning and open your blinds, the sun will be up. So I have a black sun with a diamond in the middle."

—Christina Wilson

EXECUTIVE CHEF
GORDON RAMSAY STEAK, PARIS CASINO, LAS VEGAS, NV

CHRISTINA WILSON has earned national recognition as the winner of Season Ten of *Hell's Kitchen*. With her win, the thirty-two-year-old chef from Philadelphia earned a $250,000-a-year job at chef Gordon Ramsay's massive steakhouse at Paris Las Vegas, but this chef walked a long road to get there.

Christina's first job was at McDonald's, where she discovered her hate of front of house and begged her bosses to let her work the flattop. Then, in February of 2005, she took on an unpaid apprenticeship working under Chef Michael Favacchia at Stella Blu outside Philadelphia. She later took a role as kitchen manager of Gypsy Saloon, the sister restaurant of Stella Blu, located in West Conshohocken, PA, a 20-minute drive northwest of Philadelphia, to pay her way through Temple University, where she worked on a degree in English Education, thinking she would eventually teach middle school. In 2009, she moved to Philadelphia to become sous-chef at Lolita, which was a three-time Citysearch "Best Mexican Restaurant" (2005–2007). While there, Christina worked under owners Marcie Turney, one of *Philadelphia Style* magazine's Top 10 Chefs of 2007, and Valerie Safran and their chef de cuisine, George Sabatino, who was a deciding factor for Christina to take the job. She says, "George was unlike any chef I'd ever worked for. He was patient and knowledgeable, creative and driven. . . . I had this need to work with George and being at Lolita satisfied that, and my craft has become stronger as a result." Later, Christina worked at Mercato, a top 50 Philadelphia restaurant, as chef de cuisine. She took her leave from Mercato to compete on and win *Hell's Kitchen*.

Christina got her first tattoo when she was home in New Jersey on Thanksgiving break. One of her older brothers is pretty heavily tattooed and got Christina her first tattoo for her eighteenth birthday. She says, "The guy had a little room office at his house that was his shop. I remember watching Penn State play Notre Dame, and I thought [getting the tattoo] was going to hurt so bad . . . but three or four minutes in I thought, this doesn't hurt, and just relaxed and watched the game." She got a black sun with four points on her left shoulder. The four points represent her three siblings and herself.

After moving to Las Vegas to work for Gordon Ramsay, Christina wanted to finally get a tattoo she had been thinking about for a while. Through a connection of Andi Van Willigan, the sous-chef from *Hell's Kitchen*, she was introduced to famed Vegas tattoo artist Clark North, whom she contacted with her idea. After a phone interview, North agreed to do the tattoo. The tattoo on Christina's right ribcage has a Latin quote from the book *The Sociology of Taste*, which reads "*De gustibus et coloribus non est disputandum*," meaning "In matters of taste there can be no dispute." This idea that there is no right or wrong when it comes to what you like has always stuck with Christina, and it's a theory that she lives by whether it comes to her cooking or her ink.

" I REMEMBER WATCHING PENN STATE PLAY NOTRE DAME AND I THOUGHT [GETTING THE TATTOO] WAS GOING TO HURT SO BAD . . . BUT THREE OR FOUR MINUTES IN I THOUGHT, THIS DOESN'T HURT, AND JUST RELAXED AND WATCHED THE GAME. "

Pan Roasted Fillet, Glazed Heirloom Carrots, and Gorgonzola Potato Purée, with Red Wine Bone Marrow Sauce

YIELDS 4 SERVINGS

FOR FILLET:

4 (8-ounce) center cut fillets
1 tablespoon kosher salt
1 tablespoon ground black pepper
1 tablespoon blended oil
1 tablespoon unsalted butter (optional)
1 sprig thyme (optional)
2 garlic cloves, crushed (optional)

FOR BONE MARROW SAUCE:

2 pieces beef marrow bones
Kosher salt, to taste
Ground black pepper, to taste
1 tablespoon blended oil
1 carrot, peeled, roughly chopped
1 bunch celery, cleaned, vines removed,
    roughly chopped
1 Spanish onion, peeled, roughly chopped
1 bunch rosemary
½ bunch thyme
6 garlic cloves, crushed
4 ounces tomato paste
1 bottle merlot
1 cup beef stock

FOR GORGONZOLA POTATO PURÉE:

2 Yukon gold potatoes, peeled and cubed
4 ounces Gorgonzola cheese
½ cup whole milk
½ pound unsalted butter, divided

1 **For Fillet:** Preheat oven to 400°F. Season the beef evenly on all sides with salt and pepper. Coat ovensafe pan with oil and place over medium-high heat. Sear fillets evenly on all sides, approximately 2 minutes per side. Place pan uncovered in oven and roast to desired temperature, about 8 to 10 minutes depending on the thickness of the meat. Internal temperature should read 135°F for medium-rare. Remove pan from oven, remove fillets from pan, and place them on a resting rack for 5 minutes.

2 The following steps are optional but recommended for flavor. In a new pan over medium heat, add butter, allowing it to melt and start to bubble. Place fillets in pan with thyme and garlic. Tilt the pan and, using a spoon, continually coat the beef with the melting butter until butter begins to brown. Remove the fillets, dabbing excess butter off with paper towels before plating.

3 **For Bone Marrow Sauce:** Evenly season beef bones with salt and pepper. Place marrow-side down in heated, oiled skillet over medium-high heat. After reaching a hard sear, add the carrots, celery, and onion. Season evenly with salt and pepper and incorporate the vegetables with the marrow. Cook for about 10 minutes, stirring occasionally until caramelized. Add rosemary, thyme, and garlic. Cook another 2 minutes. Add tomato paste and cook another 3 minutes. Deglaze the pan with 1 bottle merlot and reduce by half. Add beef stock and reduce by half. Remove beef bones and pass the remainder through a strainer. Discard vegetables, place jus in a pan, and reduce by half. Scrape the bone marrow and add to reduced sauce. Season with salt and pepper, to taste.

4 **For Gorgonzola Potato Purée:** Place potatoes in an 8-quart pot of salted water over medium-high heat. Bring to a constant slow boil uncovered and simmer uncovered until potatoes are fork-tender. Drain the potatoes and set aside. In a saucepan, steep cheese in milk over medium-low heat, whisking occasionally until cheese is almost fully melted. Pass through a strainer. In original pot, melt half the butter over low heat. Pass potatoes through a

FOR GLAZED HEIRLOOM CARROTS:

1 pound heirloom carrots, blanched

1 tablespoon blended oil

Salt and pepper, to taste

4 ounces chicken stock

2 teaspoons unsalted butter

¹/₈ cup finely cut chives

food mill. Return potatoes to pot and slowly stir in strained milk using a rubber spatula. Slowly add remaining butter while stirring until desired texture is achieved. Keep in mind that the potatoes should be a little loose and smoother than mashed potatoes. Check for seasoning and adjust to taste.

5 **For Glazed Heirloom Carrots:** Add carrots to heated, oiled pan. Sauté lightly over medium heat and season with salt and pepper. Deglaze with chicken stock. Reduce liquid almost fully, add butter, and toss continually. Once butter is melted and forms a glaze on the carrots, check for seasoning and finish with chives.

6 **To Complete:** Using a tablespoon and starting at the left edge of the plate, put one spoonful of Potato Purée on the plate. Using the round edge of the spoon, swipe the Potato Purée to the other edge of the plate. This will create a valley of sorts in the middle. Using a full tablespoon of Bone Marrow Sauce, fill the "valley" now made by the Potato Purée. Place the Glazed Heirloom Carrots on the right or at the end of swooped purée. Place the Fillet in the center of the plate.

MARC FORGIONE

"I use [my tattoos] almost like a roadmap of my life."

—Marc Forgione

MARC FORGIONE has had some big shoes to fill on his way up the culinary ladder. His father, Larry Forgione, a member of the first graduating class of the Culinary Institute of America, is often called "the godfather of American cuisine," due mostly to his work with his New York City restaurant An American Place, which opened in 1983 and closed in 2003. Larry was one of the first chefs to pay close attention to where his ingredients came from and worked with as many purveyors as it took across the country to find the perfect ingredients. Larry's close friend and mentor James Beard, the founder of the James Beard Foundation, suggested the name for the restaurant during one of their long discussions about the new menu for An American Place.

At age sixteen, Marc started working at his father's restaurant, but even at a young age he worked hard to step out from under his father's shadow. Marc went on to get a degree in hotel and restaurant management from the University of Massachusetts, and after stints in several great restaurants around New York City, he met Laurent Tourondel, the founding chef behind the BLT Group, a restaurant group that now spans seven different restaurant concepts with more than twenty restaurants worldwide. Laurent recruited Marc to help develop his flagship restaurant, BLT Steak, where Marc took over as sous-chef. Wanting to continue to gain more experience, Marc left BLT Steak to spend some time cooking in France. There he took a series of small jobs for Michel Guérard, a Michelin three-star chef, author, and one of the founders of nouvelle cuisine, a groundbreaking

CO-OWNER/CHEF

RESTAURANT MARC FORGIONE, NEW YORK CITY, NY

French culinary style. Marc left France with an even greater appreciation for great ingredients as well as the nuances of classic French cooking.

Upon Marc's return to NYC, Laurent invited him to step into the leadership role of chef de cuisine at BLT Prime, which opened in 2006. There he developed the recipes and headed the kitchen, leading the restaurant to receive a 27 out of 30 in the Zagat guide, making it the highest-ranking steakhouse in the history of New York City.

In 2008, Marc and his business partner Christopher Blumlo went on to open Forge, which would later be renamed Forgione. The restaurant earned the distinction of a two-star *New York Times* review and was named "Key Newcomer" by *Zagat Guide 2009*, one of the "Top 25 Restaurants in NYC" by *Modern Luxury* magazine, and "All Star Eatery" by *Forbes* magazine. In 2010, Forgione received a Michelin star, making Marc the youngest American-born chef/owner to receive the honor. That same year, Marc was also awarded the "Star Chefs Rising Star of the Year Award 2010" and won the third season of *The Next Iron Chef*. The final challenge on the show was to create the ultimate Thanksgiving meal. To commemorate the achievement, Marc immediately went out and got 1621—the year of the first Thanksgiving—tattooed on his arms. This success marked a big moment for him, and he felt that he had finally come into his own. After winning, he said, "My father, Larry Forgione, is one of the reasons that Americans recognize chefs these days. Being in this competition is my opportunity to be seen as Marc Forgione and not as the son of the godfather of American cuisine."

But while the 1621 tattoo is incredibly important to Marc, it isn't the only ink that is very meaningful to him. While visiting the Museum of the American Indian in Washington, D.C., Marc saw a piece of Navajo art known as the "Man in the Maze." While there is no known precise meaning to the Man in the Maze, the most common interpretation is that the maze signifies the difficult journey toward finding deeper meaning in life, a concept that spoke deeply to Marc as he moved through the trials of becoming a successful chef. Marc went straight from the museum to a tattoo parlor in Georgetown. He only tattooed the symbol on his left arm at first, but he says he "felt out of balance. Balance is very important to me. It is how I try and live my life and how I try and cook." Eventually he had the same image tattooed on his other arm. Marc also has tribal pattern tattoos on his left and right shoulders, which he got as birthday gifts from his parents on his eighteenth birthday.

Marc has come a long way from cooking in his father's restaurant, and he continues to keep pushing himself. In 2012, he opened his second restaurant, a classic American steak house in Atlantic City called American Cut. He has also started work on his first cookbook.

> **"BALANCE IS VERY IMPORTANT TO ME. IT IS HOW I TRY AND LIVE MY LIFE AND HOW I TRY AND COOK."**

Veal Tenderloin, Boudin Noir, Fingerling Potatoes, Grilled Green Garlic, Pearl Onions, and Porcini Mushrooms, with a Mustard Reduction

This recipe is a favorite on the menu at Restaurant Marc Forgione in New York City.

SERVES 4

FOR TENDERLOINS:

1 (454-gram; 1-pound) pork belly
2 garlic cloves
100 grams pork blood (ask your butcher)
20 grams kosher salt
20 grams Vadouvan Curry (from La Boîte)
15 grams Chios (from La Boîte)
20 grams ground cinnamon
3 tablespoons chopped fresh curly parsley
120 grams Activa, optional
2 (283-gram; 10-ounce) veal tenderloins
Canola oil
43 grams (3 tablespoons) unsalted butter
3 garlic cloves, unpeeled
2 sprigs fresh thyme
1 sprig fresh rosemary

FOR MUSTARD REDUCTION:

3 tablespoons canola oil
Veal scraps from Tenderloins
¾ cup chopped button mushrooms
3 shallots, sliced
1 garlic clove, chopped
2 tablespoons black peppercorns
1 tablespoon granulated sugar
½ cup red wine vinegar
4 cups dry red wine
1 cup ruby port
1 sprig fresh thyme
1 fresh or ½ dried bay leaf
4 cups veal stock
1 cup chicken stock
Salt, to taste
1 tablespoon whole grain mustard

1 **For Tenderloins:** Using a meat grinder or a meat-grinding attachment to your stand mixer, grind the pork belly and garlic to a medium grind. (Alternatively, you can ask your butcher to grind your pork and combine it with finely minced garlic when you bring the meat home.)

2 In a stand mixer, fitted with a paddle attachment, whip the ground pork and slowly add the blood to emulsify. Add the salt, curry, Chios, cinnamon, parsley, and Activa, if using, and mix for another 5 seconds or so.

3 Trim the tails and tops off the tenderloins so that they resemble one consistent, log-shaped loin (reserve scraps for the following Mustard Reduction recipe). Place a large piece of plastic wrap on the counter. Make a 7" × 3" rectangle out of the blood sausage meat on the plastic wrap. Place one tenderloin in the center and sprinkle enough Activa, if using, to cover the meat. Roll the meat into a tight cylinder and tie the ends tightly. Repeat with the other tenderloin.

4 *Sous Vide Instructions:* Fill an immersion circulator with water and preheat to 140°F. Place the tenderloins in 2 vacuum-seal bags, seal the bags, and poach in the immersion circulator for 2 hours. Transfer the tenderloins to a bowl filled with ice water (an ice bath) and allow the meat to cool, in the bag, for at least 10 minutes, or until ready to assemble the dish.

5 *Sous Vide Alternative Instructions:* Wrap the tenderloins in plastic wrap so that the cylinder resembles a sausage. Place the wrapped tenderloins into a resealable plastic bag and squeeze out as much air as possible. Fill a pot halfway up with water and, over medium heat, bring the water to 140°F. Decrease the heat to its lowest setting, place the resealable bag in the water, and carefully watch the thermometer, making sure the temperature of the water remains around 140°F. Have a bowl of ice cubes ready so that you can add them to the water when the temperature starts to go above 140°F. Cook for about 2 hours; then transfer the bag to a bowl filled with ice water (an ice bath) and allow the meat to cool, in the bag, for at least 10 minutes, or until ready to assemble the dish.

6 When ready to serve, in a large sauté pan set over high heat, warm enough oil to cover the bottom of the pan until just before it starts to smoke. Remove the tenderloins from the sealed bags, pat dry, and add them to the pan seam-side down. Reduce the heat to medium and add the butter, garlic, thyme, and rosemary. Baste the tenderloins for 2 minutes and remove from the pan. Let the meat rest for 10 minutes before slicing. Reserve some of the pan drippings and discard the rest.

FOR PEARL ONIONS:

1 cup red pearl onions, peeled and halved

½ cup red wine vinegar

1 tablespoon cracked black pepper

2 teaspoons kosher salt

1 teaspoon granulated sugar

1 fresh or ½ dried bay leaf

FOR FINGERLING POTATOES:

1 pound fingerling potatoes

8 sprigs fresh thyme, divided

3 fresh or 1½ dried bay leaves

2 ounces (4 tablespoons) unsalted butter

5 garlic cloves, unpeeled

2 tablespoons blended oil

Kosher salt, to taste

Freshly ground black pepper, to taste

FOR MEAT MARINADE:

1 cup chopped fresh curly parsley

3 tablespoons minced shallot

2 tablespoons chopped fresh rosemary

1 tablespoon chopped fresh thyme

1 garlic clove, minced

1 teaspoon pink peppercorns, crushed

Extra-virgin olive oil

7 **For Mustard Reduction:** In a 3-quart saucepot set over medium heat, warm canola oil. Add the veal scraps and cook until nicely browned, 5 minutes. Add the mushrooms, shallots, and garlic and cook until the shallots are translucent, about 4 minutes. Add the peppercorns and cook for 1 minute. Stir in the sugar and cook 1 more minute. Add the vinegar and deglaze the pan, scraping the brown bits off the bottom of the pan using a wooden spoon. Cook until the pan is dry; then add the wine, port, thyme, and bay leaf. Increase the heat to medium-high and cook until the liquid has reduced by about half, about 20 minutes. Add both the veal and chicken stocks and cook until the liquid has reduced to about 2 cups and is the consistency of syrup. Strain through a fine mesh strainer, return the reduction to the stovetop, and over medium heat, skim off any excess fat. Season to taste with salt and taste for balance—you may want to add a bit more vinegar depending on your preferences. Strain the sauce again and set aside. You will need 1 cup of sauce for this recipe (you will have 3 cups or so)—the rest can be frozen and used another time you make the dish or served with another meat dish.

8 When ready to serve, warm the reduction over medium heat and stir in the mustard until fully incorporated. Set aside. If freezing for later, add mustard just before serving.

9 **For Pearl Onions:** Add the onions to a nonreactive bowl. In a nonreactive saucepot, combine the red wine vinegar, pepper, salt, sugar, and bay leaf, with ¼ cup of water, and bring to a boil. Pour the marinade over the onions and let stand at room temperature for at least 1 hour before serving.

10 **For Fingerling Potatoes:** Bring a medium pot of salted water to a boil. Add the potatoes, 4 sprigs of thyme, and bay leaves and cook at an active simmer uncovered, over medium heat, until the potatoes are fork-tender. Strain and, while the potatoes are hot, peel the potatoes using a paring knife (you may need to wear rubber gloves). Transfer the potatoes to a large skillet, add the butter, garlic, and blended oil, and raise the heat to medium-high. Once the butter begins to brown, lower the heat to medium so it does not burn, add the remaining thyme, and roll the potatoes in butter, so that they are browned all the way around. Season with salt and pepper and, once the potatoes are crispy all the way around, remove from the heat and set aside.

11 **For Meat Marinade:** Combine the parsley, shallot, rosemary, thyme, garlic, and peppercorns in a small bowl. Add enough extra-virgin olive oil to cover the mixture and create a slurry. Set aside while you prepare the garlic.

FOR GRILLED GREEN GARLIC:

4 stalks green garlic
1 recipe Meat Marinade
Extra-virgin olive oil, to coat
Kosher salt, to taste
Freshly ground black pepper, to taste

FOR PORCINI MUSHROOMS:

1 pound small porcini mushrooms or other
    small mushrooms, cleaned and halved
Kosher salt, to taste
Freshly ground black pepper, to taste
Canola oil
1½ ounces (3 tablespoons) unsalted butter
1 head garlic, halved
3 sprigs fresh thyme
1 fresh or ½ dried bay leaf
½ cup dry white wine
½ cup chicken stock

TO COMPLETE:

1 ounce (2 tablespoons) unsalted butter
1 tablespoon chopped fresh curly parsley
12 celery leaves
Flaky sea salt, such as Maldon

12 **For Grilled Green Garlic:** Trim the garlic stalks, removing any dirt and tough outer layers. Cut the stalks into 5-inch pieces. Rinse the garlic under cold, running water and transfer to a container or a resealable plastic bag. Add the Meat Marinade and let the garlic sit at room temperature for 1 hour.

13 Remove the stalks from the marinade and season with olive oil, salt, and pepper. Light a grill or preheat a grill pan. Grill the garlic over high heat, turning occasionally, until slightly charred and cooked through, 4 to 6 minutes. Alternatively, place the garlic under a broiler for 1 minute, or until slightly charred. Remove from the heat, cut on the bias into 1-inch pieces, and set aside.

14 **For Porcini Mushrooms:** Season the mushrooms with salt and pepper. In a large sauté pan set over high heat, warm enough oil to cover the bottom of the pan until just before it starts to smoke. Add the mushrooms and reduce the heat to medium. Once the mushrooms begin to sear, about 1 to 2 minutes, add the butter, garlic, thyme, and bay leaf and toss together to combine. Cook, stirring from time to time, until the butter begins to brown, about 2 to 3 minutes. Add the wine and deglaze the pan, scraping the brown bits off the bottom of the pan using a wooden spoon. Cook until the pan is dry, 5 to 8 minutes; add the stock and cook until the stock reduces and the pan is dry, 5 to 8 minutes. Transfer the mushrooms to a parchment paper–lined tray and set aside in a warm place until ready to use.

15 **To Complete:** When ready to serve, while the tenderloins rest, return the sauté pan to the stovetop and, over medium heat, add 1 ounce unsalted butter, the Porcini Mushrooms, and the Fingerling Potatoes, stirring gently from time to time until warmed through. Add the Grilled Green Garlic and Pearl Onions and cook, stirring gently, until warmed through. Toss in parsley and set aside. Slice the tenderloins into 12 pieces and divide evenly across 4 warmed plates. Add the Fingerling Potatoes, Grilled Green Garlic, Pearl Onions, and Porcini Mushrooms. Drizzle the Mustard Reduction and tenderloin pan drippings over the tenderloin and vegetables, garnish with the celery and sprinkle with flaky sea salt to finish.

NOTES FROM THE CHEF

Vadouvan Curry and Chios can be ordered directly from La Boîte's website, *www.laboiteny.com*.

TOMAS CURI

"Ganesh is my right-hand man."

—Tomas Curi

THERE ARE MANY CHEFS who have always known they wanted to be chefs. Tomas Curi wasn't one of them. Born in Washington, D.C., and raised in Texas, after college Tomas found himself back in D.C. working in management consulting on a project for Homeland Security. He says, "We helped them do airport security, things like how to best set up checkpoints and layers of security." But after a few years, Tomas realized that he didn't find the work he was doing fulfilling. He says, "I wanted to do something that allowed me to use my hands, as well as my other senses, since I am a more tactile learner." Tomas grew up not only cooking, but woodworking, hunting, fishing, and gardening. Cooking seemed like the culmination of all of those. Tomas had

always been interested in Italian culture, so he gave up management consulting to move to Florence, Italy, where he started his culinary education at Apicius International School of Hospitality. An American tattoo artist gave Tomas his first piece on his left shoulder while he was still living in Florence. Tomas describes the tattoo by saying, "I wanted something in a traditional Asian style, so I got the tree with the cherry blossoms because I'm from D.C."

After completing culinary school, Tomas moved to New York City. A newcomer to one of the greatest culinary cities in the world, he didn't have a job or a home, and was staying at a friend's place. Feeling intimidated by starting his new career, he wanted someone to watch over him, and he "thought of [the Hindu god] Ganesh because of how he is described as our lord and protector." Less than two weeks after his arrival, he met Su Houston, a tattoo artist who worked at the Electric Dragon, and had Ganesh tattooed on his right forearm. The Hindu god did what Tomas was hoping he would, and his career took off. He spent time working with a list of great Italian restaurants in New York City, including Bar Milano, Falai, 'inoteca liquori, and A Voce. And thanks to his boyish grin, he even gained a little notoriety in 2009 when he was awarded the title of Eater's "hottest male chef." Today, Tomas is the executive chef at Corsino, where he continues to develop his passion for Italian cooking.

Crispy Braised Mangalitsa Belly with Bitter Greens and Citrus

YIELDS 6 SERVINGS

½ cup mustard seeds

1 cup sherry vinegar

1¼" piece of pork belly, the meatier the better, skin-on

Salt and pepper, to taste

2 oranges

2 lemons

Olive oil

8 cups of bitter greens, such as dandelion, mustard, radicchio

Lemon zest, for garnish

1 In a saucepan, combine mustard seeds and sherry vinegar. Bring to a boil and remove from heat.

2 Clean belly of all sinew and excess fat; it should be nice and smooth. Aggressively salt and pepper it. Let it sit at room temperature until it starts weeping, about 20 to 25 minutes.

3 Preheat oven to 300°F. Cut oranges and lemons into ½" slices and reserve.

4 Place belly, skin-side up, in an ovensafe pan just barely big enough for it. Add enough olive oil to cover it by ½" and the citrus. Place in oven uncovered and cook for about 3 hours or until tender. (The citrus will caramelize and turn brown. That's okay.) Remove belly from the oil and let it rest, for about 30 minutes. Then, place in another shallow pan, skin-side up, and crank the oven up to 500°F. Cook the belly in the oven until the skin starts to blister and become crisp, about 10 to 15 minutes longer. Remove from oven, let it cool a little, and cut into portion sizes.

5 Sauté the greens in olive oil over high heat until they wilt, about 1–2 minutes, remove from heat, and add a spoonful of the mustard and sherry mix. Plate the greens, place a piece of belly (best if warm, not super hot) on top, and drizzle with the mustard-sherry mix. Grate zest of lemon on top to garnish.

CHEF/OWNER

LE PIGEON AND LITTLE BIRD, PORTLAND, OR

GABRIEL RUCKER

> "I would go to raves all night and then go straight from the party to making a bunch of bagels. So I did that . . . but I kind of ended up by accident doing the cooking thing."

—Gabriel Rucker

GABRIEL RUCKER started his culinary career by making bagels at his high school job at a local bakery in Napa, CA, but after a rocky start, he's come a long way in the culinary world. Once he graduated from high school in 1999, Gabriel enrolled at Santa Rosa Junior College, but on the first day started to realize it might not be for him when he read through the math requirements of a liberal arts degree. A counselor suggested he try a two-year vocational program, and he chose cooking. Gabriel says, "I kind of ended up by accident doing the cooking thing. . . . It was exciting to me and made sense to me, and at eighteen years old, I was good at something." Less than a year into the program, he decided to drop out. He explains the decision by saying, "I wanted to get into the kitchen and work." When he was nineteen, he took a job at Napa's Silverado Resort & Spa. He was there less than a year before moving to Santa Cruz, where he took a job at Southern Exposure Bistro. He started out making desserts and salads, which, while not the highest ranked role in the kitchen, gave him creative control. Though it took him several tries, he taught himself how to make crème brûlée on the first day, and that was when he started to experiment and not fear mistakes, but learn from them.

In 2003, looking for a change, Gabriel moved to Portland, Oregon. Portland wasn't his first choice—Gabriel says, "I wanted to move to San Francisco, but I couldn't afford it"—but he had friends living in Portland who told him how affordable the city was and how there were a lot of restaurants looking for good chefs. After moving to Portland, Gabriel landed a job as a line cook at Paley's Place Bistro & Bar, a highly respected Pacific Northwest–focused eatery. Here, Gabriel worked under Vitaly Paley, 2005 James Beard Award–winner for Best Chef Northwest. Gabriel credits Paley with teaching him discipline. But he and fellow chef Jason Barwikowski were soon poached away to help open Gotham Building Tavern, a unique Portland-favorite restaurant and bar. However, Gabriel was too strong-willed and creative to remain a sous-chef forever, so in 2006, at the age of twenty-five, he opened his own place. Le Pigeon, in the southeast side of Portland, gave Gabriel a venue to serve French-inspired dishes with his own twist. The restaurant also takes its name from one of his favorite tattoos. Wrapping around his right forearm are several flying pigeons with "le pigeon" written in cursive.

Since opening Le Pigeon, Gabriel has received his fair share of accolades, including *The Oregonian*'s Rising Star of 2007; *Food & Wine* magazine's Best New Chef of 2007; *The Oregonian*'s Restaurant of the Year in 2008; and the James Beard Awards's Rising Star Chef of the Year in 2011, being the only chef from Oregon to ever receive the award. In 2010, Gabriel opened his second restaurant, Little Bird, with Erik Van Kley, his sous-chef from Le Pigeon. Finally, in 2013, Gabriel won the James Beard Award for Best Chef Northwest.

While he racked up the accolades for his cooking, Gabriel also racked up the amount of ink on his body. He didn't get his first tattoo until a friend's serious injury led Gabriel to get a shark with a bloody mouth inked across his left forearm. A friend and fellow Paley's Place alum, Jason Barwikowski, used to draw the shark on things around the kitchen when they worked together, and Gabriel would often joke it would be his first tattoo. One day in July of 2005, while swimming at Washington's Washougal River, Gabriel and Jason jumped off a rock about 60 feet into the water. Gabriel jumped first, but when Jason jumped, he glanced off a rock ledge, breaking his back in two places, shattering his tailbone, lacerating his liver, and collapsing his lung. Gabriel says, "I pulled him out of the water and just sat with him while waiting for the paramedics to come. I told him, man if you just make it through this time, then I'll get the poorly drawn shark." Jason would later recover after months of physical therapy, and Gabriel would get the shark tattoo.

Gabriel didn't stop there. Not wanting a chef knife tattoo but still wanting something that spoke to his profession, he got the Le Pigeon tattoo. "In France, the pigeon is the person who has to do all of the dirty jobs—peel the garlic, clean and shuck the mussels. I still do all of that—we all do—no one is too good for any job." As he has continued to get ink, Gabriel continues to put his own unique spin on his tattoos. Rather than the standard pig and fish tattoo, he got them in their processed form as cans of deviled ham and sardines on his right and left arms. The butter on his right bicep is simply one of the ingredients intrinsic to French, and thus his, cooking.

With two restaurants and a cookbook under his belt, the idea of expansion is now less exciting to Gabriel. The restaurants continue to succeed, and finally recognized for his talents, he hopes to be able to spend more time with his wife and his son.

Beef Carpaccio, Broccoli, Oysters, and Wasabi Vinaigrette

SERVES 4

FOR BEEF:

1 (10-ounce) piece center cut beef
    tenderloin
2 teaspoons kosher salt
5 cloves garlic
1 Meyer lemon
2 ounces ginger, peeled and chopped
2 tablespoons oyster sauce
2 tablespoons sriracha hot sauce

FOR OYSTER FOAM:

½ cup oysters, shucked, with their liquor
    (I like oysters from the northwest but
    use what is local to you)
¼ cup heavy cream
1 tablespoon lemon juice
2 teaspoons white soy sauce
½ teaspoon kosher salt

FOR WASABI VINAIGRETTE:

1 tablespoon wasabi paste
1 small shallot, minced
1 tablespoon white soy sauce
2 tablespoons white wine vinegar
¼ cup canola oil
½ teaspoon salt

TO COMPLETE:

½ cup chopped broccoli florets
2 tablespoons minced red onion
¼ cup chopped raw oysters
½ cup soy sauce
2 lemons, juiced
Sea salt, to taste
Petite red sorrel leaves, optional garnish

1 For Beef: Season the beef with the kosher salt. In the bowl of a small food processor, combine garlic, lemon, ginger, oyster sauce, and sriracha and pulse to create a thick and chunky rub. Liberally rub the beef with the mixture and place in a large zip-top bag. Seal bag, making sure to get as much air out as possible. Refrigerate for 12 to 24 hours, the longer the better.

2 Remove beef from the refrigerator and remove from the bag. Heat up a grill (either gas or charcoal) as hot as you can. Brush the grill with oil and place the beef on the hot grill. Grill each side for about 30 seconds—we aren't trying to cook the meat here so much as to form a crust of that great marinade. Once grilled, remove to a plate and refrigerate to stop cooking.

3 For Oyster Foam: Place all ingredients in a blender and blend until smooth. Strain and place the liquid in an iSi canister. Charge with nitrous and refrigerate until ready to plate.

4 For Wasabi Vinaigrette: Combine all ingredients with a whisk and reserve for plating.

5 To Complete: In a small bowl, combine broccoli, red onions, and chopped oysters. Dress with a little Wasabi Vinaigrette. In another small bowl, combine soy sauce and lemon juice. Remove beef from the refrigerator and, using a very sharp knife, slice into thin slices, about ¼" thick. Toss beef slices in soy-lemon mixture and then pat dry with paper towels. Arrange beef on four plates. Arrange some broccoli salad in small piles next to beef. Gently release foam from iSi canister in small piles around beef. Sprinkle with sea salt and finish with red sorrel.

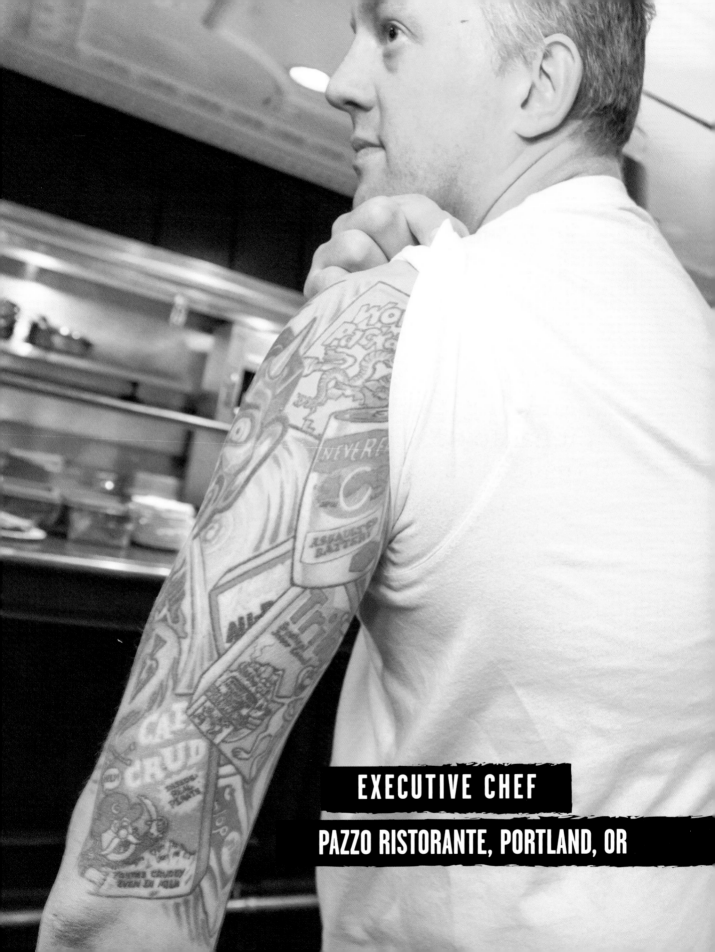

EXECUTIVE CHEF

PAZZO RISTORANTE, PORTLAND, OR

JOHN EISENHART

> "I don't know what the connection is, but it is there definitely. I don't know if it has to do with pain or what, but it really is its own phenomenon with cooking and tattoos."
>
> —John Eisenhart

JOHN EISENHART got his first restaurant job washing dishes at the Sonoma Mission Inn in the mid-1980s at the age of fourteen, and he was hooked. The job was more about earning cash to buy a 1965 Mustang convertible, but he found a calling that would stay with him the rest of his life. After graduating high school, John enrolled in the California Culinary Academy, graduating in 1991. From there, he took a position as an assistant pastry chef at San Francisco's four-star seafood restaurant Aqua. However, at the same time he was offered a position at Masa's, another four-star restaurant specializing in new French cuisine. Wanting to gain as much knowledge as he could, he took both jobs. He says, "I had two full-time jobs, and I was just going crazy. I did it for about a year, but eventually got tired of it." John got his first tattoo—the logo for the band God Bullies, a crown of thorns and three spikes, on his upper chest—when he was eighteen and living in Healdsburg, California, but got most of his work done in San Francisco when he was working at Aqua. He says, "I lived with some tattoo artists for a while, so I didn't have to pay for them. . . . It was interesting, all the people you meet. It's just like cooking in a way. You meet all these interesting personalities and misfits of society." John's left arm is covered in Wacky Packages, parody stickers of packaged foods released by the Topps Company since 1967. Much of the art was done by artists from

> **66** I lived with some tattoo artists for a while, so I didn't have to pay for [my tattoos]. . . . It was interesting, all the people you meet. It's just like cooking in a way. You meet all these interesting personalities and misfits of society. **99**

Mad magazine, and the images always stuck with John. "I'm kind of a smart-ass by nature, so I thought they would be a good pairing to put on my arm."

All inked up, John moved to New York around Christmastime in 1994 to become the saucier at La Grenouille. He says, "That was actually a really good experience. I had to make thirty different sauces every day . . . that was quite a chore." Soon after, in 1998, John took a sous-chef job at the newly opened Babbo, where he worked under famed chef and TV personality Mario Batali. After working at Babbo for a few years, John moved to Italy with Mario's blessing to further develop his skills. While there, he learned the subtleties of Italian cooking as he staged (worked as an unpaid intern) a few months at a time with top chefs in some of the finest kitchens in Lucca, Venice, and Alba. The job wasn't always easy though. John says, "I worked there for three different restaurants for room and board." Language was also a barrier. Even though he learned some words in the kitchen, they would often

be in the local dialect, so when he moved on to the next job, much of what he had learned to say was worthless. Regardless of the challenges, the experience was something he would never give back, and it cemented a love of Italian cooking in him.

When John returned to the United States, he looked to move away from the intensity of New York City and chose the more laid-back atmosphere of Portland, Oregon. After two years as sous-chef at the Heathman Restaurant & Bar, in 2003 he became the executive chef at Pazzo Ristorante, one of the largest restaurants in Portland, where he manages a staff of thirty people just for the back of house. He says, "Everyone is opening these little places, which is great, but I don't know if I could do it. Thirty seats? I think I would just go crazy." For ten years now, John has been at the helm of Pazzo, and for a chef that usually gets "itchy feet," he has found contentment in the Rose City.

Batsoa

John collects old cookbooks, and loves old Italian cookbooks the best. To find an old traditional dish and bring it out of hiding is one of the signatures to his cooking. Batsoa is one of the earliest recorded dishes from Piedmont, Italy.

FOR BATSOA:

8 black peppercorns
4–6 coriander seeds
1 fresh bay leaf
5 pounds pig's feet, about 6 pig's feet
2 teaspoons sea salt
2 tablespoons honey
1 tablespoon cider vinegar
2 fruits from the "seeds" of a tamarind pod
1 teaspoon grated fresh ginger

FOR PUMPKIN MUSTARD:

4 ounces pumpkin, roasted (no color), meat only
¼ teaspoon Marsala wine
½ teaspoon high-quality sherry vinegar
1 tablespoon Olio Verde olive oil (any high-quality extra-virgin olive oil will suffice)
1 tablespoon unsalted butter
1 pinch of salt
1 teaspoon honey
1 teaspoon plus 1 tablespoon grain mustard, divided

TO COMPLETE:

1 cup all-purpose flour
4 tablespoons tapioca maltodextrin
2–3 tablespoons olive oil
10 ounces Brussels sprouts

1 **For Batsoa:** Place the peppercorns, coriander seeds, and bay leaf in a tied cheesecloth pouch (sachet). Place sachet in a large pot; add pig's feet and enough water to cover the feet by about 3 to 4 inches. Add sea salt, honey, cider vinegar, and tamarind fruits. Place pot on stove, uncovered. On medium-high heat, bring to a simmer; then turn heat to medium-low to gently cook ingredients for 5 to 6 hours, until "fall-apart" tender. Remove from heat and set aside in the cooking liquid until cool enough to handle, but still quite warm.

2 Gently pull apart trotters, setting aside strained cooking liquid, and add skin, meat, and tendon (removing broken fat and bones) to a perforated mold set inside a container. (Note: If trotter meat gets dry and sticky while you're pulling it apart, rehydrate it with the reserved cooking liquid.) Mix microplaned ginger into meat mixture. Taste the mixture for seasoning and press (4 to 5 pounds works well; we use a large can of tomatoes) the meat inside the terrine mold. Place in the refrigerator overnight. This will drain the excess liquid.

3 **For Pumpkin Mustard:** In a blender, mix all ingredients except 1 tablespoon grain mustard on high until very smooth. Add 1 tablespoon grain mustard on low speed and refrigerate, about 30 minutes.

4 **To Complete:** Combine and sift flour and tapioca maltodextrin. Lightly bread the Batsoa in the flour mixture. On medium-high heat, add olive oil to a frying pan and fry floured Batsoa for 1½ to 2 minutes on each side. The Batsoa should feel soft at the center. Slice Brussels sprouts with a mandoline. Plate Batsoa with raw Brussels sprouts and a spread of Pumpkin Mustard.

NOTES FROM THE CHEF

Tamarind is a pod that contains about 6–7 "seeds." Each seed is covered with a sour, fruity paste. You'll use 2 seeds' worth of paste for this recipe.

BEN DE VRIES

"It's this trading of art; my food for his ink. I always think I get the better end of the deal."

—Ben de Vries

BEN DE VRIES'S mother and grandmother raised him in Ann Arbor, Michigan, which is where he first fell in love with food. Helping his grandmother often in the kitchen, Ben was only six when he announced he would like to be a chef and own his own restaurant. Then, Ben spent his junior year of high school in Paris, where he was introduced to the culinary arts at a friend's restaurant. After high school, Ben moved to Vermont to study at the New England Culinary Institute; he then went on to staging, similar to a culinary internship, at restaurants on Cape Cod and Nantucket and in New York City. He eventually moved to San Francisco to continue his culinary career in a city he wanted to live in, a decision that quickly paid off. He says, "I got off the plane New Year's Day 1994, and within an hour I got a job offer, got an offer for a place to stay, and met my current wife."

As Ben settled into San Francisco, he also took a position as a sous-chef at LuLu, a Provençal restaurant serving simple rustic foods family-style from a wood-fired oven. Ben also helped launch Scala's Bistro and Vertigo before becoming opening sous-chef at the French-Japanese restaurant mc2. In 2004, Ben worked as an executive chef at Andalu, a restaurant focused on an eclectic mix of small plates to share with the goal of having interaction among the guests be as important as the food. Andalu caught the attention of *The New York Times*, *Bon Appétit*, *Food & Wine*, and *Gourmet*, among other national media outlets. That same year, Ben went on to open his own restaurant, Luella.

CHEF/OWNER

LUELLA, SAN FRANCISCO, CA

With Luella, Ben was finally free to explore his style of cooking. He says, "I appreciate food that doesn't try to be something it's not." Luella's menu can best be described as contemporary American, with roots in Italy, Spain, and France. Dishes are robust and straightforward and not complicated by heavy sauces. Luella's modern California cuisine acquired a Bauer two-and-a-half-star review from the *San Francisco Chronicle* in 2009 and has also received many accolades from *Northside San Francisco*, Gayot, 7x7, and *San Francisco* magazine.

Ben started to get his very organized culinary tattoos almost nine years ago. His right arm starting at his wrist showcases the ingredients for bouquet garni, the bundle of herbs usually tied together with string and used to prepare soup, stock, and various stews. Moving up his arm is a picture of the knife kit that Ben uses in the kitchen, followed by the butcher charts for pig, chicken, cow, and sheep. The last tattoo on this arm is the definition for confit—"con•fit [con fée, kawN fee] (*plural* con•fits) meat cooked and preserved in fat: such as goose, duck, or pork that has been cooked and preserved in its own fat"—followed by vegetables. Ben's largest tattoo showcases a leg of jamón ibérico, Spain's famous cured ham made from pigs raised on acorns, that runs down his right thigh. Next to it sits his pinup girl chef with her own "I heart pork" tattoo. Ben also has several religious symbols from various religions wrapping his ankle, as well as many classic herbs around his calf like parsley and rosemary.

Ben attributes his ink to two people: Renee Silvestri, a good friend and a hostess at Luella who drew most of the art, and Greg Rojas, a tattoo artist from Seventh Son Tattoo in San Francisco. Ben says, "[Rojas] and I have sat for a total of over one hundred hours. It's a good thing that he likes food because otherwise I could never afford it." Over all that time, Greg and Ben have become good friends. "It's new age-y to a certain degree, but if someone is putting something permanent like that on your body, there is a certain energy that comes with it, and to have somebody you like and feel good with makes a whole world of difference."

> "IT'S NEW AGE-Y TO A CERTAIN DEGREE, BUT IF SOMEONE IS PUTTING SOMETHING PERMANENT LIKE [A TATTOO] ON YOUR BODY, THERE IS A CERTAIN ENERGY THAT COMES WITH IT, AND TO HAVE [A TATTOO ARTIST] YOU LIKE AND FEEL GOOD WITH MAKES A WHOLE WORLD OF DIFFERENCE."

Luella's Coca-Cola Braised Pork Shoulder

This dish has been a signature dish for Luella since it opened. Ben has tried to pull it from the menu a few times, but each time enough customers have asked that he has had to put it back on. Like a band that has a song fly to the top of the charts but has long since written new material, sometimes chefs can't escape certain dishes.

SERVES 12, WITH LEFTOVERS

FOR PORK:
8 pounds boneless pork shoulder
Salt and pepper, to taste
Oil, for searing
2 liters regular Coca-Cola
1 gallon low-sodium chicken stock or broth

FOR WHITE BEAN PURÉE:
3 cups dried cannellini beans (about 1½ pounds)
Olive oil
Salt, to taste
White pepper, to taste

NOTES FROM THE CHEF

Sometimes what seems like an incongruous ingredient can make the most spectacular dish. The secret: Coca-Cola. People may not be able to pick out its distinctive flavor, but it brings out the best in this cut of pork. Cooling the meat overnight: After cooking, the meat is left in the braising liquid, which intensifies the flavor and tenderness.

1 **For Pork:** Season the pork with salt and pepper. Drizzle oil onto the bottom of a deep pan to barely cover; then set the pan over high heat. When the oil is hot, add the meat and sear on all sides until golden brown, just a few minutes per side. Remove the pork from the pan and set aside. Preheat the oven to 450°F. Pour the Coca-Cola into the pan and bring to a boil over high heat. Boil, scraping up any stuck bits of meat from the bottom of the pan, until the liquid is reduced to about 3 cups, about 25 minutes. Add the chicken stock, bring to a boil again, and cook until liquid reduces by about a quarter, about 10 minutes. Carefully place the meat into the liquid, cover, and bake for about 2 hours, or until the meat falls apart easily. Remove the meat from the oven and let it rest, still covered and in its liquid, for at least 1 hour. If making ahead of time, cool and refrigerate overnight.

2 To finish the meat, remove from the liquid (save the liquid in the pot), and remove and discard any visible fat that settles on the top. Preheat the oven to 400°F. Bring the pot of liquid to a boil on the stove; then return the meat to the pot. Bake, uncovered, until the meat is warmed through, about 1 hour. Remove the meat from the pan and let rest 10 to 15 minutes. Meanwhile, bring the sauce (braising liquid) to a hard simmer and cook until it reduces to a light syrup (slightly thinner than maple syrup), approximately 10 to 15 minutes.

3 **For White Bean Purée:** Soak the beans in water overnight. Drain; then place the beans in a medium saucepan. Cover with water, add a splash of olive oil, and bring to a boil. Reduce heat and simmer uncovered until very soft, about 1 hour, adding more warm water as needed. Drain the beans, reserving some of the cooking liquid, and purée in a food processor until smooth, adding enough olive oil (and some of the cooking liquid) until the beans have a mashed potato–like consistency; season with salt and white pepper to taste. Set aside. (The purée can be made up to a day ahead. Before serving, rewarm over medium-low heat, stirring frequently. If made ahead and refrigerated, you may need to adjust the consistency with a little more oil.)

FOR PICKLED RED ONIONS:

1 large red onion (about 12 ounces), sliced
    lengthwise about ¼" thick

1½ cups red wine vinegar

¼ cup sugar

TO COMPLETE:

½ cup julienned mint leaves

4 **For Pickled Red Onions:** Combine the onions, vinegar, and sugar in a nonreactive saucepan. Bring to a boil, lower heat, and simmer uncovered for 5 minutes. Remove from heat and let cool. Adjust flavor with more vinegar or sugar as desired; then refrigerate until chilled. (The onions can be made up to a week ahead.)

5 **To Complete:** Spoon warm White Bean Purée onto a plate; top with Pork and drizzle with sauce. Drain the Pickled Red Onions and combine with mint; use to garnish the Pork. Serve immediately.

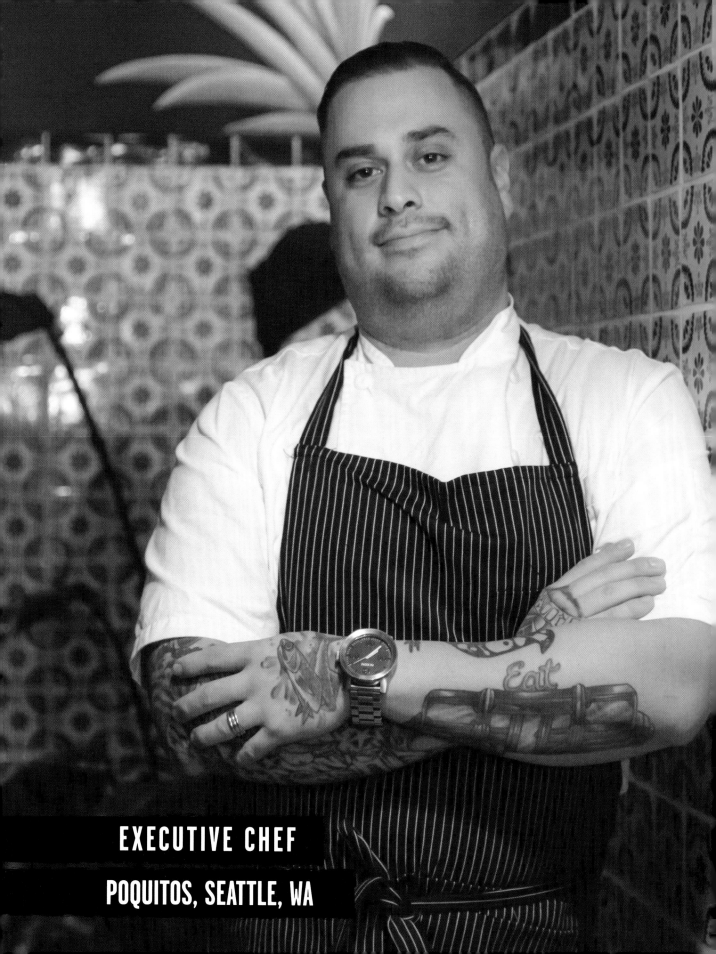

EXECUTIVE CHEF

POQUITOS, SEATTLE, WA

MANNY ARCE

> "I wasn't happy being a clipboard chef that just managed a lot of people, so I decided to get back into the kitchen."

—Manny Arce

MANNY ARCE grew up in San Diego, CA. He started culinary school at Le Cordon Bleu in San Diego but dropped out, eventually finishing his culinary degree at Mesa College in San Diego. During travels to Spain and Italy, Manny reignited his passion for the culinary arts by completing two culinary internships. In 2003, spurred by his wife, Manny moved to Seattle and eventually fell into corporate dining, working for the Compass Group, a massive food service company that has over 180,000 employees across forty-eight states and Canada. There, he did contract food service for large corporations; at one point he was running seventeen cafés for the manufacturer Boeing. Though the work paid well, Manny

says, "it's not romantic at all," so he left his job at the Compass Group and went back on the line in the kitchen. This may seem like a demotion, but Manny says, "I just thought, I don't need a title right now. I just want to cook again."

After a short time cooking on the line at La Spiga, which earned a mention in Citysearch's "Best Italian Food 2008," Manny found a job at Bastille Café & Bar. Bastille, a casual French dining concept that has a strong emphasis on sourcing from local food purveyors, was opened in 2009 by Deming Maclise and James Weimann. Bastille even converted their roof into a heated herb garden,

> **❝ The French have bistros, and the Italians have trattorias. Diners are the only locations that are representative of the working class and accessible to everybody. ❞**

gaining them attention in *Bon Appétit* magazine in 2010 as one of the "Top 10 Best Roof-to-Table Dining." The article praises urban restaurants for their innovations in bringing farming closer to them. In 2011, spurred by the success of Bastille, Deming and James wanted to open their Mexican concept Poquitos. Manny, with his culinary skills and familiarity with the cuisine from his time in San Diego, was the natural choice for the executive chef position. Since opening, Poquitos has received two-and-a-half out of four stars from the *Seattle Times*, one of the highest ratings for a Mexican concept, and has been featured in multiple articles in *Sunset* magazine for Manny's fresh takes on classic Mexican dishes.

Manny got his first tattoo, the logo for the band Black Flag, when he was eighteen. He has since covered it up and gotten quite a few more. His left arm has the silhouette of the pigeon logo from fellow *Eat Ink* chef Gabriel Rucker's restaurant Le Pigeon in Portland, OR (see info for Rucker in this part). Manny never worked at Le Pigeon, but "I just thought it was a really neat piece of artwork. It's not exactly their logo, but it is a pretty strong representation of their logo." Next to the pigeon is his tribute to American cooking: a tattoo of a classic American diner. "The French have bistros, and the Italians have trattorias. Diners are the only locations that are representative of the working class and accessible to everybody." While Manny is certain that he wants more experience before he is ready to take the risk of opening his own place, he has always dreamed of running his own restored 1930s-style diner. For this chef, who has already taken a big chance by leaving a secure job to pursue his passion for cooking, a Manny's Diner is a very strong possibility for the future.

Tamarind Braised Short Ribs with Sweet Potato Purée, Arugula, Golden Raisins, and Spiced Pumpkin Seeds

YIELDS 8 SERVINGS

FOR SHORT RIBS:
4 pounds boneless short rib plates, cleaned and seared
10 chiles de árbol
5 dried chipotle chilies
½ of an onion, diced
½ of a carrot, diced
3 bay leaves
1 cup balsamic vinegar
1 cup white wine
3 tablespoons chopped garlic
½ cup tamarind paste
Salt and pepper, to taste
2–4 cups water

FOR SWEET POTATO PURÉE:
3 pounds peeled sweet potatoes, diced
Milk, to cover potatoes
¼ cup sliced garlic, slowly cooked in oil
Salt and pepper, to taste
Splash of lime juice

FOR GOLDEN RAISINS:
1 cup raisins
1 cup dry white wine

FOR SPICED PUMPKIN SEEDS:
1 cup shelled pumpkin seeds
1 tablespoon olive oil
¼ teaspoon ground pequin chili
Salt, to taste

FOR ARUGULA SALAD:
8 cups arugula
1 tablespoon olive oil
½ tablespoon lime juice
Salt and pepper, to taste

1 **For Short Ribs:** Take all ingredients besides ribs, salt, pepper, and water and blend in blender or food processor. Preheat oven to 350°F. Place ribs in a roasting pan, pour blended liquid over ribs, add approximately 2 cups water, (but make sure ribs are barely covered), and cover pan with parchment paper and foil. Place on stovetop over high heat. Bring covered meat to a boil; reduce heat to medium-low and simmer for a few minutes. Place pan in oven and cook 2½ to 3 hours, until tender but not falling apart. Remove ribs from liquid and lay on parchment paper–lined sheet pan. Season well with salt and pepper, wrap with plastic wrap, and cool in refrigerator until cold, 2 to 3 hours. Divide into 6-ounce portions. Skim fat from braising liquid, reduce sauce over medium-low heat for about 20 minutes, remove, and let cool. Before serving, place short ribs in a large sauté pan. Add reduced braising liquid and cover with lid. Place on stove over medium heat until short ribs are heated through, about 10 to 12 minutes.

2 **For Sweet Potato Purée:** Place sweet potatoes in large pot. Cover with milk and slowly cook over medium heat until cooked through, about 15 to 20 minutes. Remove sweet potatoes from milk. In small batches, place potatoes and garlic in a blender and purée until smooth. Season with salt and pepper and a splash of lime juice.

3 **For Golden Raisins:** Place raisins and wine in a saucepot on low heat and slowly heat to a simmer. Remove and allow to cool. Remove raisins from liquid; drain well.

4 **For Spiced Pumpkin Seeds:** Preheat oven to 350°F. Place pumpkin seeds on a sheet pan and toast for 10 minutes. Remove from heat, toss with olive oil and ground chili, and season with salt to taste.

5 **For Arugula Salad:** Toss salad ingredients together. Don't overdress the greens.

6 **To Complete:** Place a spoonful of Sweet Potato Purée in the bottom of a bowl. Place one Short Rib portion on top of the purée and drizzle with a spoonful of reduced braising liquid. Add Golden Raisins and Spiced Pumpkin Seeds to the Arugula Salad, toss to combine, and place on top of the Short Rib.

DUSKIE ESTES

"I had no ink until that point. I'm someone who doesn't sign up for pain."

—Duskie Estes

DUSKIE started at Brown University as premed but eventually graduated with a prelaw degree in 1990. She realized that law was not her calling either and took the first semester of her junior year off to explore her passion for cooking and attend the California Cooking Academy. When she returned to Brown to finish her degree, she took a job as a pastry chef at Lucky's, which featured wood-grilled rustic fare, and the owners' other location, Al Forno, in Providence, RI. This was Duskie's first taste of a professional kitchen. Duskie says of her time as a pastry chef at Lucky's, "It was a line position because the desserts were all made to order—folks ordered their desserts when they ordered their entrées. That meant everybody ordered dessert because it was so special. I made cakes, soufflés, crepes, tarte tatins, and even spun ice cream to order. I got a taste of the adrenaline rush I adore to this day."

After graduating from Brown, Duskie moved to Washington, D.C., to work for Robert Kinkead at 21 Federal and, after it closed, at his new restaurant, Kinkead's, when it opened in 1993. Soon after opening, the restaurant was named one of the "25 Best New Restaurants in America" by *Esquire* magazine. Duskie started in the pantry and finished as Kinkead's lead sauté cook. Eventually Duskie felt the pull to come back home and returned to San Francisco for a short time before moving to Seattle in 1994. There, Duskie took a job working for famous Seattle chef Tom Douglas (James Beard Award winner, 1994). She was his corporate sous-chef for all three of his restaurants—Dahlia Lounge, Etta's, and Palace Kitchen—for three years. Despite all her culinary success, Duskie was still thinking about returning to law school when she was offered the executive chef job at Palace Kitchen. She decided to work at Palace Kitchen, and has never regretted her decision to become a chef. During her two years as head chef at Palace

CHEF/CO-OWNER

ZAZU RESTAURANT & FARM AND BLACK PIG MEAT CO., SONOMA COUNTY, CA

a passing comment to her mother that if she and John ever owned a restaurant, this is what she would want it to feel like. Not long after the wedding, the restaurant went up for sale, but Duskie was eight months pregnant so she couldn't fly down to see the space or negotiate the deal. Not knowing enough about the location, she made a low offer that was refused. But the day they returned from the hospital with their first child, there was a message on their answering machine accepting the offer. "It happened all very fast. We moved down here with a three-month-old baby and opened the restaurant within a month."

In 2002, Zazu was named a "Top 10 Best New Restaurant" and was listed in the *San Francisco Chronicle*'s "Top 100 Restaurants" in 2003, 2004, and 2005. *San Francisco* magazine also rated the restaurant as one of the "Top 50 Restaurants in the Bay Area," and the accolades continued to pile up. Based on the buzz the restaurant created, Duskie was chosen to compete on Food Network's *The Next Iron Chef* in Seasons Three and Five.

In between competing on her seasons of *The Next Iron Chef*, Duskie kept herself busy winning other competitions. There is a nationwide pork cooking competition called Cochon 555, where the winners of each regional competition compete at Grand Cochon in Aspen, Colorado. In Napa, up against teams like Thomas Keller's Bouchon that had deep pockets and PR teams behind them, underdogs Duskie and John never expected to win, yet in 2011 they did just that. Duskie says, "When we won that, it was a total shocker. . . . We were in T-shirts [instead of chef whites], and we didn't even have enough labor to send so we got our plumber to come help." They were so certain they wouldn't win, that John joked that he would get a crown tattoo if they managed to pull off a victory and were crowned the king and queen of pork. After they won, John remained true to his word. Since they won together, Duskie felt she needed to get one as well. It is her first and only tattoo.

Kitchen, she was voted Citysearch's Seattle Best Chef in 2000, and Palace Kitchen was rated as one of the top five Seattle restaurants in 2000 by *Gourmet* magazine.

While working for Tom Douglas, Duskie met John Stewart, her now-husband and business partner (see his entry in this part). Duskie says, "I was John's boss, but when we started dating, he had to get a job somewhere else." The two married in 2000 and, in 2001, opened Zazu Restaurant & Farm in Santa Rosa in a spot that they found while in California for their wedding. When she saw the spot, originally named the Willowside Café, Duskie made

Brussels Sprouts, Gravenstein Apple, and Black Pig Bacon Salads

Zazu focuses on whole-animal cooking, showing respect for the ingredients, and wasting as little as possible. In addition to the restaurant, John and Duskie raise heritage-breed pigs and offer the meat for sale through their company Black Pig Meat Co. You can purchase the bacon for this dish and several other great cuts from *www.blackpigmeatco.com*.

SERVES 4

4 ounces Black Pig bacon, or other quality bacon, cut into lardons

4 cups Brussels sprouts, quartered

1 shallot, minced

¼ cup sherry vinegar

1 head frisée, cleaned

1 Gravenstein apple, diced

3 tablespoons roughly chopped Marcona almonds

1 tablespoon quality extra-virgin olive oil

Kosher salt and freshly ground black pepper, to taste

1 In a large sauté pan on medium-high heat, render the bacon until slightly browned, a few minutes. Add the Brussels sprouts and cook until browned on at least one side, about 3 minutes.

2 Add the shallots and open up their fragrance, about 1 minute. Add the vinegar, remove from heat, and toss. Return the pan to the heat until the Brussels sprouts are just tender, about 3 to 5 minutes. Remove from heat.

3 Add the frisée, apples, almonds, and extra-virgin olive oil and toss. Season to taste with salt and pepper. Plate or eat right out of the pan!

CHEF/CO-OWNER

ZAZU RESTAURANT & FARM AND BLACK PIG MEAT CO., SONOMA COUNTY, CA

JOHN STEWART

> "I think some of the creativity comes from being stuck with all the odd parts you're not sure what to do with. You're not going to throw them out, so you are going to figure it out."
>
> —John Stewart

JOHN STEWART grew up in Mount Kisco, New York, in a culinary family. He is the fourth generation of his family's catering company, Thomas Fox & Son, which was founded in 1919 by his great-grandfather. By the time John was seven years old, he had been put to work helping polish silver and folding catering boxes in the family business. He continued to work in the family business during summers and vacations through college. He graduated in 1990 from the University of Colorado at Boulder with a degree in political science and a minor in Russian history. He says, "I have always been interested in political history." After visiting a friend in Seattle, he moved there in 1994. He was drawn to the low cost of living at the time and the great jazz and bar scene. John loved the city as well as the access to both the ocean and the mountains. In Seattle, John worked at Tom Douglas's restaurant Etta's, an upscale seafood restaurant, before taking a job at Palace Kitchen. While at Palace Kitchen, he met his wife, Duskie Estes. Duskie, his boss at the time, didn't want to date an employee, but John was fortuitously offered the position of sous-chef at the well-known Italian restaurant Cafe Lago. Once John started working there, he and Duskie started dating, and John fell in love twice, first with Duskie and second with all things Italian.

> **When I finally started making things like prosciuttos, really big things that require a lot of patience and a lot of skill, I think that is where I transferred over into fanatical. I was like, I'm going to get this [pig] tattooed on my arm now.**

John is now an avid salumist, someone who makes his own cured meats from scratch, an art that has seen a small revival in recent years with the help of a small handful of chefs. However, curing meat improperly can have consequences (from simply spoiling food to cultivating deadly bacteria) and, because of this, has come into conflict with the FDA and modern food safety regulations. John continues to work with prominent chef Mario Batali and at Iowa State University's Meat Lab to better understand his craft and promote safe practices. He has started a company called Black Pig Meat Co. where you can purchase their line of Black Pig meats, bacon, and salumi made from pasture-raised, heritage-breed, antibiotic- and hormone-free pork. In 2010, *Men's Journal* named John's Black Pig Bacon as one of its "Top Bacons."

Since moving to Sonoma and opening Zazu Restaurant & Farm in Santa Rosa, CA, John and Duskie live John's convictions by raising chickens, pigs, goats, turkeys, and rabbits in four locations across Sonoma, including in their own backyard. Much of what they raise can be found on the menu at Zazu. Since John and Duskie are so deeply involved in the process of raising what goes onto the table at their restaurant, they really believe in using whole animals at Zazu, even going so far as to put a notice on their menu saying that the cuts of meat in each dish may change mid-service as they work their way from snout to tail.

John's tattoos reflect his passion for using whole animals in his restaurant. He has several tattoos, including a rooster on his left forearm, but the one that might define him best is the pig cutting chart across his right arm, just above the crown he got for winning Grand Cochon, a national pork cooking competition. The pig is the logo for Salumi, an artisan cured meat shop in Seattle owned by Armandino Batali, father of Mario Batali. John had wanted to work for Armandino while he was living in Seattle, but the timing never worked out. John finally met Mario at a food festival called the Aspen Food and Wine Classic in Colorado and ended up helping Mario because "the people who were assigned to him weren't all that qualified." Ever since then, Mario has been "sort of a mentor" to John. Through his relationship with Mario, John became friends with Armandino. John says, "When I finally started making things like prosciuttos, really big things that require a lot of patience and a lot of skill, I think that is where I transferred over into fanatical. I was like, I'm going to get this tattooed on my arm now." Today, John continues to help Duskie run Zazu Restaurant & Farm, which has expanded into a new location. In addition, he continues to be an advocate for butchery, and though he swears he doesn't want to be a pig farmer, the space between farm and table becomes ever smaller when it comes to John's work.

Black Pig Bacon and Duck Egg Carbonara

Why this recipe? John says, "We make our own bacon from pasture-raised pork, so we like to highlight it in everything. We use our own farm eggs in the pasta and in the sauce. Quality bacon makes or breaks this dish! Carbonara gets its name from carbon, that is, the fresh black pepper in the dish."

SERVES 4–6

FOR PASTA:
3½ cups all-purpose flour
5 duck eggs
2 tablespoons olive oil

FOR CARBONARA:
6 slices Black Pig or quality bacon, cut into lardons
4 farm eggs
1 cup freshly grated Parmesan cheese, plus more for garnish
Kosher salt and freshly ground black pepper, to taste

TO COMPLETE:
Asparagus, cut on the bias, when in season

1 **For Pasta:** In a bowl, combine flour, eggs, and oil. Knead, wrap in plastic, and let rest for at least half an hour. Roll out in pasta machine three times at each setting, folding it each time (this gives it the tooth). Bring to desired thickness (this depends on your machine, but it's usually two notches above the thinnest setting). At the desired thickness, roll dough through twice without any folding (which sets the thickness) and cut with tagliatelle cutter.

2 **For Carbonara:** Bring a large pot of salted water to a boil. Cook the Pasta until done, about 4 minutes. Strain the Pasta, reserving ½ cup of the pasta water for the sauce. In a sauté pan on medium-high heat, cook the bacon until crispy, about 4 minutes. Meanwhile, in a large bowl combine the eggs with the Parmesan, salt, and pepper.

3 Add the hot Pasta, some of its water, the hot bacon, and its rendered fat to the egg and cheese. With tongs, toss and add pasta water to desired consistency. Season to taste with salt and pepper. (Note: It is important that the Pasta and the bacon be hot because they are cooking the egg and thickening the sauce. It's also important to work quickly so you don't overcook the eggs or they will scramble.)

4 **To Complete:** Plate up into pasta bowls and garnish with more Parmesan cheese. Top with asparagus, if using. Serve immediately.

JONATHAN POWER

"I've spent enough time in the flash-heavy, biker-style tattoo shops that I'll take a pass on doing any more of those."

—Jonathan Power

GROWING UP IN COLORADO, Jonathan Power started out in the culinary industry behind the counter of a Subway franchise. While still working at Subway in 1998, he met a friend who helped get him a job at a new restaurant (now closed) called Bloom, which was opening in Broomfield, Colorado. After working as pantry chef for about six months, Jonathan came to the realization that "All these cooks work way too many hours for not nearly enough money." Figuring he didn't have much of a future in cooking, he took part-time jobs off and on through high school and then during college while at the University of Colorado at Boulder, as a way to make extra money and pay his bills. After graduating with a degree in philosophy, he moved to Chicago to take an executive assistant job, a job he hated every minute of. He scored well enough on his LSATs to get accepted to law school, but he had trouble finding scholarships, so he eventually moved back to Colorado.

In Denver, still toying with the idea of going into law school, Jonathan took a job at Justin Cucci's restaurant Root Down. Opened in 2008, Root Down focuses on fresh, local, and organic ingredients and globally influenced seasonal cuisine. Eventually taking over the sauté position, Jonathan realized while there that, regardless of the long hours and low pay, being in the kitchen made him happy.

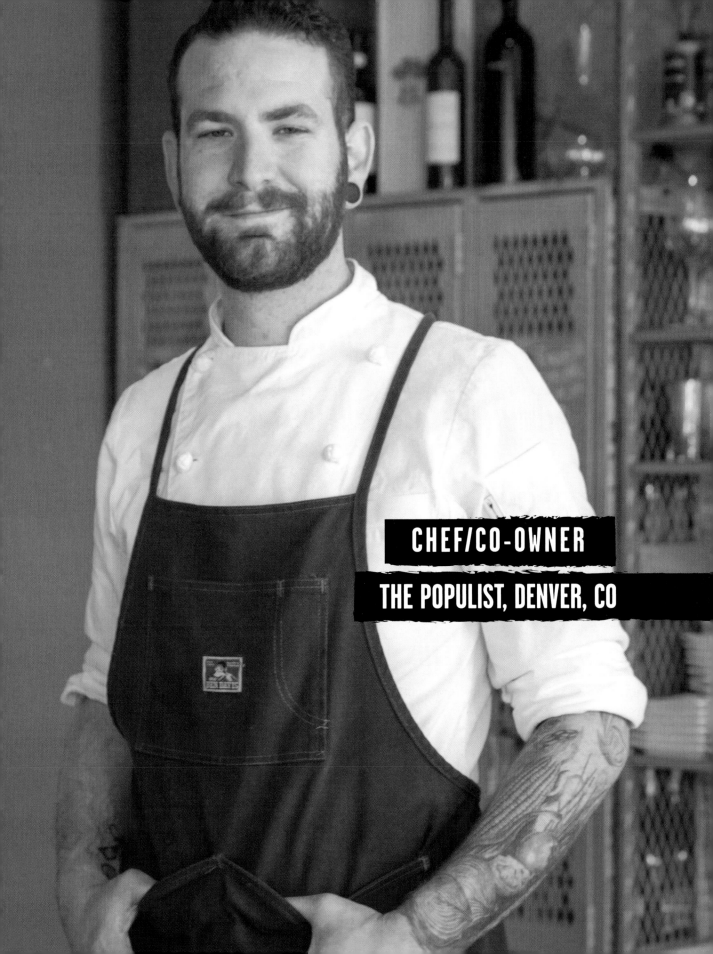

CHEF/CO-OWNER

THE POPULIST, DENVER, CO

After settling into Denver's culinary scene, Jonathan, his wife, and some friends began an underground supper club called Noble Swine. These dinners led him to Noah Price, who owned Crema Coffee House, a small coffee shop in the Five Points neighborhood in Denver. Noah's life-long involvement in the restaurant business and Jonathan's sense of Crema's potential led Jonathan to leave Root Down and partner with Noah. They built a kitchen in Crema and started turning out everything from bánh mi sandwiches to breakfast burritos. Crema's loyal, almost cultish, following led Jonathan and Noah to open a sit-down restaurant, the Populist.

A small-plate American restaurant with a seasonally influenced menu and nightly chef's tasting menu (a relic of Jonathan's Noble Swine dinners), the Populist opened to high expectations in November 2012. Soon after opening, local Colorado magazine *5280* named them as one of the top 10 new restaurants of 2012, and all signs pointed toward the restaurant being a great success.

Jonathan's culinary tattoos are the work of Karen Hall, the owner of Denver's Elemental Ink, who is working on a full sleeve of ingredients on his left arm. It's a long-term project that's based on a list he gave her that includes carrot, celery, onions, mushrooms, corn, and tomatoes. Much like his career, each new piece she adds is decided on as they go along. "It's grown pretty organically. Pun intended, I guess."

Following the vegetables up his arm (each drawn with the precision of nineteenth-century botany illustrations), Jonathan and Karen have topped the sleeve off with a primal cut roasted pig posed "pinup-style" on a platter with an apple in its mouth. Jonathan is open to other tattoos, but he has been working on his sleeve for over a year and a half, so for now he is focused on just one piece at a time. He says, "At this point I go in about once a quarter. It's not the cheapest hobby, but I don't plan on stopping."

Bacon and Egg

YIELDS APPROXIMATELY 2 CUPS, OR 8 SERVINGS

1 pound quality bacon
3 medium yellow onions, diced
1 cup sugar
½ cup sherry vinegar
Salt, to taste
Pepper, as needed
4 eggs
Splash of white vinegar
4 slices ciabatta bread
10 very thin slices lardo (available at many high-end delis)
Hot smoked paprika, to garnish
Thinly sliced scallion, to garnish

1 Cut bacon into lardons. In a cast-iron skillet, render slowly over medium heat until crisp, about 10 to 15 minutes. Remove from pan and drain off all but 2 tablespoons fat.

2 Add yellow onions to skillet and sweat in bacon fat over medium heat until translucent, about 5 to 7 minutes. Add the sugar and a pinch of salt and continue cooking for 10 minutes. Add sherry vinegar and bacon back to pan and continue cooking for roughly 90 minutes, or until liquid has reduced and mixture has caramelized and thickened. Adjust seasoning with salt and pepper as needed.

3 When jam is ready, gently poach eggs in simmering water with a splash of white vinegar. Meanwhile, toast ciabatta bread and top with paper-thin slices of lardo. Serve the egg on a bed of the jam with the lardo toast on the side. Add a touch of paprika to the egg and top with a slice or two of scallion. Serve immediately.

EXECUTIVE CHEF

FABBRICA, BROOKLYN, NY

MICHAEL BERARDINO

> "I'm very into the Kustom Kulture art that sprang up around the California hot rod scene in the late '50s, early '60s. Artists like Ed Roth, Robert Williams, Kenny Howard, Crumb."
>
> —Michael Berardino

MICHAEL BERARDINO started his culinary career in Detroit, Michigan. Starting as a dishwasher, he advanced his career the old-school way, by working his way up the kitchen ranks, learning every station along the way. After moving to New York City for the first time, he was exposed to a more traditional type of Italian cuisine—simple, rustic foods that grabbed his attention and remain his culinary passion to this day.

After working at a variety of positions in Ann Arbor, MI, and Boston, MA, where he continued to hone his Italian cooking skills, Michael eventually returned to NYC. He was hired as sous-chef at 'inoteca, the well-known Lower East Side wine bar, and began to work closely with owner Jason Denton and chef Eric Kleinman on their new fine-dining Italian concept, the now-closed Bar Milano. After leaving Bar Milano, he moved to dell'anima, a small Italian restaurant in the West Village where he worked closely with rising restaurateur star Joe Campanale. Michael and Joe worked hard to make dell'anima a restaurant industry hot spot by keeping the kitchen open late, and it worked. dell'anima was and still is one of the best places in the West Village to get great Italian food at 2:00 A.M.

Michael's tattoos reflect his Motor City roots, and he is covered in pinup girls and a hot rod motif. Michael says, "My first tattoo was of the dead man's hand, aces and eights, spades and clubs." As he continued to get ink, he found inspiration in Kustom Kulture, a name used to describe the group of modern-day admirers of the hotrod and custom car culture of the 1950s.

The bulk of Michael's work was done by fellow Kustom Kulture enthusiast Jeff Shea of Wholeshot Tattoo in Detroit. Michael says, "He would always be striping or screen printing when he wasn't tattooing. He's only doing custom work and wouldn't deal with flash pieces, so any time we would talk about doing a piece, there would be a discussion, he would draft something up, if we both liked it, we went with it. He's a very talented artist. I had seen someone with a relatively fresh piece he had done and knew I'd like his style."

And Michael does have his own sense of style, whether you're talking ink or food. Today, Michael continues his love of Italian cooking. Most recently as executive chef for Fabbrica, which is Italian for "the factory." The large industrial-looking restaurant in North Williamsburg, Brooklyn is his focus as he overhauls the kitchen and puts his own brand of traditional rustic Italian dishes on the menu. While Michael continues to make his mark helping restaurants establish themselves with authentic Italian cooking, he admits that opening his own place is likely in the near future.

After leaving dell'anima, Michael consulted with a few smaller Italian restaurants before taking the executive chef position in 2011 at the Cannibal. The small restaurant on East 29th, with a beer-centric bar and a focus on whole-animal cooking, gave Michael a chance to explore the world of craft beer and practice his butchery. Michael acted both as butcher as well as chef and reaped positive press from *The New York Times* and *The Wall Street Journal*. In 2012, he left the Cannibal, deciding he wanted to cook Italian food again, and became the executive chef of Angolo SoHo, a modern Italian restaurant in SoHo.

Malloreddus

SERVES 8–12

FOR BRINE:
½ teaspoon coriander
1 cardamom pod, crushed
1½ sprigs rosemary
¾ cup salt
⅓ cup sugar
2½ gallons water, divided

FOR MIREPOIX:
1 carrot
1 onion
3 stalks celery

FOR GOAT:
5 pounds goat shoulder and neck
1 carrot
1 onion
2 stalks celery
1 cup tomato paste
¼ cup plus 3 tablespoons olive oil
2 cups red wine
½ lemon
½ orange
2 red jalapeños
1 tablespoon rosemary
3 bay leaves
3 quarts water, to cover

FOR MALLOREDDUS:
2½ cups semolina flour
1½ cups 00 flour
1 cup hot water
½ teaspoon salt

TO COMPLETE:
Pecorino Romano, grated, for garnish
Extra-virgin olive oil, for garnish

NOTES FROM THE CHEF

"00 flour" is a very finely milled flour commonly used in Italy.

1 For Brine: Bruise the coriander, cardamom, and rosemary and combine with the salt and sugar in 1½ gallons of water. Bring to a boil to dissolve the sugar and salt. Back out the brine with remaining gallon of cold water.

2 For Mirepoix: Chop all ingredients into a small dice and combine. Set aside.

3 For Goat: Add the goat to the Brine, making sure that the meat is completely covered. Brine for 1 to 2 days covered in refrigerator. Remove the goat from the brine. Preheat oven to 325°F. Roughly cut all vegetables and place in a deep hotel pan. Cook the tomato paste in 3 tablespoons olive oil in a large sauté pan over medium heat until it develops a rusty color; then add the red wine. Leave the pan on medium heat and slowly reduce the wine by half, about 25 to 30 minutes; then transfer it to the hotel pan. Place the goat on the vegetables, add the citrus fruit, jalapeños, rosemary, and bay leaves to the pan, and then add 3 quarts of water to cover the vegetables. Cover and cook in oven for about 3 hours, or until tender. Remove from the oven and allow to rest uncovered at room temperature until cool; then cover and refrigerate overnight in the braising liquid.

4 The next morning, remove the goat from the cooking liquid. Pick all of the meat off of the bones. Strain the cooking liquid through a China cap and reserve. In a large rondeau over medium heat, warm ¼ cup olive oil. Add the Mirepoix to the rondeau and sweat until soft. Add the goat and cook for 10 minutes, stirring constantly. Add the braising liquid and lower the heat to maintain a light simmer. Cook for 45 minutes to an hour, or until tender.

5 For Malloreddus: Combine both flours, water, and salt in a bowl and mix by hand or with a mixer until a smooth, firm dough is formed. Cut the dough into a few pieces, wrap with plastic, and allow to rest for 15 minutes. Roll the dough into pencil-thick logs, cut those into 1" segments, and form Malloreddus with fingers or take the logs of dough and run them through a cavatelli maker.

6 To Complete: Bring a large pot of heavily salted water to a boil. Add the Malloreddus to the boiling water and stir vigorously. Cook the Malloreddus until tender, approximately 6 minutes. Drain the pasta, combine with the braised goat, and allow to simmer in the sauce for 1 to 2 minutes. Portion the pasta onto plates, and top with grated Pecorino Romano and a few drops of extra-virgin olive oil.

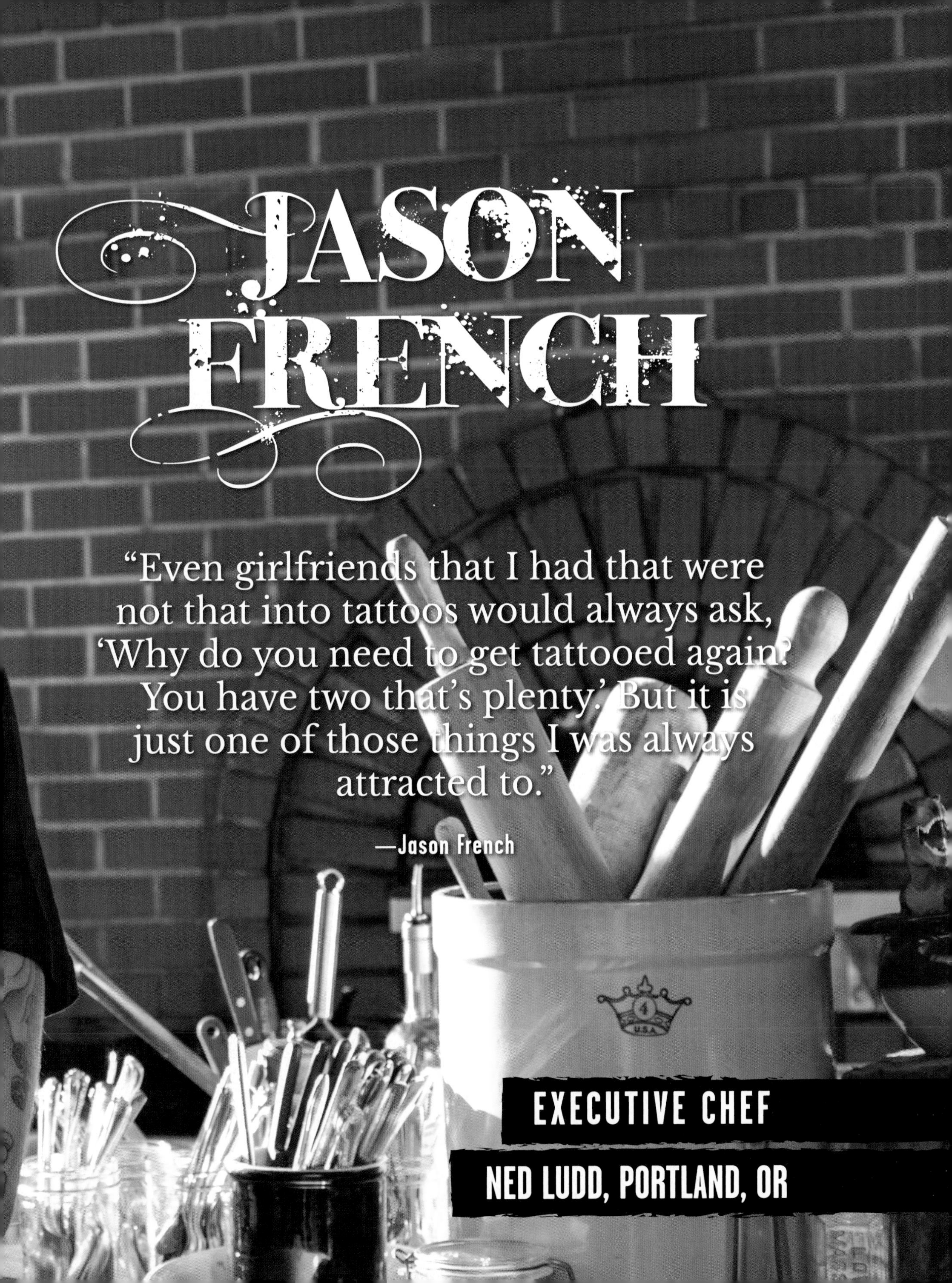

JASON FRENCH

"Even girlfriends that I had that were not that into tattoos would always ask, 'Why do you need to get tattooed again? You have two that's plenty.' But it is just one of those things I was always attracted to."

—Jason French

EXECUTIVE CHEF

NED LUDD, PORTLAND, OR

JASON FRENCH took a long road to owning his own restaurant in Portland, OR. After high school, this East Coast native found himself desiring to explore the western United States and, in 1988 he found himself in Telluride, CO, where he worked in his first restaurant job washing dishes. This was soon followed by a bakery gig. After some time in Taos, he returned east for college, where he focused on liberal arts at Skidmore College in Sartoga Springs, NY, all the while working in restaurants for money. Jason found the pace, excitement, and even the stress and the physicality of working in a kitchen fit him well. in 1996 Jason enrolled in culinary school in at L'Academie de Cuisine in Gaithersburg, MD, and went on to work in the Washington, D.C., area, honing his skills by working at Vidalia, a nationally recognized modern American cuisine restaurant under Jeffrey Buben.

Over the years, Jason has worked a variety of culinary jobs, doing everything from catering to selling wine and cheese to teaching culinary school in Boulder, CO. Finally, in early 2000s, Jason began looking for a place to open his own restaurant and decided on Portland, Oregon. The community of local farmers and the opportunity to work in a producing area not tied to the four seasons made it a nearly irresistible place to relocate. He speaks of his adopted home with love: "The intensity of the farming and the wine community and the cheese makers . . . the producers themselves and the fact that there are mountains, beautiful orchards, and the coastline with amazing seafood and oysters. All that cemented for me finding a home where I would be satisfied as a chef."

In Portland, Jason worked for several notable Portland chefs who influenced his cooking style along the way. He worked with Chef Vito Dilullo at Cafe Mingo, where despite not getting along that well with Vito he admired his ability to create a dish and for the care and focus of how he ran a kitchen. He also worked with Morgan Brownlow (now co-owner of Tails and Trotters) at Clarklewis, who impressed him and influenced him through his sheer cooking talent.

When Jason finally opened his restaurant Ned Ludd in 2008 he wanted it to embody all the principles of seasonal and locally sourced cooking that drew him to Portland in the first place. Ned Ludd offers seasonal menus with dishes sourced from artisanal local producers from the Northwest and West Coast areas. The restaurant also has no gas line, instead cooking everything from a wood fired oven or in a smoker he has behind the restaurant.

Jason sees a kitchen's pain and pleasure principle as part and parcel of the heightened sense of pain involved in getting tattooed. His brother once asked him, "How can you call it art or a craft when all they're doing is putting a picture on you and jamming it with ink? It's like tracing." Jason identifies it as an art form, much like cooking—an effort to constantly push yourself to do better. Jason admits that Portland's tattoo culture is one of the things that ultimately attracted him to the Pacific Northwest. He'd gotten a lot of tattoos when he was living in New Mexico and regularly stopped by parlors to look at local artists' work, but he rarely returned to them. Not so in Oregon. Atlas Tattoo in Portland became the rare parlor he regularly visits. The shop has drawn in artists from around the city, and Jason describes it as a "phenomenal all-around shop, whatever style you're into." A combination of Atlas artists has inked both his arms, Lewis Hess has done his full right arm, a traditional Japanese style tattoo with falling cherry blossoms. The left arm is a combination of Dan Gilsdorf, Jerry Ware, and Cheyenne Sawyer and is a black and white medley of items that reflect Jason's culinary interests from a rooster, a pig, and a chain of garlic to a meat grinder and green beans. Jason is currently designing a large chest piece with another Atlas artist, Corey Crowley.

One of Jason's most prominent tattoos is a trio of stars that represent the Michelin stars, an ultimate goal of quality that Jason sought when he was coming up. "The three stars are my ever-humbling quest," he says. "It's funny too now, because I don't really care about any of that, but it's always important to know where you came from and what inspired you to start your career. To a lot of people it's like, 'well this is my job. It's the only thing I know.'" To that Jason says, "Wow, I'm sorry. This is a really brutal industry. . . . You don't know why you're doing it?"

Pastured Pork, Sauerkraut, and Whey Sauce

SERVES 4

FOR SAUERKRAUT:
2 heads cabbage
Salt
3 bay leaves
6 whole juniper berries
1 tablespoon caraway seeds

FOR PORK BRINE:
2 quarts water
½ cup sugar
½ cup salt
1 cup apple cider
1 cup dry white wine
2 cinnamon sticks
1 tablespoon ground black pepper
4 bay leaves
1 bunch thyme
1 onion, sliced

FOR PORK BELLY AND RIBS:
2 pounds pork belly, skinned and slightly
    scored
1 rack of spare ribs
2 cups apple cider
1 bunch thyme

FOR SPICED PORK SAUSAGE:
Salt, to taste
6 cloves garlic
1 teaspoon brown mustard seed
1 teaspoon ground ginger
1 tablespoon caraway seed
2 teaspoons white pepper
2 teaspoons coriander seed
3 tablespoons winter savory, stemmed
2 pounds pork trim and fatback
½ cup heavy cream
Cleaned pork casing

1 **For Sauerkraut:** Pack the cabbage into a ceramic jar in three layers, seasoning each layer with salt, a bay leaf, 2 juniper berries, and a sprinkling of caraway seeds. When done, press down the ingredients and then insert a heavy-duty trash bag the way you would in a garbage can with the top open and the excess folded back down around the side. Then fill the trash bag with water so it is pressing down on the ingredients and against the sides so the surface is not exposed to air. Allow to sit out for several days or until the juices and cabbage ferment.

2 **For Pork Brine:** Place all the ingredients in a pot and bring to a boil. Simmer uncovered on low heat for 45 minutes. Remove from heat and allow to cool.

3 **For Pork Belly and Ribs:** Place the belly and ribs in Pork Brine for one week covered in the refrigerator. Remove both belly and ribs from the brine. Preheat oven to 280°F. Braise pork belly in a roasting pan with cider and thyme, making sure the cider fully covers the belly. Cover and cook for 4 to 6 hours until fully tender. Hot smoke ribs for 8 hours at 165°F in your choice of smoking apparatus.

4 **For Spiced Pork Sausage:** Mix the salt, garlic, spices, and pork together and allow to marinate covered in the refrigerator overnight. Grind the sausage twice on a large die and then on the next smallest one. Whip lightly and add the cream to emulsify. Pump into cleaned pork casing and twist into 4 sausages.

NOTES FROM THE CHEF

You can also make the sauerkraut over several months in your refrigerator. Check daily and adjust seasoning.

FOR WHEY SAUCE:

1 gallon goat's whey
1 quart cream
3 bay leaves
Salt, to taste

TO COMPLETE:

2 cups stock, cider, and/or wine
Coarse sea salt, to garnish
Chives, to garnish
Parsley, to garnish

5 **For Whey Sauce:** Reduce the whey by ¾ in a saucepan over medium heat, approximately 30 minutes. The sugars will caramelize, and it should look broken and funky. Add the cream, some salt, and the bay leaves and allow to reduce a few minutes further until saucy. Remove from heat.

6 **To Complete:** Heat the Spiced Pork Sausages and Ribs in the Sauerkraut in a skillet on medium heat for 20 to 30 minutes, adding liquid in the form of stock, cider, wine, or all three. Roast the belly in the oven on a baking sheet on high heat until well browned and crispy. Heat the whey sauce until warm but not boiling in a sauce pan. Place the Sauerkraut in the center of the plate and top with all of the pork. Spoon the Whey Sauce over the meat and garnish with coarse sea salt, chives, and parsley. Enjoy with friends and a great bottle of Riesling!

KEITH FULLER

"I was in the punk rock scene and very rebellious as a kid, so since I was 14, I wanted to be completely covered head to toe."

—Keith Fuller

CO-OWNER/CHEF

ROOT 174, PITTSBURGH, PA

KEITH FULLER was born in Wilmington, Delaware, but began his culinary career in his hometown of Hudson, Ohio, a small town about a thirty-minute drive south of Cleveland. Starting at age fifteen, he took a job at a McDonald's but quit after only three weeks, opting instead to work in a family-run restaurant called Yours Truly. There, Keith worked the stove for five years through high school and into his time at Rice University, where he started a two-year degree in polymer science but dropped out after the first year. Keith jokes, "Basically *Tony Hawk Pro Skate* and *Legend of Zelda* came out at the same time so what was I to do?" Needing to figure out what to do next, Keith moved to Dayton, OH, and begged his way into the kitchen of L'Auberge. The white tablecloth, fine-dining French restaurant was opened in 1979 and was *Mobil* (now *Forbes*) Guide's longest-running four-star eatery in Ohio until it closed its doors in 2012. Keith says, "the place was basically 1970s food, suit and jacket, Dover sole done tableside. I actually love that stuff, but the restaurant was dated and Dayton was a dying town." Despite L'Auberge's dated style, it was where Keith learned his foundations for French cooking.

In 2000, after a year there at L'Auberge, Keith moved to Philadelphia, where he joined the team at Jake's and Cooper's Wine Bar, a four-star restaurant focusing on American cuisine. Keith originally thought that he would also go to culinary school while in Philadelphia, but the chef at Jake's convinced him he was better off just learning in the kitchen and not spending the $40,000 on school. Keith spent six years at Jake's, moving from line cook to saucier and eventually taking a sort of "junior sous-chef" position where he where he filled in for any of the head chefs when they weren't available. While he was there, Jake's was continually honored as one of the top dining destinations in the city, having the "Best Brunch" and "Best Crab Cakes" as recognized by *Philadelphia* magazine.

While Keith was working at Jake's he spent a few months living in a house in Delaware with the members of the punk band Boysetsfire. The large house was the stage for many big parties with many members of the post-hardcore/punk scene, and even after moving out, Keith frequently returned for the blowouts. After they had to give up their lease in 2003, they threw one last bash where they dragged all their belongings into the yard and lit a huge bonfire. The cops were eventually called but not before Keith blew out his knee during the ruckus. That same year, all the people who lived in the house got tattoos of praying, which are now known as the "Big House" tattoos. Keith, a lover of religious art who is not particularly religious, got Darth Vader prayer hands.

While he had a great time in Dayton, in 2005 Keith was recruited to be the opening executive sous-chef of Six Penn Kitchen, an open-kitchen restaurant that focused on American comfort food prepared well but served in a casual setting. The restaurant was in Pittsburgh, PA, and Keith packed up his bags and moved. When the executive chef moved to Brooklyn in 2008, Keith took over as executive chef. He stayed in this position for more than three years and then decided it was time to try to open his own restaurant. However, the road to fulfilling this dream wasn't easy.

Keith found a location, but also found that all the people who told him they wanted to invest suddenly didn't have any money. As he asked around, a mutual friend from Pittsburgh told him that Patrick Bollinger, the drummer of punk rock band Anti-Flag, was interested in opening a place. Keith had met Patrick year prior at the parties at the Boysetsfire house in Delaware, and they soon met for a meeting to discuss their mutual desire to open a place. Keith says, "Patrick is great. He is straight-edge and very together." Patrick agreed to back Keith, and in 2011 they opened Root 174 in Pittsburgh, PA.

Root 174 takes its name from the square root of the neighborhood's two zip codes. There, Keith does what he calls "modern rustic" food, where he focuses on taking what he thinks most people see as waste or leftover parts and turning them into gourmet dishes. He says, "Shit you throw away can make a great meal." Since opening the restaurant, Keith has become an area favorite and received a great review in 2011 from *Pittsburgh Magazine*, prompting Restaurant Critic Valentina to write "Imagine a restaurant where you might fight over the last Brussels sprout (this happened to me) . . . "The following year in 2012 *Pittsburgh Magazine* honored them again naming them one of the top 25 restaurants of Pittsburgh. Keith was even interviewed on CNN for one of his more adventurous dishes, swordfish fish marrow; his was one of only two restaurants in the United States serving it at the time.

Keith isn't just adventurous when it comes to cooking. He got his first tattoo the day he turned eighteen, a tribal arm band around his right arm. Over the next three years, he got a lot more ink, and by the time he was twenty-one, he felt he was ready to ink up his neck and knuckles. He laughs, "I kind of wanted to fuck myself and see how far I could get on just my personality and charm." He got a sacred heart on the center of his neck with a fire-themed sparrow on the left side of his neck and an ice-themed sparrow on the right to complement it, but when it came time to do his knuckles, he had second thoughts. He made several appointments to get his knuckles done but kept changing his mind at the last minute. Finally, the artist told Keith that no one was going to be looking at his hands because everyone would already be staring at his neck. Keith agreed and finally got "GAME NERD" tattooed across his knuckles. This may seem out of character, but while much of Keith's ink is inspired by religious art, his body also showcases his love of games and science. He even tends to combine these two ideas in his tattoos. For example, he has zombie Pikachu and Ash Ketchum from the game *Pokémon* on his chest and a Darth Vader sacred heart on his left arm. In 2010, he got a portrait of actor Steve Buscemi as Darth Vader on the back of his left leg. After posting a picture of it to ugliesttattoos.com, the photo received a ton of notice and was the number one viral photograph of 2010 on Geekologie's website.

Keith continues to collect ink, getting the Root 174 logo behind his left ear, and he is now working to do a cover-up piece of an octopus and shipwreck on his right arm, but the original dark band was tattooed so heavily that it is raised and has been a difficult piece to cover. Keith is currently focused on continuing to run Root 174, spending more time with his wife, and teaching his son how to play all the games he loves.

Pork Belly, Scallops, and Reindeer Lichen, with an Elderberry Gastrique

This recipe was served at one of Keith's CRUX dinners, a pop-up dinner on November 1, 2012, at a home in Lincoln Park, Chicago, where Keith Fuller and Brandon Baltzley (see entry in Part 4) cooked together for eleven guests.

YIELDS 35–40 SERVINGS

FOR PORK BELLY:
250 grams salt
100 grams sugar
10 grams mustard seed
20 grams Frantoia extra-virgin olive oil
1 medium red onion
1 medium carrot
1 celery stalk
1 5-pound pork belly
8–10 cups rendered fatback or lard
    (enough to cover the belly fully in a
    roasting pan)

FOR SCALLOPS:
40 scallops

FOR ELDERBERRY GASTRIQUE:
50 grams water
250 grams sugar
100 grams white wine vinegar
200 grams St. Germain liqueur

FOR REINDEER LICHEN:
1 pound Reindeer lichen (also known as
    Caribou Moss)
1 pound unsalted butter
Salt, to taste

TO COMPLETE:
1 stick butter
4 chamomile flowers, for garnish

1 **For Pork Belly:** Process all ingredients, other than the belly and lard, in a food processor. Rub belly in cure and wrap tightly in plastic wrap. Refrigerate for 4 days. Cut the belly in half perpendicularly, wash well in cold water, and pat dry. Tie belly in cheesecloth; then submerge in warm, rendered fat inside a roasting pan. Cook in a 275°F oven for 4 to 5 hours. Remove pan from oven and save 2 cups of the pork fat for assembly later. Remove cheesecloth carefully from fat while still warm. Press overnight between two half-sheet pans underneath four boxes of Diamond Crystal Kosher Salt. Cut into 2" × 2" cubes.

2 **For Scallops:** Shuck. Put scallops in a 1.5 percent salt brine for 45 minutes. Remove, pat dry, and refrigerate for 4 hours, uncovered.

NOTES FROM THE CHEF

Only purchase live, in the shell scallops.

3 **For Elderberry Gastrique:** Bring water and sugar up to a clear caramel in a sauté pan over medium heat, about 5–10 minutes. Remove from heat and add vinegar and St. Germain. Cook over medium heat until it coats the back of a spoon. Add St. Germain to taste at the end for flavor and viscosity adjustments.

4 **For Reindeer Lichen:** Soak lichen in cold water and agitate vigorously. Remove when all debris is picked out of the crevices. Lay between a lot of paper towels and apply pressure to remove all water. Heat butter until melted and drizzle over lichen. Massage butter all over lichen. Season with salt and bake in a 325°F oven for 15 to 25 minutes or until crispy.

NOTES FROM THE CHEF

Our lichen comes from a forager in Maine.

5 **To Complete:** Sear Scallops over medium heat in a sauté pan. Baste Scallops in butter, cooking mostly on one side. Sear Pork over medium-high heat in a separate pan. Baste Pork in its own fat that was saved from the baking process while cooking. Plate Elderberry Gastrique on bottom of plate. Arrange Scallops, Pork, and Reindeer Lichen how you like. Garnish with crushed chamomile flowers on top.

EXECUTIVE CHEF

VERMILION, ALEXANDRIA, VA

WILL MORRIS

"Find a place that you're comfortable with. . . . If you don't feel comfortable, even at the moment of getting tattooed, just walk away. Think about it, because it's there. They're not going away."

—Will Morris

WILL MORRIS can thank an unreliable babysitter for his passion for cooking. When he was only ten years old, his parents had dinner reservations at French chef Jean-Louis Palladin's restaurant, Palladin. Jean-Louis, who passed away in 2001, was at the top of his field and mentored some of today's most famous French chefs, including Eric Ripert of Le Bernardin; Daniel Boulud of Daniel; Christian Delouvrier of Lespinasse; and Sylvain Portay, formerly of Le Cirque and now at the Ritz-Carlton in San Francisco. Will's parents had been looking forward to that dinner, and when the babysitter canceled at the last minute, they just brought Will along. He was fascinated. "I fell in love with everything . . . I can still remember the table and

hearing the chef in the back screaming. All of a sudden, he came through the doors and [there's] this big tall French guy with a big head of hair. Boom, I was in love with it."

In his teenage years, Will worked at chain fast food restaurants and was still entertaining the idea of going to university, but eventually he decided that if he was going to become a chef as a career, he needed to do it at a certain level. Refocused on his goal of becoming a chef, he took classes to supplement what he learned on the job and threw himself into cooking with a new passion. He attributes his first big break to his job at the Tower

Club, a private club in Vienna, VA. There, he met Ciaran Devlin, the executive chef and his first great mentor. Will says, "I love him to death and still keep in touch with him, but he kicked my ass. I was so scared of him and respect him so much." As Will puts it, Ciaran was not afraid to show his displeasure, but at the same time took Will under his wing and taught him much of his restaurant foundations.

"From there, [Will] kept on pushing and pushing." Working in New York and abroad, he eventually returned to the D.C. area and was able to interview with Michael Mina, the famed chef who has built a restaurant group that spans eight states and more than twenty restaurants. Applying for a position at his signature steak house, Bourbon Steak, this interview was the one time that Will was truly nervous about his tattoos. He says, "I was in a fresh pressed suit, and I walk in there and the first thing he says is, let me see your hand. I was like, ah shit, I'm not going to get this job." Michael instead told him how awesome his tattoos were, and also gave him the job. Will has a great deal of respect for Michael and says, "You get used to it, working for him over the years, but it's Michael Mina. It's like . . . wow." During his time at Bourbon Steak, Will was inspired by how much Michael seemed to genuinely care about each person that worked for him. He drove them to work hard, but no harder than himself, who was always working.

When he was sixteen, Will got his first tattoo, a dragon that he placed on his thigh so it would be easier to hide from his parents. His father, a former marine, had gotten several tattoos during his time in the service, but had them removed. When Will's parents finally saw his dragon tattoo years later, he remembers being surprised that they weren't as upset as he thought, which was a good thing because Will now estimates that about 60 percent of his body is covered in ink.

His left arm is covered in a full sleeve of a traditional Japanese-style dragon that wraps around his arm. His right arm showcases a collection of pieces he got over the years that are part of his life's journey or things he gets excited about. He has a pig with a ribbon that says "bacon" around it, as he hopes to one day own a ranch and thinks it would be great to have a pig named Bacon there. Around his wrist are stars to represent the Michelin stars that were awarded to Nobu (one star), Le Manoir (two stars), and Oak Room (three stars), all restaurants Will staged (interned) at when first starting his career. On his left bicep are five diamonds, the highest award given by the AAA (American Auto Association) and a reminder to always strive for excellence. He also has a chupacabra, the mythical beast of Mexico, as an ode to all the Central American kitchen staff he has worked with in the restaurant business. One of his most noticeable tattoos though is also one that he likes to talk about the least. Across his hands are the words "Cancer" and "Free." In 2008, he had a difficult fight with cancer and got the tattoos the day he got his all clear.

Will has had most of his ink done in D.C. at a shop called Tattoo Paradise. The shop has an ongoing guest artist program, and it was there that Will met and befriended

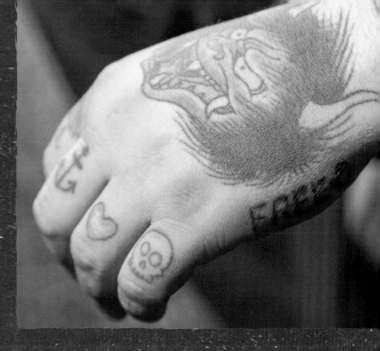

Grant Cobb, a highly regarded artist based in L.A. Grant has done some of the pieces on Will's arm, but it's the full back piece of the Virgin Mary that Will is most proud of. Grant and Will worked a long time on just what to do and how to specialize it, eventually deciding to make her dress in a Gucci print. Will says, "I thought, well the pope wears Prada, why can't she wear Gucci?" The word "Sacrifice" is scrolled across his neck above the Virgin Mary, but it was actually done years before. He says, "It's fitting at the top of the virgin, but wasn't planned." In 2008, Will got his hands and knuckles tattooed with a collection of symbols. The two skulls represent him and his brother, the heart his mother, and the crown his father. The other small symbols are ones that are meaningful to him. The decision to tattoo his knuckles, the same tattoos he was so nervous about during his interview with Michael Mina, took him a while to make. "At that point, people look at you differently. If you don't have anything on your hands or fingers, you can really disguise it. . . . But when you get your hands, then you get the funny looks and the, what are you going to do when you get older? Well, I'm doing the job I want to do and I do fairly well for myself."

Will now works as executive chef for Vermilion, where he took over at the end of 2012. The high-end modern American restaurant is just outside D.C. in Alexandria, VA, and is part of the Neighborhood Restaurant Group that owns several restaurants around the D.C. area. Will hasn't been tattooed for over a year now, a long time for him. But he still thinks he will probably get more. He jokes, "It's the one good thing about this business; you get fatter and your skin stretches, and so you have more room for tattoos."

> "BUT WHEN YOU GET YOUR HANDS [TATTOOED], THEN YOU GET THE FUNNY LOOKS AND THE, WHAT ARE YOU GOING TO DO WHEN YOU GET OLDER? WELL, I'M DOING THE JOB I WANT TO DO AND I DO FAIRLY WELL FOR MYSELF."

Crispy Pork Belly with Littleneck Clams and Trumpet Royale Mushrooms

FOR PORK BRINE:
YIELDS 2 LITERS

2 pieces star anise
0.5 tablespoon allspice
.5 cinnamon stick
2 teaspoons juniper berry
1 teaspoon whole cloves
1 tablespoon chopped thyme
1 tablespoon chopped rosemary
1 tablespoon chopped sage
0.5 tablespoon ground black peppercorns
55 grams salt
25 grams Sel Rose curing salt
1.2 liters water
0.4 liters apple cider, added when cold
0.4 liters hard cider, added when cold
1 Granny Smith apples, split in half

FOR PORK BELLY BRAISING LIQUID:

100 grams sliced shallot
100 grams julienned onion
4 grams toasted coriander
6 grams toasted whole black peppercorns
1 bay leaf
0.25 garlic head, split
12 grams parsley stems
12 grams thyme
1 liter apple cider
1 liter chicken stock
60 milliliters sherry vinegar

FOR CELERIAC PURÉE:

1000 grams celeriac
200 grams heavy cream
175 grams cold butter
Kosher salt, to taste

1 **For Pork Brine:** Toast all spices and mix with salt and Sel Rose. Add water to a large pot, add spice mix, and bring to a boil to ensure saturation; remove from heat. Chill rapidly in ice bath. Once cool, add cider, hard cider, and Granny Smith apples.

2 **For Pork Belly Braising Liquid:** Combine all ingredients in a large, ovensafe pot and bring to a boil. Remove from heat once it has come to a boil and set aside for further use.

3 **For Celeriac Purée:** Peel celeriac and dice to uniform size. In a heavy-bottomed pot on medium-high heat, sweat the celeriac. No color! Add heavy cream and butter. Cook slowly until celeriac is cooked tender to the touch and cooked through, about 5 minutes. Strain celeriac, making sure to save liquid in separate container. Blend celeriac in a blender until smooth and velvety, adding cooking liquid if needed. Season to taste with salt.

4 **For Pork Jus:** Preheat oven to 350°F. Roast bones in roasting pan uncovered in oven until golden brown. Reserve fat that comes off of bones. In stockpot, use reserved fat with the carrots, celery, and onions and cook on low heat until lightly golden. Deglaze pot with white wine and reduce almost completely. Add veal stock, onion brûlée, and bones. Cook until sauce thickens, about 10 minutes, and strain through a chinois. Cool rapidly in ice bath.

5 **For Clams:** In a large-size sauté pan over medium-high heat, sweat minced shallots until translucent. Add clams and cook for about 1 minute. Toss in mushrooms and let cook for 1 to 2 minutes. Deglaze pan with a touch of white wine and place lid over the pan until clams begin to open. Once clams start to open, remove them from pan. Add Pork Jus to pan and bring just to a boil. Remove from heat and finish Pork Jus sauce with fresh herbs and a of cold butter. Whisk until emulsified.

6 **For Crispy Pork Belly:** Soak raw pork belly for 24 hours in Pork Brine in refrigerator. Remove, pat dry, and keep in refrigerator until you are ready to use it. To cook belly, sear it in a large skillet over medium-high heat, skin-side down, until lightly caramelized, about 1 minute. Preheat oven to 300°F.

FOR PORK JUS:

2 kilograms roasted pork bones
80 grams carrots
150 grams chopped celery
150 grams chopped onion
150 milliliters white wine
0.5 liters veal stock
330 grams onion brûlée

FOR CLAMS:

500 grams minced shallots
50 littleneck clams, scrubbed and purged
225 grams trumpet royale mushrooms,
    sliced on the bias
200 milliliters white wine
0.5 liters Pork Jus
3 tablespoons cold butter

FOR CRISPY PORK BELLY:

1000-gram pork belly
2 liters Pork Brine
1–2 liters Pork Braising Liquid
1 bunch thyme

7 Place belly in braising liquid and cook, covered, slowly in oven about 3 hours, until pork is tender but still holds together. Once fully cooked, remove from oven and let cool down in liquid, so as to not dry out. Place cooled pork in between two sheet pans and press to have a piece with even thickness. Portion out squares at 85 grams each. Note: To lessen cooking time the day of serving, the previous steps can be done in advance and the belly can be kept for 2 to 3 days wrapped in plastic in the refrigerator.

8 Preheat oven to 375°F. Sear pork belly in a medium sauté pan over medium-high heat, skin-side down, until crisp. In a small roasting pan, lay a bed of thyme. Remove pork belly from sauté pan and place skin side up on bed of thyme. Place in oven and cook uncovered, until warm throughout and skin is crispy.

9 **To Complete:** While pork is in the oven, heat celeriac in small pot, thinning it out with cream if needed. It should have a light and fluffy texture to it. Place 45 milliliters of Celeriac Purée on the inner edge of a plate and drag a spoon through it to create a swoosh following the curve of plate. Randomly place 5 Clams and glazed mushrooms along the Celeriac Purée. Place Crispy Pork Belly, crisp-skin-side up, on the rest of the plate. Using the Pork Jus, sauce around the pork. Serve immediately.

PART 2
FINNED

TONY MARCIANTE

"I figured I might not be a chef forever, but it has been a huge part of my life and I would never regret any tattoo I got."

—Tony Marciante

BORN IN MILAN, ITALY, Tony Marciante moved to Bethesda, Maryland, when he was four. He started his restaurant career at a seafood restaurant called O'Donnell's Sea Grill in Washington, D.C., washing dishes, and by the time he was twenty-two, he had worked at many restaurants, honing his skills and taking on challenges, and even had a partnership in a restaurant. Tony says, "I believe that as my father wisely told me, 'learn everything, that way no one's got you by the short strings.'. . . I've cleaned out grease traps, been a waiter, busser, bar back, bartender, GM, executive chef, line cook, etc. . . . " He adds, "I would almost *demand* that anyone planning to own a restaurant one day plan to work in every position. As well, many chefs I know aren't very front of house savvy or even comfortable. A chef today needs to be a business person first, and a creative type second."

At the age of twenty-six, Tony moved to Charlotte, North Carolina, where he opened two restaurants with friends, which they sold a few years later. Tony then went back to Bethesda to head up McCormick & Schmick's, a seafood and steak restaurant, as executive chef. In 2007, after eight years at McCormick and Schmick's, he opened Chef Tony's. Tony envisioned a home to locals, a relaxed setting for business dinners, and a spot for great quality seafood, and that's exactly what Chef Tony's is. Since opening, the restaurant has been featured on Channel 9 locally, on CNN nationally, and in several trade magazines.

Tony got his first tattoo—Italian and American flags inked beside his name—in his early twenties when he was in Miami on vacation with a few friends. The tattoos are a tribute to his heritage. "It went over really well with the parents," Tony says sarcastically. Several years later, he commissioned Miami-based artist La Ron Burke to do a back piece inspired by Roger Blachon's *The Kitchen*,

a painting depicting a caricature-like view of the many different chaotic happenings in a busy kitchen. A print of the painting hung in the office of a restaurant he worked at in Baltimore. Tony liked it so much he eventually got a version of the painting inked across nearly his entire back. Tony combined the painting with his love of hip hop by adding the words "Chef Life" in true Tupac style above the painting across his shoulders. He says, "It pretty much represents my daily life, not as much literally, but every day is just a humongous mishmash of events, phone calls, e-mails, prepping, line cooking, guest interactions, and such." The entire piece took more than twenty hours to complete. Tony says, "It's funny because most people who know me, like my staff, don't think I have any tattoos because I don't have any visible ink. Then when they find out that I have a tattoo and ask to see it, I'm like yeah, here you go . . . boom."

Today, Tony's commitment to his craft is unwavering. He continues to delight the palates of his diners and to teach and inspire upcoming chefs. He is taking on more challenges, developing a line of bottled sauces and online cooking lessons, as well as online training for people who plan to open restaurants. He says, "Another location of Chef Tony's would be great as I get investors. We'll just have to see what God has planned out for me. . . . " Tony hasn't been inked in five years, but there is definitely more to come, maybe something visible this time on his arms.

"IT'S FUNNY BECAUSE MOST PEOPLE WHO KNOW ME, LIKE MY STAFF, DON'T THINK I HAVE ANY TATTOOS BECAUSE I DON'T HAVE ANY VISIBLE INK. THEN WHEN THEY FIND OUT THAT I HAVE A TATTOO AND ASK TO SEE IT, I'M LIKE YEAH, HERE YOU GO . . . BOOM."

Pan-Seared Diver Scallops with Seasonal Vegetables and Crispy Sweet Potatoes

Tony says, "In my restaurant, the results are from quality ingredients, not over-the-top presentations or overthought flavor combinations. 'Rustic gourmet' is what I like to call my style. For this dish, you'll need to buy excellent 'dry pack' scallops from a quality fishmonger to make sure it tastes its best."

FOR BASIL OIL:
10–14 basil leaves, fresh
2 cups olive oil
1 teaspoon salt
Pinch of red pepper flakes
1 bunch fresh parsley (only curly top part)

FOR SIMPLE GARLIC MASHED POTATOES:
2 cups heavy cream
1 teaspoon chopped garlic
Salt and pepper, to taste
2 tablespoons butter
2 tablespoons chopped parsley and/or green onion
2 pounds red potatoes, quartered

FOR CRISPY SWEET POTATOES:
1 cup shredded sweet potatoes (matchstick size is best)
Oil, for frying (you want to have about 2" of oil in the pan, or use deep fryer if possible)
Salt and pepper, to taste
½ tablespoon honey
Pinch of ground cumin

FOR VEGETABLES:
½ cup zucchini
½ cup carrots
½ cup potatoes
½ cup sweet potatoes
1 cup fresh spinach
1 tablespoon olive oil or butter
Salt and pepper, to taste

FOR SCALLOPS:
1 tablespoon vegetable oil/olive oil blend
8 (U-10, under 10 per pound) scallops
Salt and pepper, to taste

1 **For Basil Oil:** In a blender (Vitamix works best) or using an immersion blender, combine all ingredients and blend on medium-high for 2 minutes until puréed. Oil may look cloudy but will settle over time. Keep refrigerated until ready to use. Allow to come to room temperature before using.

2 **For Simple Garlic Mashed Potatoes:** In a small pot over medium heat, heat up cream, garlic, salt and pepper to taste, and butter. Once bubbling gently, turn off heat and add parsley and/or green onion. Fill a large pot with cold, salted water and add quartered potatoes. Boil until fork-tender; then drain. Put back in cooking vessel and pour cream-garlic mixture on top. Mash with either a fork or potato masher until just combined. Overmashing will tend to produce "sticky" mashed potatoes instead of fluffy and nice ones. Leave some chunks in the mix and check seasoning. Keep warm on stovetop or in oven.

3 **For Crispy Sweet Potatoes:** Shred sweet potatoes using a mandoline slicer (can buy a cheap one at an Asian grocery store) and soak in water for 30 minutes. Add 2" of oil to deep pot and heat to 350°F. Fry in batches, until crispy, about 5 minutes. Sprinkle with salt and pepper as they come out of fryer; then drizzle with honey and top with a pinch of ground cumin. Set aside.

4 **For Vegetables:** Julienne vegetables and sauté uncovered in a sauté pan with olive oil or butter for approximately 2 minutes. Season to taste with salt and pepper. Cook until vegetables are just wilted, approximately 3 to 4 minutes.

5 **For Scallops:** Heat an aluminum sauté pan over high heat; then drizzle vegetable oil/olive oil blend into the pan. Season scallops very lightly with salt and pepper to taste (they have natural salt content). Lay scallops in pan (you should hear sizzling) and cook approximately 2 minutes, until caramelized. Then flip over, cook for another 2 minutes or so, turn off heat, and begin plating. This will give you a nice "medium" doneness. Great scallops like these should not be overcooked!

6 **To Complete:** Plate your Simple Garlic Mashed Potatoes in a line down the middle of the plate, topping with the seared Scallops. Add two mounds of sautéed Vegetables and top Scallops with the Crispy Sweet Potatoes. Drizzle Basil Oil around outside of plate, in a circular fashion, to finish the presentation.

NOTES FROM THE CHEF

While the Crispy Sweet Potatoes will be delicious made on your stovetop, they're absolutely amazing when done in a deep fryer. Try it this way if you have one available.

JUSTIN WARNER

"All mayo everything."

—Justin Warner

JUSTIN WARNER is a native of Hagerstown, Maryland, and has had a different road than most in becoming a chef. With no formal training as chef, most of Justin's restaurant experience was working the front of house. When Justin came to New York he eventually found himself working as a dinning captain at the Modern. The Modern is a Michelin star restaurant located in the Museum of Modern Art owned by famed NY restaurateur Danny Meyer. Working in the dining room Justin met his future business partners George McNeese and Luke Jackson.

In 2010 Justin competed on *24-Hour Restaurant Battle* in August 2010 with his then-girlfriend J.J. Pyle. They won the episode with their brunch restaurant concept, but never opened it. Instead, Justin along with George and Luke teamed up with local Brooklyn artist Perry Gargano

and opened Do or Dine in 2011. Far from the wealthy elite of midtown scene, they opened the restaurant in a Brooklyn neighborhood known as Bedford-Stuyvesant or "Bed-Stuy," a neighborhood made famous by Spike Lee films and countless rap lyric references. The neighborhood was referenced in the film *Notorious*, where The Notorious B.I.G., played by Jamal Woolard, states that he was growing up in "Do or Die Bed-Stuy." Hence the name Do or Dine. Though Bed-Stuy has slowly gentrified since the early 2000s, it is still not the location you would expect to find such an eclectic dining experience.

Justin Warner and the team at Do or Dine have seemed to defy definition since the beginning. This culinary destination showcases their unique culinary take by combining fine dining and an irreverent regard to

CHEF/OWNER

DO OR DINE, BROOKLYN, NY

culinary tradition, mixed with a bit of not taking oneself too seriously. You can see Justin's culinary sense of humor on the menu, which ranges from "A fish and some chips" to "Frog Legs with Spicy Dr. Pepper Glaze" to the now infamous "foie gras doughnut," the dish that perhaps has brought Justin the most notoriety. After an article about the pastry ran in the *Gothamist*, a petition signed by hundreds asked the restaurant to stop serving the controversial dish. Despite that, the foie gras doughnut remains on the menu.

Since its opening, the restaurant has been become known for many things aside from the edgy menu, including the disco ball in the dining room, the mosaic tile skull and cross bones in the entrance, as well as the hip-hop-heavy playlist. Justin and Do or Dine continue to gather success. In September of 2011, Do or Dine received a great review from *The New York Times*, and

the same year Justin was named *Forbe's Magazine's* 30 under 30 in Food and Wine. In 2012 Do or dine made the Michelin Guide's Bib Gourmand list and Justin Warner won Food Network's eighth season of *Next Food Network Star*, making the restaurant officially a destination for "teens and middle American housewives."

Like his cuisine, Justin's only tattoo is edgy, eclectic, and unexpected. He has the logo for Kewpie mayonnaise from Japan, his favorite brand of mayonnaise, inked on his right forearm. Kewpie is also the name of his dog.

In March of 2013, Justin's show *Rebel Eats* premiered on the Food Network. In addition, when not in the restaurant, he makes several appearances at various food festivals and events around the country for the Food Network.

Frog Legs with Spicy Dr. Pepper Glaze

This is one of the original recipes served at Do or Dine when they first opened.

YIELDS 24 FROG LEGS

FOR GLAZE:
2 cups Dr. Pepper
1 cup gochujang (hot pepper paste)
½ cup caper brine
1 teaspoon xanthan gum, to stabilize

FOR FROG LEGS:
1 dozen pairs (24) frog legs, frozen and
  skinned
1 quart buttermilk
Oil, for frying (you want to fill a deep 14"
  pot with about 4" of oil)
2–3 cups rice flour (enough to fully coat
  the legs)

TO COMPLETE:
Fresh black pepper, to taste
Cilantro leaves, to taste

1 **For Glaze:** Combine all ingredients in a blender and blend until thoroughly mixed.

2 **For Frog Legs:** Soak legs in buttermilk until you are ready to fry them, at least 6 hours. Add 4" oil to a deep pan and heat to 350°F. Dip the frog legs in rice flour and fry, about 8 minutes, until golden brown and delicious. Remove to a paper towel–lined plate to cool.

3 **To Complete:** Put ½ of the Glaze in a bowl, add the fried Frog Legs, and coat the legs with the Glaze. Place glazed legs on serving plates. Top with fresh black pepper and cilantro leaves before serving.

EXECUTIVE CHEF

NORTHEAST KINGDOM, BROOKLYN, NY

KEVIN ADEY

"Commis for life, man."

—Kevin Adey

KEVIN ADEY grew up in Rome, New York, outside of Syracuse, but moved away to Florida when he was twenty. There, he spent over a decade working in kitchens along the West Coast. He focused on working at the best places he could find, eventually rising to sous-chef at contemporary American restaurant Derek's in Sarasota, FL. Chef and owner Derek Barnes was a semifinalist for the 2009 James Beard Awards, "Best Chef South." Kevin continued to work in Florida but wanted to test himself in a bigger market and eventually was pulled back to New York.

Soon after returning he took a line cook position at three-Michelin-star restaurant Le Bernardin, the fine dining restaurant considered one of—if not the best—seafood restaurant in the country. Kevin says, "I knew on the third day that this was not what I want to do with the rest of my life." Running a kitchen with fifty employees did

not fit with his management style. He needed a more intimate work environment. But the fifteen months he spent at Le Bernardin, working for the legendary chef Eric Ripert, continues to influence him as a chef to this day. Kevin says, "I credit knowing the difference between good and bad to that place. The good and bad is kind of complicated, but basically working at a top restaurant in a small town is not even close to working at a top restaurant of the world."

Since taking over as executive chef at Northeast Kingdom, a contemporary American restaurant in Brooklyn, NY, in an outer area called Bushwick, Kevin has slowly changed the menu from jalapeño poppers to something truly special. Focused on seasonal foraging and strong relationships with local farms and organic gardens (including their own rooftop garden), Northeast Kingdom allows Kevin

> **❝** You shouldn't stop learning when you're the chef. You shouldn't stop learning when you're a line cook and the chef de partie and the sous-chef. You always have to believe that there's more. There's a better way to do this. **❞**

to create menus that extend his love for food out of the kitchen. Showing respect for the care it takes to raise animals, Kevin has slowly committed the restaurant to buying full animals, forcing them to learn how to not waste any food. He say "Every week we get a goat, a pig, and a quarter cow and that's it." The menu can rotate daily based on what parts are left as they cook through each cut.

Although Kevin has a lot of tattoos, none of them were food-related until his wife surprised him on his birthday by bringing him to a tattoo parlor. He had the word "commis" tattooed on his wrist. The word refers to the lowest person in the kitchen, a reminder to be a perpetual learner. Kevin firmly believes that we are learning every day, and his tattoo reminds him that no chef is that far from being just any cook and to not stop learning. He says, "You shouldn't stop learning when you're the chef. You shouldn't stop learning when you're a line cook and the chef de partie and the sous-chef. You always have to believe that there's more. There's a better

way to do this." The spirit of his tattoo is a reminder that he is a "commis for life."

On Kevin's left forearm is a tattoo of a pig's head with angel's wings. The tattoo represents Arthur, a pig that Kevin raised from his birth in October of 2011 and eventually slaughtered himself in 2012. The experience changed his perspective on how to run a restaurant. He had toyed with the idea of using whole animals before, but then became fully committed to using every part of the animals served at Northeast Kingdom. He says of slaughtering Arthur, "That moment set us on this roller coaster to deal with one animal at a time. Every week we get one pig, and we have to figure out how to use that pig because there is another one coming next Thursday." Reflective of a less introspective side (and his love of rabbit), Kevin also has a tattoo of the Holy Hand Grenade from *Monty Python and the Holy Grail*, a time-honored tool for killing voracious rabbits. He says, "That movie will always make me laugh."

Roasted Scallops with Sunchoke Purée, Wilted Spinach, and Walnut Salad

SERVES 4

FOR SUNCHOKE PURÉE:
2 pounds sunchokes
1 quart milk (enough to cover)
Salt and pepper, to taste

FOR WILTED SPINACH:
1 teaspoon butter
1 pint spinach
Salt and pepper, to taste

FOR WALNUT SALAD:
20 paper-thin slices of raw sunchoke
1 scallion, sliced
Juice of 1 lemon
Zest of 1 lemon
1 teaspoon walnut oil
¼ cup walnuts
Salt and pepper, to taste

FOR SCALLOPS:
⅛ cup canola oil
16 (U-12, under 12 per pound) scallops
Salt and pepper, to taste
2 tablespoons butter

TO COMPLETE:
½ cup toasted walnuts

1 **For Sunchoke Purée:** In a pot, cook sunchokes in milk, covered, over medium heat until soft, about 20 minutes. Purée all the ingredients, except salt and pepper, in a blender. Season with salt and pepper and keep warm in pot on very low heat.

2 **For Wilted Spinach:** Melt butter in a pan over medium heat. Add and lightly warm spinach, uncovered, until wilted, about 4 minutes. Season with salt and pepper. Keep warm.

3 **For Walnut Salad:** Dress sunchoke slices and scallion with lemon juice, lemon zest, and walnut oil. Toss in walnuts. Season with salt and pepper and set aside.

4 **For Scallops:** In a pan over medium-high heat, add canola oil. Season scallops with salt and pepper and sear in hot pan for about 3 minutes. When brown, flip over and add butter. Baste scallops in the melting butter for 30 seconds. Remove from heat and set aside for plating.

5 **To Complete:** To plate, place Sunchoke Purée and Wilted Spinach on the plate. Add the Scallops and Walnut Salad and finish with toasted walnuts.

NOTES FROM THE CHEF

Seafood sellers use a range of numbers to describe the size of a the scallops based on how many it would take to equal a full pound. "U12" is less than 12 scallops to weigh a pound.

DEREK SIMCIK

"I like clean lines and clean flavors."

—Derek Simcik

DEREK SIMCIK'S younger years were a life on the road. His father worked for the CIA and was assigned all over the world during Derek's youth. Derek lived in Tunisia and Germany and eventually ended up spending his high school years in Japan, where he received his first tattoo. "My grandfather called me monkey, so when I was around sixteen or seventeen, I got the Japanese character for monkey on my back shoulder." The legal age to get a tattoo in Japan is twenty, but as Derek explained, "The culture is based on morals. They would never ask you for ID, and you would never be there if you weren't supposed to be."

After high school, Derek completed a fine arts degree at the Art Institute of Washington in Arlington, Virginia, but he eventually found food to be a better match for his artistic sense and creativity. After graduating from the Art Institute, he moved to Vienna, Austria, but after returning to the D.C. area, he took a job as sous-chef at D.C. hot spot Cafe Milano and eventually found a home at the Kimpton Hotel & Restaurant Group, a hugely

successful organization that runs hotels and restaurants in more than twenty cities across the United States. His first position at Kimpton was as pastry chef at the Grille at Morrison House, and he then joined the team at Jackson 20 as executive pastry chef, before being promoted to chef de cuisine in early 2009. Soon after, in the spring of 2010, he accepted an executive chef position at Atwood Café in Chicago. Derek attributes much of his culinary success to his travels both early on in life and as an adult, using cuisine as a window into other cultures.

Many of Derek's tattoos reflect his love for cooking—and his sense of humor. His right arm sports a butcher girl surrounded by roses, which were just filler. Also on his right arm is his younger brother's name. His brother is exactly four years, four days, and four hours younger than him and has an identical tattoo, except his brother's tattoo is Derek's name. Derek says that he and his brother are extremely close. On Derek's left arm is a Mexican Day of the Dead skull rocking a chef's hat and a realistic heart. Derek's left foot is topped with two fried eggs. One

EXECUTIVE CHEF

ATWOOD CAFÉ, CHICAGO, IL

morning while making breakfast in his home kitchen, he dropped an egg on his bare foot. Thus, the idea for the eggs tattoo was born. The right side of his neck is inked with a chili pepper covered in flames that showcases his love of spicy food and hot rods. To balance out the chili pepper tattoo, Derek got the ice cube on the left side of his neck as a play on fire and ice. On his left finger is the character for love with a fork and spoon that he says shows how much he loves to eat.

Derek plans to finish off his sleeve in the near future and is teaming up with his tattoo and chef buddies to do an "ink" dinner for his thirtieth birthday, "where artists are tattooing and then the chefs are doing dishes with 'ink' in them [i.e. squid ink or fruit purées]."

Although Derek jokes that he will be retired by forty-five, he can't see himself outside of a career in food.

> " My grandfather called me monkey, so when I was around sixteen or seventeen, I got the Japanese character for monkey on my back shoulder. "

Sautéed Red Snapper with Purple Cauliflower Medley and Cauliflower Purée

The colors in this dish match the colors in Derek's tattoos. He says, "[I] love the use of color and how it just pops."

SERVES 4–6

FOR CAULIFLOWER PURÉE:
1 head white cauliflower
1 clove garlic
3–4 cups whole milk, or a little more if needed to cover the cauliflower
Salt and white pepper, to taste

FOR PURPLE CAULIFLOWER MEDLEY:
1 tablespoon oil
1 head cleaned purple cauliflower florets
1 pound lobster mushrooms, chopped
½ pound corn kernels, cleaned and blanched
2 teaspoons minced garlic
2 teaspoons minced shallot
Butter, to taste
Parsley, finely minced, to taste
1½ teaspoons finely chopped chives
Salt and pepper, to taste

FOR RED SNAPPER:
1 tablespoon oil
4–6 (6-ounce) red snapper fillets, skin-on (striped bass may be substituted as well)
Salt and white pepper, to taste

TO COMPLETE:
Turnip oil, to garnish (may be purchased at a specialty store)
8–12 long chives, for garnish

1 **For Cauliflower Purée:** Cut off the florets of the cauliflower and place in a heavy-bottomed saucepot. Add the clove of garlic and cover with whole milk. Bring to a simmer and cook on medium heat, about 10 to 15 minutes, until florets are soft. Strain but keep the milk to the side. Add the cauliflower to a blender. Blend on medium-high speed, slowly adding milk to blender—enough to purée the cauliflower but not to liquefy it too much; you don't want a soupy consistency. Season with salt and white pepper to taste.

2 **For Purple Cauliflower Medley:** In a hot sauté pan over medium heat, add oil and coat the pan. Add the cauliflower and mushrooms to the pan and allow to cook for a few moments, about 1 to 2 minutes. Add the corn, stir, and then add the garlic and shallots. Allow to cook on the stovetop over medium heat, stirring occasionally for 5 minutes. Then add butter and herbs to coat the vegetables and season to taste with salt and pepper.

3 **For Red Snapper:** Preheat oven to 400°F. In an ovensafe sauté pan over medium-high heat, add oil to coat the pan. Season the fillets with salt and white pepper. Add fillets to pan, skin-side down, pressing down into the pan slightly. After a few moments, about 2 minutes, place in oven uncovered and cook for 12 minutes or so, until fish meat is flaky but still shiny.

4 **To Complete:** On each plate, place a dime-size swirl of Cauliflower Purée and a spoonful of the Purple Cauliflower Medley. Top it with the fillet of Red Snapper slightly off-center and drizzle the turnip oil tightly around the dish. Garnish with two long, beautiful chives for presentation.

MICHAEL FIORELLI

"No matter who you are,
it comes from the classics."

—Michael Fiorelli

MICHAEL FIORELLI found cooking through books. Born and raised in Long Island, NY, he majored in English in college with a minor in journalism. Early on, Michael aspired to be a writer for *Saturday Night Live*, which was at the top of the ratings at the time, but then his passion for reading turned to cookbooks and he never looked back. Michael still recommends two of the books that affected him the most to aspiring chefs to this day: *Culinary Artistry* and *Becoming a Chef*, both by Andrew Dornenburg and Karen Page.

Michael began his culinary career as chef de partie at Susanna Foo, a traditional Chinese restaurant in Philadelphia, PA, working under the tutelage of Foo, a James Beard Award–winning chef. He says, "I had no

idea what I was doing. If I wasn't eighteen, I never would have had the balls." While there, he had the opportunity to cook with renowned chef Thomas Keller; he made a dinner with Keller to promote Keller's newly launched book, *The French Laundry Cookbook*. While cooking, Michael received some words of wisdom from Keller himself. Keller encouraged Michael to decide what he wanted to do and then find the person who was doing it best and work with him or her. According to Michael, the advice Keller gave him "was groundbreaking," and for the next several years, Michael did just that.

Not long after that conversation with Keller, Michael was offered the position of lead chef under European master chef Peter Timmins at the Greenbrier, a five-star resort

"THE ONLY TWO INGREDIENTS YOU NEED TO MAKE GREAT FOOD ARE LOVE AND SALT."

in West Virginia. During the off-season, Michael worked as a chef at five-star, five-diamond hotel the Little Nell in Aspen, CO. Next, he took a job as chef de partie at the Inn at Little Washington in Washington, Virginia, working under chef Patrick O'Connell, winner of the James Beard Award for Outstanding Chef. Michael then moved to Florida to take an executive chef position for yet another James Beard Award winner, Mark Militello, at Militello's highly touted Mark's at the Park. While there, *CitySmart* magazine named Michael the "South Florida Rising Star Chef."

Finally, Michael ended up in Los Angeles, recruited by celebrity chef Kerry Simon to take the chef de cuisine position at Simon's restaurant Simon LA. After great success there, he went on to become chef de cuisine at mar'sel, the signature restaurant at Terranea Resort and Spa, eventually becoming the executive chef of the entire property. The menu at mar'sel reflects Michael's culinary focus of sourcing fresh organic ingredients from a close radius around the restaurant whenever possible. The Terranea property is also a perfect environment for a large outdoor garden, which provides many fresh ingredients for his recipes. Michael is currently working on a cookbook based on the cuisine at Terranea.

Michael wears his love of food on his sleeve, literally. His right forearm has the word "love" and his left has a blue salt molecule because "the only two ingredients you need to make great food are love and salt." Above the salt molecule is a banner that reads simply, "Hard Work," to remind Michael of what it took to get him to where he is today and to stay humble. On his right arm, under the word "love," are two fighting phoenixes that were inspired by Michael's father Steve's phoenix tattoo. Michael says, "Every seven years they light themselves on fire and rise from their own ashes. The idea is that it's a never-ending battle."

Grilled Spanish Octopus with Salsa Verde, Fried Potatoes, Piquillo Peppers, Green Onion, Preserved Lemon, and Chorizo

SERVES 6–8

FOR SOFRITO:

½ cup quality extra-virgin olive oil

1 teaspoon kosher salt

4 Spanish onions, thinly sliced

2 (12-ounce) cans plum tomatoes, drained from the liquid

8 cloves garlic, minced

1 teaspoon red chili flakes

FOR SALSA VERDE:

1 cup Italian parsley leaves

1 cup basil leaves

1 tablespoon capers

2 tablespoons roasted garlic

3 anchovy fillets

2 tablespoons Marcona almonds

1 teaspoon chili flakes

1 teaspoon kosher salt

2½ tablespoons extra-virgin olive oil

FOR FINGERLING POTATOES:

1 tablespoon chopped bacon

2 tablespoons chopped Spanish onion

2 tablespoons chopped garlic

16 fingerling potatoes, a little smaller than thumb-size

2 sprigs fresh thyme

1 sprig fresh rosemary

1 quart chicken stock or water

1 teaspoon kosher salt

1 teaspoon cracked black pepper

FOR OCTOPUS:

2 whole Spanish octopuses, defrosted (about 2–3 pounds each)

Kosher salt, to taste

Cracked black pepper, to taste

2 large vacuum seal bags

1 lemon, cut in half

2 tablespoons paprika

2 garlic cloves, smashed

½ cup olive oil

1 **For Sofrito:** In a heavy-bottomed saucepot set over medium-low heat, add the oil, salt, and onions. Stirring frequently, allow onions to caramelize until very deep golden brown, about 1½ hours. Add the canned tomatoes and bring to a simmer, stirring well to incorporate. Turn heat to low and simmer uncovered for an additional 1½ hours. Add the garlic and the chili flakes. Remove from heat and purée mixture, in batches, in a high-speed blender. At this point, you can cool and store in the refrigerator for up to 1 week.

2 **For Salsa Verde:** Blanch the parsley and basil in rapidly boiling water for 2 minutes and then plunge into ice water to stop cooking and preserve the color. Squeeze out all of the excess water. Add all of the ingredients to a high-speed blender and blend until smooth. At this point, you can refrigerate in an airtight container for up to 3 days.

3 **For Fingerling Potatoes:** In a heavy-bottomed 2-quart saucepan, over medium heat, render the bacon until almost crispy, about 5 minutes. Add the onions and garlic and sauté until soft and translucent, about 3 minutes. Add the rest of the ingredients and bring to a simmer. Turn the heat to low and simmer uncovered, until the potatoes are just tender or when a toothpick will pierce with little resistance about 10 minutes. Check frequently to prevent overcooking. Remove the potatoes from the broth. Set aside to cool. You may cool the broth, keep refrigerated, and use for another application within 3 days. Once cool, take the fingerling potatoes and flatten them with the palm of your hand so they look smashed. Fry them in a deep fryer set to 350°F or in a large heavy-bottomed pot of canola oil, fitted with a thermometer. When the potatoes are golden brown and crispy, about 3 to 4 minutes, remove them from the oil and drain on paper towels, reserving for the finished dish.

4 **For Octopus:** Rinse the octopuses thoroughly. Season both of them liberally with salt and pepper. To each bag, add 1 octopus, 1 lemon half, 1 tablespoon of paprika, 1 smashed garlic clove, and ¼ cup of olive oil. Seal the bags in a vacuum seal and shake thoroughly to distribute ingredients. Refrigerate until chilled, about 1½ to 2 hours.

5 Set an immersion circulator to 195°F. When the water is up to temperature, place the bagged octopuses in the water bath and circulate for 5 hours. Remove the bags from the water and allow to rest, just until cool enough to handle. Remove the octopuses from the bags, discarding the liquid. Using a kitchen towel, gently slide the tentacles off of the octopus legs (optional). Remove the legs from the octopuses, discarding the heads or reserving for another use. Once the octopuses are cleaned and cool, marinate them in the Sofrito for at least one hour.

TO COMPLETE:

1 pound cured Bilbao chorizo links, cut into
    1-ounce slices

8 piquillo peppers, removed from oil and
    halved

8 green onions, washed, trimmed, and cut
    in half

1 tablespoon preserved lemon, thinly
    sliced

6 Preheat a grill to medium-high heat. Place your marinated octopus on the grill and grill on one side until slightly charred, about 3 minutes. Turn the octopus and repeat on the other side. Remove the octopus from the grill and set aside.

7 **To Complete:** In a large sauté pan coated with a thin film of olive oil, set your chorizo over medium heat and cook until deep brown and caramelized, flipping the pieces halfway, about 1 minute each side. Add the piquillo peppers, Fingerling Potatoes, green onions, and Octopus. (Note: You can use the saucepan used for the earlier steps of the dish. It's good to let the flavors meld together and makes it easier to plate up.) Turn heat to low and lightly toss until everything is heated through. On a large oval platter, spoon a generous helping of the Salsa Verde, spreading the sauce from one end of the plate to the other. Add the Fingerling Potatoes, chorizo, and peppers. Place the Octopus on top of that. Evenly distribute the green onions and preserved lemon on top of the Octopus.

NOTES FROM THE CHEF

Once the octopus is marinated in the Sofrito, you can grill it immediately or cover in an airtight container and refrigerate for up to 3 days.

EXECUTIVE CHEF/OWNER

ED'S LOBSTER BAR, NEW YORK CITY, NY

ED McFARLAND

> "I got the logo tattooed the second year we were open. I had to make sure we would stand the test of time before I got something that big. Maybe if we went out of business I would have got a smaller one somewhere."

—Ed McFarland

ED McFARLAND started cooking in the classic Staten Island pizzerias near his home on Staten Island, and never stopped. In 1995, he joined the French Culinary Institute and, after graduating, worked beside culinary masters in the kitchens of Le Cirque and Picholine, two of the top New York City kitchens at the time. He says, "I bounced around for a while after that at a bunch of no-named restaurants before I ended up at Pearl Oyster Bar." Ed spent more than six years at Pearl as sous-chef, and the experience helped Ed develop his love of seafood and New England cuisine.

In 2007, Ed opened Ed's Lobster Bar in SoHo, New York. He says, "I just really have an affinity and a drawing to lobster. While I find it to be very elegant and light in flavor, I find it has so many more uses than just making a lobster roll." Ed uses his own homegrown vegetables and herbs in the summer months and draws from his Italian

> **"I JUST REALLY HAVE AN AFFINITY AND A DRAWING TO LOBSTER. WHILE I FIND IT TO BE VERY ELEGANT AND LIGHT IN FLAVOR, I FIND IT HAS SO MANY MORE USES THAN JUST MAKING A LOBSTER ROLL."**

heritage to make homemade pastas like lobster ravioli and lasagna, which he offers along with specials like lobster meatballs and lobster pot pie. He's even made a lobster ravioli with lobster infused directly into the pasta.

The logo for Ed's Lobster Bar was the inspiration for Ed's boldest tattoo, a prominent lobster inked on his left forearm. However, Ed didn't get the tattoo until the second year the bar was open. He says he "had to make sure we would stand the test of time before I got something that big. Maybe if we went out of business I would have got a smaller one somewhere." The ink on his right arm is nearly ten years old and shows three koi fish swimming in the same direction, a token for good luck.

Ed is still in love with his Lobster Bar and continues to get tattooed to this day. He's actually thinking about adding a tattoo with a combination of Jameson whiskey and his pit bull terrier, also named Jameson.

Lobster Rolls

One of Ed's Lobster Bar's most popular menu items is Ed's take on the classic Maine delicacy, the lobster roll.

SERVES 4

FOR LOBSTER SALAD:
4 whole (1¼- to 1½-pound) lobsters
1 cup Hellmann's mayonnaise
½ stalk celery, finely minced
1 tablespoon freshly squeezed lemon juice
Salt and pepper, to taste

FOR ROLLS:
⅓ cup butter
4 top-split hot dog buns

TO COMPLETE:
½ bunch chives, finely chopped, for garnish

1 For Lobster Salad: Boil whole lobsters in heavy stockpot uncovered over high heat until they float, about 15 to 20 minutes. Remove from water and place in ice bath. When chilled, shell the meat, clean by removing any cartilage in claw, and devein the tail. Chop lobster into bite-size chunks. Mix with remaining Lobster Salad ingredients in large bowl.

2 For Rolls: Melt butter in small sauté pan on medium-high heat. Place hot dog buns in sauté pan and toast in butter until golden on each side, about 5 minutes each side.

3 To Complete: Stuff each Roll with a generous portion of Lobster Salad and top with a sprinkle of chopped chives.

NOTES FROM THE CHEF

Ed says, "[This dish] is served with French fries and pickles. [You can also serve with a fresh salad, but] the salad is just a bouquet and is not necessary."

JESSE SCHENKER

> "I wanted to put something on my arm to brand me in my craft. . . . It was probably impulsive, but I guess most tattoos are."
>
> —Jesse Schenker

GROWING UP IN FLORIDA, Jesse Schenker always loved to cook. At an early age, he began requesting menus from his parents' dinners and began to invest in a cookbook collection that has since grown to more than 300 titles. His first official kitchen job was at the age of fifteen working the line at a McDonald's. Bitten by the "cooking bug," Jesse enrolled in vocational school for cooking and has been in the kitchen ever since.

After graduating from vocational school, Jesse began building his resume in great kitchens in Florida and helped open City Cellar Wine Bar & Grill, a large upscale wine bar in Palm Beach, FL. After learning the ropes of a high-volume restaurant, the corporate chef urged him to challenge himself and move to New York, where he would learn the techniques of culinary perfection while surrounding himself with some of the best chefs in the world. Although the chef didn't want to lose him in the kitchen, he knew Jesse was destined for bigger and better things.

Upon moving to New York, Jesse accepted a position as chef de partie at the two-Michelin-star rated Gordon Ramsay at the London and found time to stage at Per Se and Jean-Georges. But after a year at the London, Jesse began to set his sights on a restaurant of his own. In January of 2010, at the age of twenty-seven, Jesse (along with his girlfriend and now-wife Lindsay Schenker and Christina Lee, a pastry chef) started Recette, a small thirty-five-seat restaurant in Manhattan's West Village. He also enlisted the talents of Savoy Bakery owner Brian Ghaw. Together they created tasting menus for exclusive

private parties. Since opening Recette, Jesse has been a finalist for the James Beard Award for Best New Chef in 2011 and was named one of *Forbes's* "30 under 30" in the Food and Wine category. At the end of 2011, he was invited to compete on *Iron Chef*, where he took on and beat Iron Chef Geoffrey Zakarian.

Although Jesse thoroughly enjoys life in his kitchen, he still needs an outlet to change things up and push some boundaries. Out of this need came "Mondays with Jesse." This monthly culinary event is a chance for Jesse and his kitchen to get creative and experiment. They take about half of the seats out of the dining room and prepare ten-plus-course tasting menus on the second Monday of every month. The dinners have grown in popularity, and some of the favorite dishes have even made their way onto the daily menu.

This passion for cooking extends into Jesse's tattoos. He got his first tattoo, a tribal image on his left shoulder, in 2002, and over the next two to three years, he built on it, adding a T-bone steak skewered with olive, lettuce, and tomato and expanding the tattoo to the back of his arm, where you'll find a skull breathing fire, holding ice.

Jesse eventually got a chef's knife on his left arm and, in 2006, started wrapping it in tattooed caul fat. He even brought a piece of fat into his preferred tattoo parlor, Addictions on St. Marks in New York's East Village, where they stretched the fat around his arm and, with ink, essentially left it there forever. Jesse also tattooed lyrics from his favorite band Pearl Jam (from the song "Indifference") around his thigh in 2007. Along his wrist, traced out in his own handwriting, are the words "All or None." It's a reminder to this determined chef of how he wants to live his life. Do it to the fullest or don't do it at all. After the birth of their son Eddie, in 2011, Jesse and Lindsay both got his name tattooed on their right shoulders.

While not ruling out more tattoos, Jesse admits they aren't really a focus for him anymore. Instead, his attentions are set on his new family and his restaurant. Recette is now running smoothly, and Jesse and Lindsay aspire to open a bigger restaurant somewhere in Manhattan.

Roasted Red Snapper, Corn Purée, Fresh Corn, Rock Shrimp, and Lobster Butter

YIELDS 4 SERVINGS

FOR CORN PURÉE:
1 tablespoon butter
2 cups fresh corn kernels, about 3 cobs
½ teaspoon salt, or to taste
2 cups heavy cream

FOR LOBSTER BUTTER:
½ cup dry white wine
½ pound butter, chilled and cut into small
   blocks
1 tablespoon lobster roe

FOR SNAPPER AND SHRIMP:
2 tablespoons canola oil
5 pounds red snapper
Salt, to taste
1 tablespoon butter
2 tablespoons fresh corn
8 pieces rock shrimp (or any kind of desired
   shrimp)
1 cup Corn Purée
8 cherry tomatoes, cut in half
Pinch of chopped parsley

TO COMPLETE:
16 arugula leaves, for garnish
Fresh cherry tomatoes, for garnish

1 **For Corn Purée:** In a medium saucepan over medium heat, melt butter and add fresh corn kernels. Roast the corn for about 2 minutes; then add some salt. Add the heavy cream and reduce to low heat. Let it simmer uncovered for about 30 minutes. When it's done cooking, blend it in a blender and pass it through a chinois. Set aside to cool.

2 **For Lobster Butter:** In a saucepan, reduce white wine until almost dry, about 5 to 8 minutes. When it has reduced, add cold butter slowly until it emulsifies. Add the lobster roe and whisk until mixture is smooth. Pass it through a chinois and set aside.

3 **For Snapper and Shrimp:** In a medium-size pan over medium heat, add canola oil; wait for about 2 minutes or until the pan is hot enough. (Note: You don't want the pan to be extremely hot because it will burn the sides of the fish if you start with a super hot pan.) Season both sides of the fish with salt and place in pan to sauté about 5 minutes. (Note: Do not cover the fish while sautéing; it will build moisture and you won't get the perfectly brown seared crispy side of it.) While the fish is cooking, place another medium-size pot over medium heat. Melt butter, wait for about 2 minutes, and then add the corn and rock shrimp and sauté for about 3 minutes. Remove from heat. Add Corn Purée and cherry tomato (make sure to remove it from the heat so what you're really doing is folding the tomato into the corn mixture). Add salt and pepper to taste and pinch of parsley to finish.

4 **To Complete:** Place the corn/shrimp mixture on the bottom of the plate and the fish on top. Drizzle the Lobster Butter on top of the fish and around the plate. Use arugula leaves and fresh cherry tomatoes to garnish. Serve immediately.

NOTES FROM THE CHEF

When buying fish in the market, make sure to tell them that you want your fish skin-off. It's just easier for cooking.

CHEF/OWNER

GRAFFIATO, BANDOLERO, KAPNOS, AND G, WASHINGTON, D.C.

MIKE ISABELLA

"My mouth has definitely gotten me into trouble my whole life. I'm a New Jersey Italian who comes from a broken family, and I had to fight my whole life to get where I am."

—Mike Isabella, from a 2011 interview in the *Chicago Tribune* after his second-place finish on *Top Chef Masters*

CHEF MIKE ISABELLA was named *Food & Wine*'s "The People's Best New Chef Mid-Atlantic" in 2012, but he is probably much better known for his appearances on Bravo's *Top Chef*. He was first on the show during Season Six in 2009, where he finished sixth, and was also on Season Eight (the All-Stars edition), where he finished second. Yet, long before his TV notoriety, Mike spent years working with some of the most respected chefs in the country. Born and raised in New Jersey, he started his formal training at the Restaurant School in New York City, taking classes while working in restaurants around the city. One of his first jobs in the city was working for fellow *Eat Ink* chef Ed Witt (see entry in this part) as a line cook at the now-closed Nicole's on the Upper East Side. Mike eventually moved to Philadelphia to work with Starr Restaurants, which now operates twenty-three restaurants across Philadelphia, New York, Atlantic City, and Washington, D.C. Mike worked at a number of Starr restaurants, and it was there that he saw what it took to run a multilocation restaurant group. His first position was as a sous-chef for James Beard Award–winner Douglas Rodriguez at the modern Latin restaurant Alma de Cuba. His time at Alma de Cuba and the time he later spent working for Iron Chef Jose Garces at his modern Mexican restaurant El Vez was when Mike learned true Latin cuisine. This eventually led him to the position of executive sous-chef on the opening team of Top Chef Master Marcus Samuelsson's Washington Square restaurant. There, Mike saw what it takes to open a fine-dining restaurant from the beginning.

Continuing to seek out his culinary passion, Mike left Philadelphia in 2005 and moved to Atlanta, GA, to work as the chef de cuisine of the seafood-inspired Kyma, one of the top Greek restaurants in the country. While working at Kyma and after traveling to Greece, the Mediterranean, and parts of the Middle East, Mike developed his love and understanding of Greek cuisine. In the spring of 2007, he continued his Greek focus by moving to Washington, D.C., to work as executive chef of José Andrés's Zaytinya, a Greek/Mediterranean tapas restaurant. During Mike's three years at Zaytinya, the restaurant was consistently ranked as *Washingtonian* magazine's "100 Very Best Restaurants," and Mike was named as a "Rising Culinary Star of the Year" nominee by the Restaurant Association of Metropolitan Washington in both 2009 and 2010. During this time, Mike was urged by José Andrés to try out for *Top Chef*.

Eventually, Mike decided that he wanted to get back to his Italian-American heritage from his days growing up in the suburbs of New Jersey. He says, "I wanted to go back to my roots and get away from Greek for a little while." To fulfill this dream, Mike opened Graffiato, an Italian-inspired restaurant in D.C.'s Chinatown, in June 2011. In May of 2012, Mike opened Bandolero, a modern Mexican-style restaurant serving mostly small plates, in the Georgetown neighborhood of Washington, D.C. In 2012, Mike released his first cookbook, *Crazy Good Italian*.

Mike's tattoos are almost all tied to his culinary endeavors. He tattooed an evil eye on his right hand to protect him from evil spirits before going on *Top Chef* Season Six, and he has a "badass pizza cutter" across his right forearm, next to his star tattoo, to commemorate the opening of Graffiato. Mike's Hawaiian-themed tattoos on his left leg in a way are responsible for how he happened to open Bandolero. After being tattooed at Jinx Proof Tattoo in Georgetown, Mike ran into restaurateur Jonathan Umbel, who ran the recently closed Hook. After looking over the space that once housed Hook that day, they would eventually partner on Bandolero in the same spot. Mike's left upper arm is now tattooed with a Day of the Dead–style bandolero, the namesake for the restaurant in Georgetown.

Today, Mike continues to get tattooed and continues to open restaurants. In the spring of 2013, he opened G, an Italian deli and sandwich shop, in Edison, NJ. However, Mike is most excited about his return to Greek food with his new restaurant, Kapnos.

Kapnos Octopus

YIELDS 5–6 SERVINGS

FOR LARGE OCTOPUS:

1 teaspoon peppercorns
1 star anise
1 teaspoon coriander
1 teaspoon fennel seed
1 teaspoon allspice
2 sprigs thyme
1 garlic clove
1 bay leaf
1 large octopus, 6–8 pounds
1 ounce red wine vinegar

FOR BABY OCTOPUS:

1 teaspoon peppercorns
1 star anise
1 teaspoon coriander
1 teaspoon fennel seed
1 teaspoon allspice
1 teaspoon thyme
1 garlic
1 bay leaf
1 baby octopus, 1–1½ pounds
1 ounce red wine vinegar
1 cup water

FOR GRAPEFRUIT CELLS:

1 grapefruit
1 cup olive oil

FOR VEGETABLES:

1 cup sugar
2 cups red wine vinegar
3 cups water
2 pearl onions
2 ounces sea beans
1 English cucumber
1 Fresno chili
1 baby fennel

1 For Large Octopus: Preheat oven to 350°F. Place peppercorns, star anise, coriander, fennel seed, allspice, thyme, garlic, and bay leaf in a piece of cheesecloth. Tie the cloth tightly with a piece of string, making a sachet. Take large octopus, cut off all tentacles, and throw away head. Once the head is cut off, you'll see the circular beak directly in the middle of the octopus. Remove beak. Add sachet, red wine vinegar, and octopus to hotel pan and cover with aluminum foil. Place hotel pan in oven and cook for 45 minutes to an hour, or until no chewy bite is left. Line a terrine mold with plastic wrap and stab a few holes in plastic wrap. Once cooked, remove octopus from braising liquid and stuff into the terrine mold. Be sure to pack in as many octopus tentacles as possible. Then place mold in the refrigerator and place a large, weighted object (like a gallon of milk or a case of beer) on top of the mold, making sure it pushes all the tentacles down into the mold. Allow the terrine to press for about 6 hours, until octopus completely cools down. Once cooled, wrap in plastic and freeze in freezer overnight, until completely frozen.

2 For Baby Octopus: Place peppercorns, star anise, coriander, fennel seed, allspice, thyme, garlic, and bay leaf in a piece of cheesecloth. Tie the cloth tightly with a piece of string, making a sachet. Cut head off of baby octopus and throw in trash. Once the head is cut off, you'll see the circular beak directly in the middle of the octopus. Remove beak. Place octopus into a small pot with your sachet of spices, vinegar, and water. Place into oven at 350°F and check after 30 minutes. The only way to find out if it is cooked is by biting it: Octopus should be tender and chew easily. Allow octopus to cool and set aside.

3 For Grapefruit Cells: Supreme the grapefruit. Place in bowl. Heat oil in a pan to 300°F, then pour the oil over the grapefruit. Constantly stir the grapefruit, causing the cells to break apart. Strain into chinois.

4 For Vegetables: Place sugar, vinegar, and water into a pot. Bring to a boil. Place pearl onions in a bowl or plastic container. Once pickling liquid is boiling, pour onto onions. Allow the onions to cool down in liquid at room temperature. They can be left in pickling liquid until ready to use. Fill a medium-size pot with water and bring to a boil. Place sea beans into boiling water for about 10 seconds. Immediately remove sea beans from water and submerge into ice water. Cooking the sea beans is mainly done to remove impurities and to bring out the bright green color. The texture will still have a little bite to it. Peel and cut cucumbers in a baton shape. Thinly slice chilies with a sharp knife. Thinly shave fennel with mandoline.

TO COMPLETE:
2 ounces olive oil
1 bunch dill
1 ounce lemon juice

5 To Complete: Remove Large Octopus terrine from freezer. Slice octopus with a meat slicer very thinly and lay onto plate very flat. It's important that the Large Octopus terrine is frozen solid. Brush olive oil on top of the sliced frozen octopus; then apply a thin layer of Grapefruit Cells. Take the braised Baby Octopus and cut tentacles apart. Preheat a large sauté pan coated with oil on high heat and char the Baby Octopus tentacles. Be sure to rotate tentacles to char completely. Add cucumbers, Fresno chilies, fennel, pickled onions, sea beans, and dill into a bowl with lemon juice. Toss the salad with charred Baby Octopus. Place salad and Baby Octopus onto the middle of the thinly sliced Large Octopus terrine. The terrine is meant to be cold and the Baby Octopus is to be eaten hot.

ED WITT

"I think the whole thing is of the same mentality. Chefs have this at a certain point. If you sit there and you aren't picky, you'll eat better. If you sit there and you trust an artist that is tattooing you, you'll end up with a better tattoo."

—Ed Witt

CHEF/OWNER

8407 KITCHEN BAR, SILVER SPRING, MD

> **❝** I ended up having to travel back and forth from New York to Jersey. [My tattoo artist] would pick me up from the bus stop, we would go get brunch, and then he would tattoo me for six hours. **❞**

ED WITT wasn't always sure that he wanted to be a chef. In fact, he majored in electrical engineering, mechanical engineering, and physical therapy at the University of Maryland before he finally dropped out of college to attend the Culinary Institute of America in New York. Since then, Ed has become a veteran of several great restaurants—and has gotten a lot of ink.

Ed was part of the opening team in 2005 for French fine-dining restaurant Jardinière's, one of four restaurants owned by chef Traci des Jardins in San Francisco. He then moved to New York to help move Daniel Boulud's French restaurant Daniel (a three-Michelin-star Relais & Châteaux restaurant) to its new 65th Street location. He continued to work around New York City until the recession hit, which motivated Ed to move again. After leaving New York City, Ed moved to Washington, D.C., and soon found himself working at 701 Restaurant, known for its contemporary continental cuisine. There, he earned two-and-a-half stars from the *Washington Post* before moving to 8407 Kitchen Bar in Silver Spring, MD, where he is currently the executive chef. 8407 Kitchen Bar is *Washingtonian* magazine's "Editor's Pick" and one of its "100 Best Restaurants" of 2013. Ed is passionate about local and seasonal food, which is offered at 8407 Kitchen Bar in creative, contemporary meals.

Ed estimates that he's spent more than 300 hours getting tattooed and is certainly in the running for most tattooed chef. Ed got his first tattoo, a dolphin on his back, when he was twenty while attending the University of Maryland. It would be nearly four years before he would get more ink. After moving to San Francisco in 1996 he met well known Bay area musician and tattoo artist Jeff Whitehead. There, he got his back piece and half sleeves done. The connected themes of his back piece and sleeves are the ocean and space, two elements that Ed has always been interested in. His back piece draws inspiration from traditional Japanese tattoo art but is done as a city and landscape. When Ed moved to New York, he connected with painter and tattoo artist Kevin LeBlanc, who did most of his work for the next ten years. Kevin was living in New York City when he and Ed met, but later moved to New Jersey, which made things hard for Ed. He says, "I ended up having to travel back and forth from New York to Jersey. [Kevin] would pick me up from the bus stop, we would go get brunch, and then he would tattoo me for six hours."

At this point, Ed has nearly has a full suit and has a continued theme of ocean and space. One leg features mermaids, and a crumbling Atlantis. Above that scene on the rib is a sea monster. On his right arm space Ed has girls and Flash Gordon rockets. The continuity of his suit has also come with giving the artist he works with a lot of freedom. He says, "I think the whole thing is of the same mentality. Chefs have it at a certain point. If you sit there and you trust an artist that is tattooing you, you'll end up with a better tattoo." Ed is running out of skin, but he still plans to find some space to get tattoos of his dogs and is trying to figure out the logistics to getting "Love" and "Hate" tattooed on each of his legs at the same time by two different artists.

Duck Fat Poached Salmon, Forbidden Rice, Plum Wine BBQ Sauce, and Snap Peas

Ed served this dish at 701 Restaurant and is now serving a salad version of it at 8407 Kitchen Bar.

YIELDS 4 SERVINGS

FOR PLUM WINE BBQ SAUCE:
YIELDS 2 CUPS

1 tablespoon grapeseed oil
50 grams shallot, brunoise
20 grams fennel, brunoise
5 grams garlic, brunoise
4 grams Thai chili, finely chopped
8 grams ginger, brunoise
375 milliliters plum wine
100 grams brown sugar
Salt, to taste

TO COMPLETE:
2 quarts vegetable broth
1 quart forbidden rice
Salt, to taste
½ stick of butter
2 quarts duck fat
4 (6-ounce) portions of salmon, preferably wild, skin-off and blood line removed
1 bunch radishes, for garnish
½ pound snap peas (4–5 per portion), for garnish

1 For Plum Wine BBQ Sauce: Add grapeseed oil to a small pot over medium heat and sweat vegetables until tender, about 5 to 10 minutes. Add wine and sugar, bring to a boil, and then turn down to a simmer. Simmer approximately 20 minutes; then season with salt and remove from heat. Sauce can be kept cool in refrigerator until ready to use.

2 To Complete: Combine vegetable broth and rice in pot and salt to taste. Heat broth over high heat to a boil. Once boiling, turn down to a simmer. Cook approximately 15 minutes, uncovered, until cooked. Rice will still be a bit firm like risotto. Strain and finish with butter. Heat duck fat to low heat in a pot large enough to submerge fish. You should still be able to put finger in fat. Submerge salmon and simmer on low for approximately 10 minutes, until medium-rare (do not turn salmon). Meanwhile, slice radishes thinly with knife or mandoline. Briefly blanch snap peas in salted, boiling water, remove from heat, and shock in ice water; then slice into 3 pieces on the bias. Spoon rice onto plate, lay the salmon on the rice, and arrange vegetables on top of salmon. Serve warm, topped with Plum Wine BBQ Sauce.

EXECUTIVE CHEF

BEUCHERT'S SALOON, WASHINGTON, D.C.

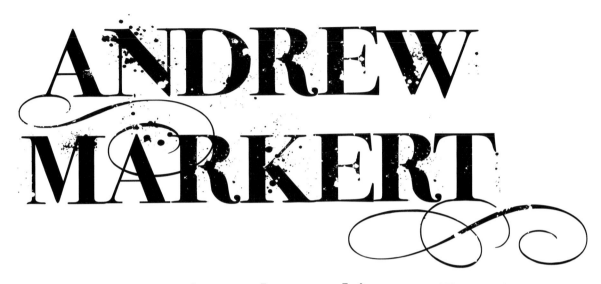

ANDREW MARKERT

"We'll see what *The Washington Post* thinks about my food."

—Andrew Markert

ANDREW'S knack for drawing flavor from even the simplest ingredients has brought him into the company of some of the finest chefs in the world and helped him place second in a bone marrow competition on his 2011 appearance on Food Network's edgy competition program *Chopped*. Andrew got his first few tattoos, which he calls "my college white boy tattoos, mostly tribal and Celtic and some Japanese symbols," while he was attending the culinary program at Rhode Island's Johnson & Wales University, and his ink—and culinary endeavors—didn't stop there.

After he graduated in 2004 with a bachelor's degree in culinary arts, Andrew moved to Washington, D.C., where he cooked under a variety of top chefs, including David Deshaies at French restaurant Citronelle and Tony Chittum at Italian restaurant Notti Bianche. Andrew

followed Tony to Vermillion, a contemporary Indian and Latin American fusion restaurant. Of his time with Tony Chittum, Andrew says, "In total I was under his training for three years. Much of my style and ideals came from Tony. He has always been a huge part of my growth as a chef, learning the ins and outs of the paperwork side of being a chef and really helping me become a better chef."

At Vermillion, Andrew was able to explore his interest in charcuterie for the first time, an experience that inspired one of his largest tattoos. He took an old-school drawing of a meat market to Fatty, the artist he'd been working with who owns an eponymous tattoo parlor in Dupont Circle. It was Fatty who showed Andrew the album cover of *Honky Reduction* by the Agoraphobic Nosebleed, a grindcore band. On the album cover, a grinning Stepford

blonde in a butcher's apron holds a slab of meat level with her head in one hand while her other hand drives a cleaver into a carving board. Although Andrew admits grindcore isn't his genre, the two concepts blended into an epic work that appears to be carved out of his chest. Andrew says the tattoo "is my inner butcher demon man. He is holding a beef rib rack covered in blood, holding a butcher knife and surrounded with meats, such as a side of cow, a pig head, sausages, and many others."

On his right arm is a sleeve that pays tribute to his godparents, both scholars, one of Dante and the other of Shakespeare, another tattoo inked by Fatty while he was working at Vermillion. It's a combination of Shakespeare quotes, references to their home, and a crumbling cathedral and setting sun to represent the end of their lives. On Andrew's left arm is an oriole that represents his past and his present: where he came from, Baltimore, and his favorite cooking ingredient, which is vanilla. Andrew says, "I started this one about four years ago [in D.C.] and have been working on it since. I am almost done with it."

The most forward-looking of Andrew's tattoos are the four empty stars on his left arm. Andrew's waiting for his first starred review as an executive chef to fill them in. He'll have the chance to earn those stars working as executive chef at Beuchert's Saloon, a "farm American" restaurant in Washington, D.C. The restaurant, located in Andrew's home state of Maryland, comes with the luxury of being able to source ingredients from the restaurant's own farm, East Oaks Organic Farm in Poolesville. You might not think working on a farm would be high on the list of priorities for a chef, but Andrew considers it to be the essence of his new menu. "Working on the farm really taught me what using local ingredients means," he says. "Providing quality, one-of-a-kind ingredients to your customers is paramount, and something I am adamant about executing."

Drew's Mama's Crab Cakes with Mustard Cider Reduction and Walnut Brown Butter

Andrew's oriole tattoo and this crab dish both show his pride for his hometown of Baltimore, MD.

YIELDS 4–6 SERVINGS

FOR CRAB CAKE MAYO:

1 egg
1 cup mayonnaise
Juice of ½ lemon
1 teaspoon Worcestershire sauce
2 tablespoons chopped parsley
2 tablespoons diced red bell pepper
Salt and pepper, to taste

FOR CRAB CAKES:

1 pound jumbo crab meat
¼ cup Crab Cake Mayo
¼ cup panko (bread crumbs)
Salt and pepper, to taste
1 tablespoon oil

FOR MUSTARD CIDER REDUCTION:

2 cups apple cider
2 cups apple cider vinegar
1 tablespoon whole grain mustard
1 tablespoon butter, cold

FOR WALNUT BROWN BUTTER:

½ cup butter
1 teaspoon lemon juice
¼ cup walnuts, toasted and chopped
Salt and pepper, to taste

TO COMPLETE:

¼ pound mixed baby greens or micro greens, for garnish

1 **For Crab Cake Mayo:** In a large bowl, crack the egg and whisk. Add the mayo, lemon juice, and Worcestershire sauce to the egg and whisk until smooth. Next, fold in the parsley and red pepper with a rubber spatula. Add salt and pepper to taste.

2 **For Crab Cakes:** Carefully remove the crab meat from the container and place in a bowl. Using your hands, gently pick through the meat and feel for shells. Try to keep the crab clusters as whole as possible as this will make for a much nicer crab cake. Put all crab cake ingredients (except oil) in mixing bowl and gently fold together—try not to break up the meat. Add salt and pepper to taste. Portion the crab cake mixture into six 3-ounce, 1"-thick cakes and refrigerate until needed. On the stove, place a large nonstick or cast-iron pan over medium-high heat. Place the oil in the pan and heat until it just starts to smoke. Gently place cakes in the pan and sear until golden brown on both sides, about 1 minute per side. Remove to a paper towel–lined plate and set aside.

3 **For Mustard Cider Reduction:** In a medium saucepan, place the apple cider and reduce by ¾ over medium heat. Next, add the vinegar and reduce again by ¾ over medium heat. This whole process should take about 20 to 30 minutes. Next, whisk in the mustard and butter over low heat until the butter is just melted; then turn off the stove. Leave the sauce in the pot until ready to plate.

4 **For Walnut Brown Butter:** In a small sauté pan, heat the butter on medium-high heat until it starts to brown, about 2 to 3 minutes. Then add the lemon juice and walnuts and mix in the pan. Add salt and pepper to taste. Turn off heat, leave in pan, and follow the plating instructions.

5 **To Complete:** Place each Crab Cake on a small salad plate and spoon 1 tablespoon Mustard Cider Reduction on the cake and around the plate. Repeat with Walnut Brown Butter, placing 1 tablespoon of the sauce on the cake and around the plate. Then take a small pinch of baby mixed greens and place them on top of the Crab Cake. Take a teaspoon of the Walnut Brown Butter and drizzle it on the greens. Lastly, pick up a fork and begin to devour your creation.

OWNER/EXECUTIVE CHEF

THE ORANGE SQUIRREL RESTAURANT, BLOOMFIELD, NJ

FRANCESCO PALMIERI

"I'm just in love with the squirrel lifestyle."

—Francesco Palmieri

FRANCESCO PALMIERI started to get interested in cooking as a child growing up in Bloomfield, New Jersey, and although his culinary path took him into New York City, it also brought him home again.

Francesco graduated from the Culinary Institute of America with his culinary degree in 2000 and, soon after, took a job at the Windows on the World restaurant in the World Trade Center in New York City. There, he trained with chef Michael Lomonaco, the TV personality and restaurateur who runs the steak house Porter House at the Time Warner Center in Manhattan. Francesco worked at Windows on the World until the tragic events of 9/11. With the restaurant he worked in now leveled, he joined Pino Luongo's team at Italian restaurant Coco Pazzo

as sous-chef. Francesco cooked for two years at Coco Pazzo, and finished as acting executive chef. He then left Coco Pazzo to take a sous-chef position at Town, a three-star restaurant (and *New York* magazine's "Best New Restaurant 2002") in the Chambers Hotel. There, he had the opportunity to work for Geoffrey Zakarian, one of Food Network's Iron Chefs. After three years, Francesco left and worked at a series of restaurants where he didn't quite fit. After the dust settled, Francesco knew that he wanted to be his own boss, and he began to form a plan to open his own place in his hometown of Bloomfield, NJ. He was able to return to Town and work the morning shift so he could pay his bills while working on his new place in the evenings.

Finally, in 2008, Francesco returned to his hometown full-time and opened the Orange Squirrel Restaurant, an Italian restaurant where Francesco serves as both executive chef and owner. He operates the small forty-seat space with the help of his chef de cuisine, Andy Watterson, whom he met while at the CIA, and a handful of servers. In this intimate setting, Francesco is able to touch everything and most nights can be seen seating a table, checking on the bar, and then hopping in the kitchen to finish a dish. This close connection to his patrons has earned him a lot of loyalty, which can be seen in the restaurant's growing collection of squirrel figurines that Francesco's patrons often bring him.

Bloomfield, NJ, is not known as the ideal place for a fine-dining restaurant. Situated just off the New Jersey Turnpike a few miles north of Newark, you could easily drive by it if you weren't looking for it. Yet the restaurant has thrived, earning a great review from *The New York Times*, which called it a "Don't Miss" and said that The Orange Squirrel " . . . is the most exciting new restaurant I've come across in 2009." Today, Francesco and The Orange Squirrel continue to build a reputation for fine cuisine and were named one of the "Top 25 Restaurants in New Jersey" by *New Jersey Monthly* in 2012. Most recently Francesco was been featured on *The Today Show* and *CBS News*.

Francesco finds inspiration for much of his tattoos in nature. When he was a young boy, he visited his father's old home in Italy and, while playing, found a crushed scorpion. He says, "I remember being fascinated by the iridescent blue of it." Jump forward to when Francesco was eighteen years old and went to a shop in New Jersey to get his first tattoo. He says, "I got the old tester tattoo on my lower stomach. You know, somewhere I could hide it from my parents." While looking at the flash around the shop, he found a scorpion, was reminded of the one he saw in his youth, and decided on that.

The magpie on his neck came soon after a trip to Colorado in 2010. He had never seen a magpie before and was fascinated by their mannerisms. They also reminded him of the old Terrytoons cartoon Heckle and Jeckle about a pair of magpies.

Francesco already has his next piece planned out, this time taking inspiration from his own garden. At his home, he grows squash and often uses the squash and their blossoms in his restaurant. He plans to work a full sleeve up his left arm of squash vines and blossoms, wrapping the design up around his shoulder and ending on his neck, with the magpie perched on a vine. Meanwhile he continues to try and improve the Orange Squirrel and speaks of maybe getting more involved in the world of television cooking.

Lobster Cobb Salad

This dish is currently on the menu at The Orange Squirrel Restaurant.

SERVES 2

FOR COURT BOUILLON:

4 gallons water

6 lemongrass stalks, bruised and sliced

3 bay leaves

4 ounces whole white peppercorns

1 (6-ounce) piece ginger, peeled and sliced

2 whole heads garlic, unpeeled and sliced
    in half horizontally

Kosher salt, to taste

FOR LOBSTER:

4 gallons Court Bouillon, divided

1 whole lobster, about 1½ pounds

FOR ROASTED GARLIC PURÉE:

2 whole garlic heads

Kosher salt, to taste

White pepper, to taste

4 ounces blended oil, divided

FOR DEVILED QUAIL EGGS:

1 pint water

1 ounce white vinegar

2 quail eggs

1 pint ice water

Dash lemon juice

½ ounce mayonnaise

¼ ounce Roasted Garlic Purée

Smoked paprika, to taste

Sel gris, to taste

Kosher salt, to taste

White pepper, to taste

1 **For Court Bouillon:** In a large pot (6 gallons), add all ingredients and bring to a boil for 15 minutes. Turn off heat, let steep for 10 minutes, and check seasoning. Strain, cool, and divide liquid in half. Half the liquid should be kept in pot to poach the lobster. The other half will be used to cool it. Place 1 gallon in ice cube trays and freeze; refrigerate the remaining gallon in a large bowl.

2 **For Lobster:** When ready to cook lobster, bring 2 gallons of Court Bouillon (CB) to a boil. Slowly submerge lobster, head first, into boiling CB. (4 minutes is the restaurant-preferred cook time—meat will be just set and translucent. You may prefer to cook up to 8 minutes.) After 4 minutes, remove lobster and place into the chilled gallon of CB with the CB ice cubes. (This ensures that you do not wash away the flavor of the CB when cooling off the lobster and stopping the cooking process.) Next, remove tail and slit in half with a large sharp knife, removing the shell and veins. With sharp kitchen shears, remove knuckle meat and carefully remove claw meat—do your best to not damage it. Place all meat into airtight container and reserve in refrigerator.

3 **For Roasted Garlic Purée:** Preheat oven to 275°F. With sharp serrated knife, slice off top of garlic heads to expose all cloves. Place in foil, season with salt and pepper, drizzle about 1 tablespoon of oil over them, and seal tightly. Roast in oven for 35 minutes or until cloves are golden and tender. Let cool; then squeeze out cloves and pass through a fine strainer into a small bowl. Whisk in remaining oil and emulsify; then place in airtight container and keep refrigerated.

4 **For Deviled Quail Eggs:** In a small pot, boil water and vinegar, carefully place eggs, and set timer for 4 minutes. Remove eggs and add to ice water. Gently peel off shells and split eggs in half vertically. Remove yolks (reserving egg whites) and pass through a fine strainer into a small mixing bowl. Add lemon juice, mayonnaise, and Roasted Garlic Purée and whip with whisk or small fork; check seasoning and adjust. Place in a small plastic pastry bag (small sandwich bag will also work) and reserve in refrigerator with egg whites. Upon assembly, this product will be piped into reserved egg white cavity.

FOR CHAMPAGNE GRAIN MUSTARD VINAIGRETTE:

½ ounce Dijon mustard
½ ounce whole grain mustard
1 ounce champagne vinegar
½ ounce honey
6 ounces blended oil
Kosher salt, to taste
White pepper, to taste

FOR BUTTERED CORN KERNELS:

2 whole ears of corn on the cob
3 ounces unsalted butter
3 sprigs thyme
2 garlic cloves, peeled
Kosher salt, to taste
White pepper, to taste

FOR PANCETTA LARDONS:

6 (¼-inch-thick) slices pancetta disks

FOR AVOCADO MOUSSE:

2 avocados, ripe
¼ ounce lemon juice
¼ ounce Roasted Garlic Purée
¼ ounce mayonnaise
Kosher salt, to taste
White pepper, to taste

TO COMPLETE:

12 leaves garden greens (Boston Bibb), cut into ¼-inch ribbons
Kosher salt, to taste
White pepper, to taste
Sel gris, to taste
Smoked paprika, to taste
¼ cup micro greens (mixed is best)

5 For Champagne Grain Mustard Vinaigrette: In a mixing bowl, add mustards, vinegar, and honey. Slowly whisk in oil to emulsify. Check seasoning, adjust if necessary, and place in airtight container. Reserve in refrigerator.

6 For Buttered Corn Kernels: On a cutting board, stand corn up and, with a firm grip and a sharp knife, slice off kernels, discarding cob when finished. In a sauté pan on low heat, add butter, thyme, and garlic until melted, about 2 minutes. Add corn kernels. Season and cook, stirring, for 10 to 15 minutes. Remove pan from heat and garlic and thyme sprigs from pan. Let corn cool down, place in airtight container, and refrigerate.

7 For Pancetta Lardons: Unroll pancetta disks, lay flat on a tray, and place in freezer for 10 to 15 minutes. (This will help ensure even cutting.) With sharp knife, slice ¼-inch pieces across. Place in sauté pan over low heat. As fat starts to melt and render, drain into a metal can. As lardons start to become golden and crispy, about 4 to 6 minutes, remove and place on paper towel–lined plate to cool. Reserve in a dry, cool place.

8 For Avocado Mousse: Remove skin and seed from avocados and squeeze the flesh through a fine strainer. Place in a mixing bowl and whisk in remaining ingredients. Season to taste and place in airtight container; reserve in refrigerator.

9 To Complete: In a small bowl, add greens, 3 ounces Pancetta Lardons, 4 ounces Buttered Corn Kernels, and 4 ounces Champagne Grain Mustard Vinaigrette. Season with salt and pepper and mix. The following steps should be done twice, once for each plate. Place half of the greens mixture inside a 3-inch round mold and pack down with a spoon. Then top with 1½ ounces of Avocado Mousse and spread evenly. Next, carefully perch half of the lobster tail on mousse and slowly raise mold. Drizzle plate with Vinaigrette and strategically place Deviled Quail Egg, after filling with the deviled yolk mixture. Season claw meat with sel gris and lay across bottom base. Finally, dress with smoked paprika and garnish with micro greens. Serve immediately.

PART 3
WINGED

RICK TRAMONTO

"Scars are not injuries, Tanner Sack. A scar is a healing. After injury, a scar is what makes you whole."

—China Miéville, *The Scar*

A THIRTY-PLUS-YEAR VETERAN TO RESTAURANTS, Rick is easily one of the most respected chefs to call Chicago home. He has published seven cookbooks; appeared on numerous television shows, including *The Today Show*, *Top Chef Masters*, and *Iron Chef*; and has worked at a very long list of highly ranked restaurants, such as Tavern on the Green; Gotham Bar and Grill in New York City; Charlie Trotter's in Chicago; Stapleford Park in Leicestershire, England; and the Criterion Restaurant in Piccadilly Circus. He has also run a variety of exclusive restaurants, including

CHEF/CO-OWNER

RESTAURANT R'EVOLUTION, TRAMONTO STEAK AND SEAFOOD, OSTERIA DI TRAMONTO, RT LOUNGE, CHICAGO, IL

the world renowned four-star fine-dining restaurant Tru, Tramonto Steak and Seafood, Osteria di Tramonto, and RT Lounge. He has worked with great European chefs, such as Pierre Gagnaire, Anton Mosimann, Michel Guérard, and Raymond Blanc.

Rick's success story is made even more amazing when you take his tough childhood into account. When Rick was fifteen, he came home to have his father tell him that he was fleeing the country for Mexico. Rick says, "He said that he was going to run away. He had embezzled a bunch of money and was in trouble with the law and needed to disappear for seven years. At first, it felt very exciting. It felt like being in a movie. It was like mafia, like growing up mafia." The next day, Rick skipped school and spent the day smoking pot with a friend across the street from his house. While there that afternoon, he saw federal agents come to his home looking for his father. His father was arrested two days later while trying to board a plane. He received five years in prison. Oddly enough, it was his father's arrest that started Rick on the road to culinary greatness. Being the only man of the house, he quit school and took a job at one of the only places he could: Wendy's.

As Rick discovered his talent for cooking and started working at better and better restaurants, he also met his first wife, Gale Gand, who is also a highly acclaimed chef. Once married, Gale and Rick went overseas to work with many of the chefs they had revered for so long including Pierre Gagnaire, Anton Mosimann, Michel Guerard, Raymond Blanc, and Alain Chapel. But after Gale's father's death, they returned to Chicago, where they decided to open their own restaurant, Tru, an upscale Mediterranean-influenced French restaurant. In the midst of opening Tru, Rick had some of the best experiences of his life—and some of the worst. While opening Tru, Gale

and Rick decided to divorce, and Rick lost his mother, his house, and even his dog. But he also signed his fourth book deal, and Tru became a world-class restaurant. Rick also rediscovered his faith that year. After his divorce, Rick spent all his time (eighty hours a week) working at Tru, and going to church. Then, out of the blue, he got a call from an old friend, Eileen Caroll. Rick met Eileen when he was working at Wendy's back in 1977. She was the sandwich girl next to his burger station. Two years after that, they were married, and Rick has never been happier.

Since food and faith are the two things that keep Rick going from day to day, they're also represented on his body. Rick is covered in tattoos, but the two that define him the most are the words down his forearms, "Chef" on his right and "Faith" on his left. His tattoos and his scars are symbols of the things that matter to him most and serve as a reminder of things he has chosen not to do anymore. Paying homage with ink to his love of food and faith, Rick's tattoos include a portrait of Jesus on his chest along with the passage from John 8:36—"If the Son therefore shall make you free, ye shall be free indeed"— on his left shoulder. He also has a knife set on his left calf; a pig and crab on his right arm; and wine, grapes, and barbed wire on his left arm. In progress on Rick's right elbow is a koi fish that symbolizes transformation and perseverance, traits that Rick knows well.

Today, Rick continues on his culinary path by travelling between Chicago and New Orleans, operating his awarded and highly popular restaurants. He has no plans to stop getting tattooed any time soon.

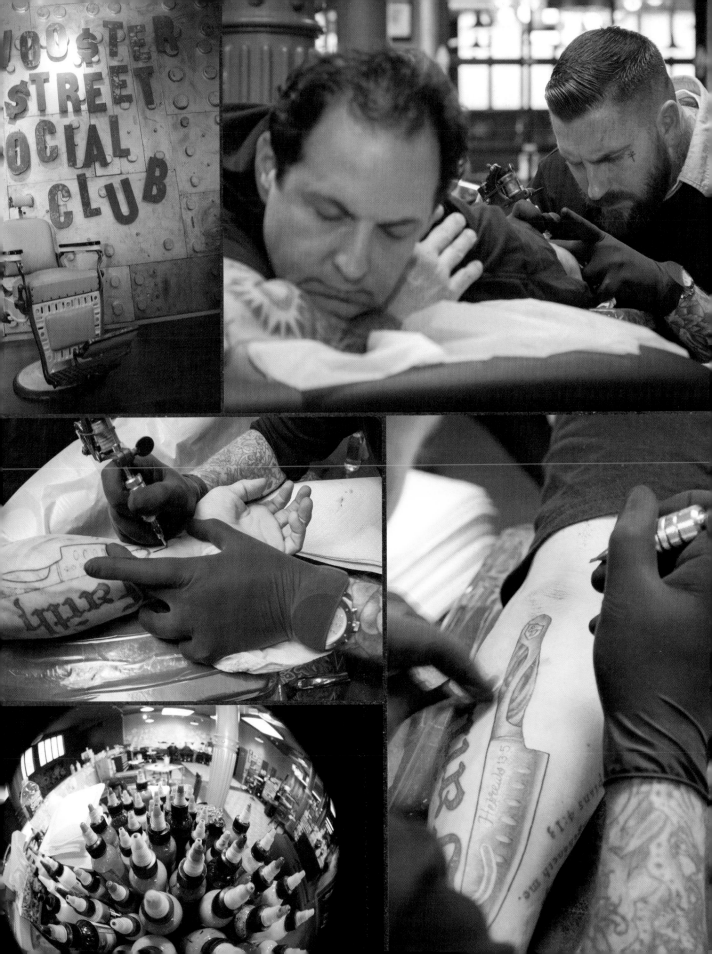

Gemelli con la Salsa dell Erba e Pollo (Gemelli with Chicken and Spring Herb Sauce)

This dish showcases Rick's Italian upbringing and heritage.

SERVES 4

FOR PARMESAN BROTH:

1 tablespoon whole peppercorns
1 teaspoon crushed red pepper flakes
1 gallon chicken stock
1½ pounds Parmigiano-Reggiano cheese rind or scraps of cheese
1 bay leaf
1 sprig fresh thyme
2 tablespoons olive oil
Kosher salt, to taste

FOR OVEN-DRIED CHERRY TOMATOES:

16 cherry tomatoes
About ¼ cup extra-virgin olive oil
Kosher salt and freshly ground black pepper, to taste

FOR SPRING HERB SAUCE:

1 cup extra-virgin olive oil
3 bunches flat-leaf parsley, stemmed
2 cups fresh basil leaves
½ cup fresh tarragon leaves
½ cup fresh chervil leaves
1 tablespoon chopped garlic
6 ice cubes
1 cup grated Parmigiano-Reggiano

TO COMPLETE:

12 ounces asparagus tips (usually 1 bunch)
1 cup torn roasted chicken meat
2 tablespoons unsalted butter
1 pound gemelli pasta
Kosher salt and freshly ground black pepper, to taste
4 ounces Parmigiano-Reggiano cheese

1 **For Parmesan Broth:** In a stockpot, toast the peppercorns and pepper flakes over medium heat for about 30 seconds or until fragrant. Add the chicken stock and cheese rind and bring to a simmer over medium-high heat. Add the bay leaf, thyme, and olive oil and simmer the broth uncovered for about 1 hour, adjusting the heat to maintain the simmer. Remove and discard the cheese rind and bay leaf. Season to taste with salt. Using a hand mixer or emulsion blender, mix the broth until smooth. Strain through a fine mesh sieve or chinois into a bowl. Use immediately or let the broth cool, cover, and refrigerate for up to 5 days.

2 **For Oven-Dried Cherry Tomatoes:** Preheat the oven to 250°F. Cut the tomatoes in half lengthwise. Set each half, cut-side up, on a baking pan and drizzle with enough olive oil to coat. Season lightly with salt and pepper. Let the tomatoes "dry" in the oven for about 20 minutes, or until they are slightly softened and the edges are slightly crispy. Let the tomatoes cool; then use immediately or refrigerate in an airtight container, covered with olive oil, for up to 7 days.

3 **For Spring Herb Sauce:** In the canister of a blender, process the oil, parsley, basil, tarragon, chervil, and garlic until smooth. Add the ice cubes and blend for 30 seconds, until the ice is crushed. Add the cheese and blend until incorporated. Cover and refrigerate for up to 2 days or until ready to use.

4 **To Complete:** Fill a saucepan with water to a depth of about 6 inches and bring to a simmer over medium-high heat. Add the asparagus tips and cook uncovered for about 1 minute, just until bright green. Place the tips in ice water to stop the cooking. Drain the asparagus tips and set aside. In a separate saucepan, bring 3 cups Parmesan Broth to a boil over medium-high heat. Add the chicken, asparagus, and butter. Return to a simmer and cook uncovered for about 5 minutes. Remove from heat and cover to keep warm. Meanwhile, cook the pasta according to the package directions until nearly al dente. Drain, reserving about ¼ cup of the pasta water. Add the pasta, 16 Oven-Dried Cherry Tomatoes, pasta water, and ¾ cup Spring Herb Sauce to the saucepan with the chicken and season to taste with salt and pepper. Bring to a brisk simmer over medium-high heat and cook uncovered for 2 minutes or until the pasta is al dente. Ladle into bowls and shave the cheese over the servings. Serve immediately.

CHEF DE CUISINE

DEPARTURE, PORTLAND, OR

GREGORY GOURDET

"I was run down from living that way
and needed a change."

—Gregory Gourdet

GREGORY GOURDET didn't start out thinking that he wanted to be a chef. Born and raised in Queens, New York, Gregory attended the University of Montana, where he studied wildlife biology and French. While there, he moved in with a roommate who turned out to be a pretty good cook. While cooking meals with his roommate, Gregory became interested in food and started working as a dishwasher at a vegetarian deli. By the time he graduated with his bachelor's degree, Gregory had decided to attend the Culinary Institute of America back in New York.

Gregory excelled at the CIA. He says, "It was the first time everything clicked and school was easy." After completing an externship with world-famous French chef and restaurateur Jean-Georges Vongerichten at Jean-Georges in New York City and graduating from culinary school, Gregory began working in the famous chef's kitchen full-time. Eventually he worked his way to chef de cuisine at 66, a former Jean-Georges modern Chinese restaurant. However, Gregory "was having way too much fun living that New York lifestyle." He was staying out all night clubbing and partying. He says, "I had major issues with substance abuse. I became unreliable and irresponsible." It took rehab and a move to Portland, Oregon, to make Gregory realize that he was missing out on the life he wanted, and that he wasn't being the person he wanted to be. Gregory says, "I got sober and quit smoking and have never looked back. In the past few years, I have accomplished goals I never imagined I wanted to achieve."

All the healthy living and hard work has paid off, and Gregory's food has received a variety of awards and accolades. In 2011, he was nominated for *Food & Wine*'s "People's Best New Chef Northwest," and in 2012, he won the Great American Seafood Cook-Off in New Orleans, becoming the first chef outside of a gulf state to win

this esteemed title. Also, his "Brussels Sprouts with Chili and Lime" was named one of the "Best Vegan Dishes in Portland" by *The Oregonian*, and he was named *Eater*'s "Hottest Chef in Portland." In addition, Gregory has completed twelve marathons, including three ultra-marathons (longer than 26.2 miles), and he has no plans to stop running. Gregory says, "There is a true sense of determination that comes with being an ultra-runner. This drive helps me in other parts of my life."

Gregory's tattoo is a tribute to the city that helped him get his big break. The tattoo is the center of a rose, the iconic symbol of the city of Portland, OR, and says, "To thine own self be true." For Gregory, it is a reminder about the good that can come when you give yourself second chances.

Curry Noodles, Slow Chicken, Pickled Mustard Greens, and Toasted Chili

This modern interpretation of a very traditional Thai dish, Khao Soi, is one of Gregory's signature dishes. At Departure, he finds inspiration in the Asian classics and updates them with modern cooking techniques and local products. Everything is connected to his tattoo: "To thine own self be true." You can't be anything or make anything without self-honesty.

YIELDS 6 SERVINGS

FOR CURRY NOODLE BROTH:
2½ ounces ginger, peeled, finely chopped
2½ ounces garlic, chopped
1½ ounces salt
3 ounces vegetable oil
1 ounce curry paste
1 ounce turmeric
72 ounces coconut milk
11 ounces palm sugar
3 chicken carcasses, roasted and chopped
36 ounces chicken stock
4 ounces fish sauce
3 ounces lime juice

FOR CHICKEN:
6 boneless chicken breasts and thighs, skin-on
Salt and pepper, to taste

TO COMPLETE:
15 ounces cooked, flat egg noodles
3 ounces toasted chili oil, to garnish (use to taste)
Pickled mustard greens, to garnish
Sliced shallots, to garnish
Cilantro leaves, to garnish
Fried, thin egg noodles, to garnish
Lime wedges, to garnish

1 For Curry Noodle Broth: In a large pot, sweat ginger and garlic in salt and oil. Cook uncovered over medium-low heat until aromatic and translucent, about 20 minutes. Add curry paste, turmeric, and some skimmed coconut milk fat and cook for 3 to 5 minutes, until fragrant and toasted. To get milk fat make sure not to shake the can of coconut milk before opening, open can, and scoop out the creamy coconut milk on top. Add remaining coconut milk, palm sugar, chicken carcasses, and chicken stock. Simmer uncovered until reduced by $1/3$ and at medium consistency, about 40 minutes. Add the fish sauce and lime juice. Bring to a quick simmer again and remove from heat. Let cool slightly and strain broth through a fine strainer. Squeeze bones and aromatic pulp well to get maximum flavor. Allow to cool completely; then refrigerate overnight. Broth stored in an airtight container will keep for 4 days in the fridge.

2 For Chicken: Season chicken with plenty of salt and pepper. Place in a large Cryovac bag with 2 cups of cold Curry Noodle Broth. Cook at 145°F in a circulator water bath for 55 minutes. If you don't have a Cryovac, season chicken with salt and pepper. In a large sauté pan, brown chicken over medium-high heat in 2 ounces of hot oil, skin-side down. Add 2 cups of Curry Noodle Broth and simmer chicken in broth until cooked and tender, about 40 minutes. Shock and cool completely in an ice bath. Dice chicken into bite-size pieces. Save and use all liquids when serving broth.

3 To Complete: In a large soup pot, add diced Chicken to Curry Noodle Broth and simmer uncovered at medium-low heat until hot. Pour 10 ounces of broth per person over blanched egg noodles. Garnish with toasted chili oil, pickled mustard greens, sliced shallots, cilantro, fried egg noodles, and a squeeze of lime wedge. Enjoy!

NOTES FROM THE CHEF

The chicken in this recipe is cooked in the broth, so when making this dish, make the broth a day ahead.

IAN MARKS

"Cooking is alchemy. I love the idea that food can be turned into gold simply by putting your soul into a dish. Be a Jack of all things food and try everything. This is the road to good cooking."

—Ian Marks

A SAN FRANCISCO NATIVE, Ian describes experiencing an upbringing of "cooking all around me." Raised by parents who nurtured an interest in cooking and baking, his older brother (who Ian still works with regularly) went to culinary school while Ian was still in high school, and Ian always felt the same calling. However, Ian didn't follow the path to culinary school that his brother took. Instead, he learned in the kitchen at Liberty Café, Hog Island Oyster Company, and Fatted Calf, where he picked up the art of charcuterie. Ian says, "It wasn't till I quit that I learned it was something I really enjoyed and missed." His experience in charcuterie came together in November 2010 when Ian and fellow Hog Island alum Dylan Denicke opened Beast and the Hare, a restaurant serving American and Italian cuisine with an Asian flair.

Ian wanted a feature of Beast and the Hare's menu to be meat cured on-premises and encouraged patrons to start with the charcuterie plate (a combination of chicken liver pâté and house-cured meat). The menu itself is "animal-focused." The numerous sandwiches on the menu reflect Ian's training at Fatted Calf, with a main feature being a daily special called the "Provisional Sandwich" based on how he's feeling each day. Ian says, "Beast and the Hare is really my start into the world of charcuterie. . . . It always amazes me every time I cure salumi. I can taste the days that passed. The natural fermentation or buildup of good bacteria that creates flavors unable to create anywhere else. Our salumi tastes like our salumi. Similar to a baker, the food is specific to the house it was made in."

Surprisingly, Ian's tattoo isn't based around his love of food. He got his first tattoo with a girlfriend when he was eighteen. He says, "I was dating this girl, and she had all these tattoos and piercings and was like, let's get a tattoo. So I said sure and we went." He ended up picking a piece of flash from a book, a "terrible tribal dragon thing." In the summer of 2011, a local artist and friend in San Francisco named Jill Bonny offered to cover it up for him. Inspired by one of Ian's favorite songs, Bob Dylan's "Lily, Rosemary and the Jack of Hearts," she designed an elaborate shoulder tattoo that evokes the song's complex lyrics. The finely shaded black ink piece focuses on a playing card–style Jack of Hearts with elaborate surrounding adornments. Ian says, "She just drew it out in a couple of seconds, and I thought, oh man that's so fucking cool." The tattoo covered up the dragon and was completed over several sessions at Jill's house. And while the tattoo doesn't showcase Ian's culinary talents, he would bring a bottle of whiskey and cook dinner for Jill after she'd finished tattooing him. Ian's next tattoo will be a scene from Jimmy Hendrix's "Long Hot Summer Night." He says it's only in his head right now, "so we'll see how it turns out."

> " I was dating this girl, and she had all these tattoos and piercings and was like, let's get a tattoo. So I said sure and we went. "

Duck Frites

FOR DUCK:
1 mallard duck breast
Salt and pepper, to taste
1 tablespoon piment d'Esplette

FOR FRITES:
Oil, to fry
2 yams, peeled and cut into fries
3 tablespoons Dijon mustard
¼ cup rice flour
Salt and pepper, to taste

FOR RAITA:
1 cup Greek yogurt
Zest and juice of 1 tangerine
Pinch of ground celery seed
Pinch of cumin
Pinch of coriander
1 clove garlic, minced
Salt, to taste

FOR SALSA VERDE:
2 small shallots, diced
1 cup white wine vinegar, enough to drown
　the shallots
3 tablespoons chopped parsley
3 teaspoons chopped marjoram
3 teaspoons chopped chives
3 teaspoons chopped mint
¾ cup quality extra-virgin olive oil

TO COMPLETE:
Parsley, to taste, for garnish
Chives, to taste, for garnish
Marjoram, to taste, for garnish

1 For Duck: Pat duck breast dry with a paper towel; then massage salt onto meat side. Score fat side with the tip of your knife to help fat render. Heat a cast-iron pan to high, add 1 tablespoon salt, place duck skin-side down, and lower heat to medium-low to slowly render the duck fat. When skin is golden brown, about 6 minutes, remove duck and wipe clean with a paper towel. Rub the piment d'Esplette on the flesh side of the duck and return to pan, skin-side up, for another 4 minutes or so to finish cooking. Cook for another 6 minutes on the flesh side. Remove duck from pan and set aside to rest.

2 For Frites: Fill a heavy-bottomed 14-quart pot with oil and heat to 325°F. Blanch fries for 5 minutes; then remove yam frites from oil and drain on a paper towel–lined plate. Mix mustard and rice flour in a bowl and toss yam frites to coat. Raise oil temperature to 350–365°F. Fry yam frites again until golden brown and crispy. This should take about 3 to 4 minutes max. Remove with a slotted spoon into a bowl with a paper towel. Toss with salt and pepper.

3 For Raita: Place all ingredients in a bowl and mix to combine.

4 For Salsa Verde: Soak diced shallots in white wine vinegar for 10 minutes; then drain. Combine shallots with remaining ingredients and mix to combine.

5 To Complete: Slice the duck breast on the bias, sprinkle with salt, and fan out on your plate. Nestle the Frites next to the Duck. Drizzle the Salsa Verde over the duck. Serve the Raita in a little ramekin on the side and garnish the dish with parsley, chives, and/or marjoram.

NOTES FROM THE CHEF

Feel free to substitute any of the herbs in the Salsa Verde for your favorite. Ian says, "Any herbs will do here. I used parsley, chives, and marjoram, but mint, oregano, or cilantro can easily be substituted."

CHEF
20 SPOT, SAN FRANCISCO, CA

ANTHONY PAONE

"I like that old-school aesthetic. I prefer pencil sharpeners to word processors."

—Anthony Paone

COMING FROM AN ITALIAN-AMERICAN FAMILY, Anthony was inspired to start cooking because of the enjoyment he found in it at home. He says, "I enjoyed the time around the table and just pursued interests that revolved around that conviviality." And pursue a culinary career he did.

After graduating from the New York Restaurant School, Anthony Paone, a Staten Island native, felt satisfied that twenty-one years on the East Coast was sufficient and, with the encouragement of friend and fellow chef Erik Hopfinger and the promise of a job, he moved to San Francisco in 1997. Once settled, Anthony worked at small restaurants, eventually working his way up to become the executive chef of both Sea Salt and T-Rex Restaurant & Bar, two of many popular Bay Area restaurants owned by restaurateurs Haig and Cindy Krikorian's K2 Restaurant Group. Anthony amicably parted with the group in 2011, and worked toward opening his own restaurant.

Anthony says, "I truly love just about every part of the job. The beginning of the day with ingredients and energy, tackling all of the tasks and obstacles to making that night's offerings the best they can be. I am also quite passionate about buying and cooking with 'clean' food. The best in animal husbandry, ocean stewardship, and organic produce are at my disposal, and I take full advantage." While he was working at both Sea Salt and

> ## " I JUST REALLY LOVE TATTOO CULTURE, SO TATTOOS MAY HAVE ALWAYS BEEN A GIVEN FOR ME. "

T-Rex simultaneously, he developed relationships with meat, fish, and produce purveyors that continue to this day, as does his dedication to sourcing the best possible product.

Anthony is now the proud owner of wine bar 20 Spot, which opened in March 2013. The restaurant has Anthony working creatively using mainly raw food and serving well-planned and thought-out bar snacks since the wine bar doesn't have a full kitchen.

Anthony is as passionate about his ink as he is about his cooking. He says, "I just really love tattoo culture, so tattoos may have always been a given for me." Many of his tattoos are food-oriented. A large wooden-handled sashimi knife, a replica of a favorite of his, adorns his right forearm. He had originally intended to have the actual knife to scale on his body, but it would have run from his wrist to his shoulder. On the opposite side of his right

forearm sits the word "cafone," Italian for a person who is ill-mannered or uncouth, and below that is "nullius in verba," which is Latin for "on the word of no one" or "take nobody's word for it." Across Anthony's left forearm is a large yellowfin tuna. Sea Salt was a completely sustainable seafood restaurant, and Anthony's time there led him to have a fascination and respect for the fish. Anthony laments that tuna is not really a sustainable fish: "Most tunas are going to be fished to extinction. Unfortunately, they're analogous to lions or tigers on the land." While it's not quite as endangered as the tuna Anthony also has a crawfish on the back of his right arm, and a large squid on his bicep. On the inside of his wrist is a naked man eating a sandwich. He says, "In 2000 I was in Holland and I bought a pencil drawing, 2" by 2", of this image. I liked it and kept it and put it near my computer for years until the drawing started to wear. I decided to get it tattooed cause I liked it so."

Anthony describes his nonculinary tattoos as embodying a spirit of "recently deceased Americana." These tattoos include a pencil sharpener, a one-cent stamp, and a cassette tape. Anthony says he's the kind of guy who'd love a coffee table book of "things people born after a certain date don't know what they are." Hopefully, the tuna won't go the same way as these tattoos.

Chef's Day-After Breakfast

How did this recipe come about? Anthony says, "I had taken a chicken home from work the night before, and because a bit of wine was consumed, the chicken was only picked at before I fell asleep. When I woke up and saw my wife off to work, I rolled a smoke and settled in for a bit of pre-shower recovery in the form of a cup of strong coffee. What I cooked to finish my recovery is pretty much what I have written here."

SERVES 1

FOR CHICKEN:
1 chicken leg, left over from roasted chicken
2 cups chicken stock (chefs tend to have chicken stock handy for moments like this)

FOR GRITS:
2 cups water
1 cup milk
½ cup Anson Mills grits, or quick grits
Salt and pepper, to taste
½ cup any cheese, grated (optional)

FOR SALSA VERDE:
1 clove garlic
Salt, to taste
1 piece anchovy
½ cup kale, left over from roasted chicken
1 tablespoon parsley
1 tablespoon mint
Marash pepper, to taste
2–4 tablespoons vinegar
California extra-virgin olive oil

FOR PICKLED ONION:
1 red onion
1 cup red wine vinegar
⅓ cup water
1 bay leaf
1 Balinese long peppercorn (can use 2 black peppercorns)
1 allspice berry
2 tablespoons sugar

1 For Chicken: Preheat oven to 300°F. Place chicken leg and stock in an ovensafe cast-iron pan and put in oven, uncovered. As the chicken leg heats through, it will go from leftover and cold, to hot and braised. This should take 20 to 30 minutes. Remove from heat and set aside.

2 For Grits: While the chicken is in the oven, combine water and milk in a pot and bring to a boil. Whisk in the grits. Season with a little salt and pepper and reduce heat to very low. Cook, whisking the whole time, until creamy and delicious, about 30 to 40 minutes if you are using Anson Mills grits. If you are using "quick cook grits," follow box instructions. Remove from heat, whisk or fold in cheese, and set aside. (Since we regularly have cheese around, I usually add some, but it is more of a gilding of the lily than a necessity.) In truth, you can cook the grits in a rice cooker while you shower and wait for the chicken, or you could use instant grits, which are easier but less satisfying.

3 For Salsa Verde: First, pound garlic, salt, and anchovy in a mortar and pestle until it forms a paste. Then add kale, parsley, mint (you can use any green herbs here, except cilantro or dill), and pepper (I use marash, but chili flakes, Aleppo, etc., are all acceptable) and grind until it is a semi-homogenous paste. Taste. Add a little vinegar. Taste again. (It shouldn't be very vinegary, but rather balanced with the herbs and garlic.) Then add enough olive oil to make the mixture "spoonable." Taste again, adjusting seasoning to your liking.

4 For Pickled Onion: Slice onion and place into large bowl. Bring vinegar, water, spices, and sugar to a boil. Pour boiling liquid over onion. Let sit for 10 minutes before using. I usually make these in batches and keep them in the fridge for moments like this. The liquid can be stored in the fridge for up to 6 months. Serve cold.

NOTES FROM THE CHEF

Making Salsa Verde is a very versatile thing. You can make any variation (add capers or nuts) for any number of dishes. Making a sauce can help you use up small amounts of leftover herbs or greens. Use it for meat, fish, eggs, or vegetables.

FOR POACHED EGG:
Large pinch of salt
1–2 tablespoons white vinegar
1 egg

TO COMPLETE:
California extra-virgin olive oil, to garnish
Arugula, to garnish

5 **For Poached Egg:** Fill a small pot ¾ full with water. Bring water, salt, and white vinegar to a simmer in an uncovered pot and poach egg to your desired doneness, about 3 to 5 minutes. (I like mine quite runny.) Remove and set aside.

6 **To Complete:** Put a large spoonful of Grits on the plate and top with chicken leg, spooning some of the reduced chicken stock from the pan over the chicken (it's nice to squeeze a little lemon in this stock just before). Place your Poached Egg alongside the chicken and spoon some of your rustic Salsa Verde on top. Then sprinkle with Pickled Onion slices and maybe drizzle some good California extra-virgin olive oil on top. Garnish with arugula (because I live in California, and we have to garnish everything with arugula—it's the law). Serve immediately.

JOHNNY CLARK

> "It was about nature and foraging and the medicinal qualities of food . . . a little bit of spiritual-ness to food."
>
> —Johnny Clark

JOHNNY'S EXTREME FASCINATION with history led him to his love of classic French food. History is the only class he consistently got A's in during high school. He says, "So I became a bit of a Francophile due to the food history. There is no other cuisine with such well-recorded food history." With his love of cooking well documented, it came as no surprise when Johnny Clark started to attend the Culinary Institute of America in 2000. After graduation, Johnny spent nearly eight years in New York working a variety of jobs, most notably under chefs Jean-Jacques Rachou and Geoffrey Zakarian at the highly acclaimed restaurant Town. Johnny says, "I've always had my own passion and drive, so I just looked for places that

I could make a living, continue my path, and hopefully learn something from others."

An opportunity came along in the summer of 2008 for Johnny to work for chef Yim Gi Ho, whom he now considers a mentor, at Sandang just outside of Seoul, South Korea, and he took it. Johnny says, "I'm interested in all food and open to all opportunities." He describes Yim Gi Ho's cooking as neither modern nor traditional, but as process emphasizing nature. Johnny says, "It was almost so old world it was modern . . . I've never worked in such a unified kitchen before. Everyone was on the same team. Just [Yim Gi Ho's] personality in general is very inspiring. Overall a really great role

model." Johnny remembers driving to the ocean for sea water (a necessary coagulant to break down proteins) to make tofu instead of using a store-bought chemical compound. His time in Korea affected him more than he expected and he returned to the U.S. deeply interested in Korean cuisine.

Johnny's time in Korea influenced more than just his cooking. Three mugunghwa blossoms (a hibiscus commonly known as "the Rose of Sharon" in North America) are inked across his inner right arm. In Korean, the flower's name is derived from the word *mugung*, meaning "eternity," and it is the national flower of Korea. They are a memento of the summer in Korea that meant so much to him.

Understandably, Johnny's return to New York resulted in a major culture shock, and he soon found himself living with his brother in Chicago. Uninspired by the heavy fat- and salt-based cuisine, he sought out chefs doing something similar to what he'd done in Korea. Johnny read an article about Beverly Kim, a chef who had worked in Korea and was interested in cooking Korean food, and wrote her. When Johnny and Beverly met, they were each in a relationship, but they started dating each other not long after and eventually married. Today, their goal is to open a place together that is not a "Korean grill" but a neighborhood restaurant that uses Korean ingredients and preparation in a cuisine that will be their own.

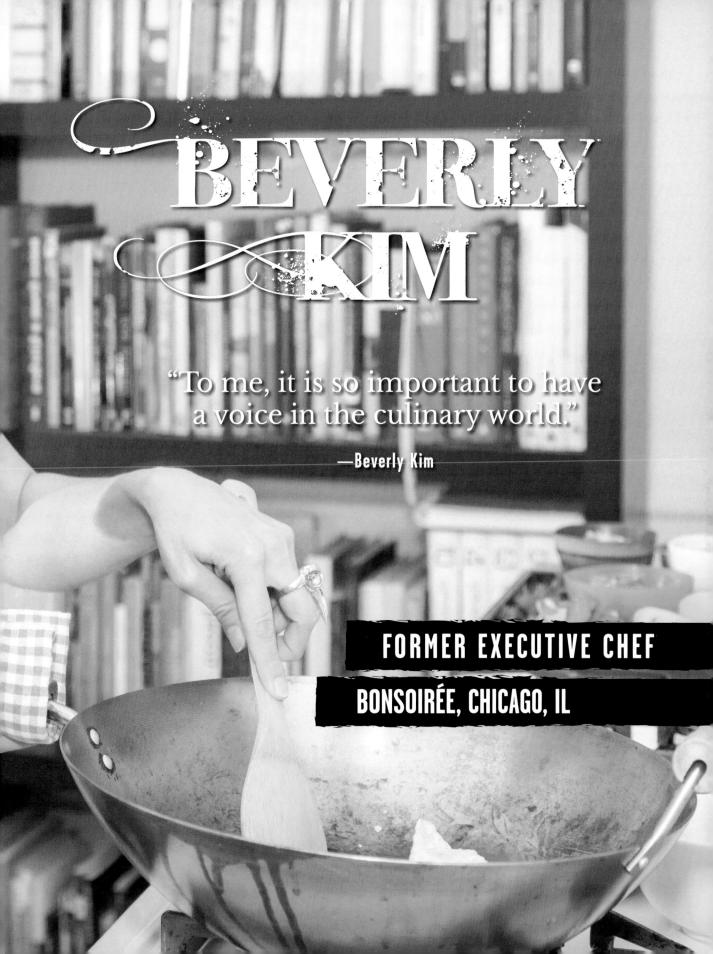

BEVERLY KIM

"To me, it is so important to have a voice in the culinary world."

—Beverly Kim

FORMER EXECUTIVE CHEF

BONSOIRÉE, CHICAGO, IL

BYPASSING AN OFFER to attend Northwestern University, Beverly decided to attend the School of Culinary Arts at Kendall College. Beverly, ever a good student, excelled in her academic classes but found herself struggling in her culinary classes. "I got a sort of rude awakening when I went to culinary school." Growing up in a Korean family and never going out to eat fine dining Western cuisine with her family growing up, she struggled to find a frame of reference to put her cooking in. She eventually found her place in the kitchen, but she had to learn to fight for it. After graduating with a culinary arts degree in 2000, she took advantage of Chicago's top-notch restaurant industry and started working on the line under George Bumbaris and James Beard Award–winning chef Sarah Stegner in the Ritz-Carlton right out of culinary school. Sarah became a mentor to Beverly and helped her expand her professional knowledge.

Wanting to expand her experience Beverly left the Ritz-Carlton to take a cook position at the famed Charlie Trotter's under chef Matthias Merges and stayed for a year and a half. She then did a stint in catering and worked her way up to sous-chef at J and L Catering, but Beverly confirmed her identity as a restaurant chef and returned to work for chefs Sarah Stegner and George Bumbaris at their "home-cooking with flair" restaurant Prairie Grass Cafe in Northbrook, Illinois.

After a life-changing car accident, Beverly decided to spend her savings and travel for two months in Korea. She had never been and, while there, she experienced her family's native cuisine firsthand by taking Korean Royal Cuisine classes, and staging at Shilla Hotel and Top Cloud restaurant. This experience led her to approach American cuisine with the Korean "refreshing," "earthy" flavors and textures she grew up with and explored on her trip. She says, "Growing up with more out-there kind of flavors is something I crave, so I bring that into my food a little."

When Beverly returned to Chicago she found another mentor in Chef Jackie Shen at Chicago's Red Light. There Beverly learned how to truly run a kitchen, and was also able to explore her family's cuisine in the modern Asian fusion restaurant. She started at Red Light on the grill and was promoted to sous-chef, but she soon had the opportunity to be the chef de cuisine at Opera (a sister restaurant) under Chef Paul Wildermuth. Ever looking to learn and gain experience she would move on to work briefly on the hot line at Takashi, a French-Japanese fusion restaurant, but would soon have to leave her position and the Chicago culinary scene.

While working at Takashi Beverly learned she was pregnant and continued to work on the line until she was six months pregnant and finally had to step down. After that change, she moved to Cincinnati and took a job with Whole Foods. At the same time she got married to Johnny Clark. While she felt like it was the right thing for her family, she worried she was moving away from her dream of being a chef. Then one day, a headhunter called her randomly to work at Aria, a fine dining Asian restaurant in the Fairmont Hotel.

The renewed confidence she felt returning to work, combined with the news that she had been selected to appear on Season Nine of *Top Chef*, inspired the phoenix tattooed on her left arm. She says, "It was this aha moment where I felt like I didn't have anywhere to go and then this rebirth happened." Although she didn't win her season of *Top Chef*, she was the first chef to win *Last Chance Kitchen*, the Bravo web series from *Top Chef* that puts eliminated chefs in head-to-head challenges for a chance to return to the main competition. Today, Beverly lives in Chicago with her husband and fellow chef Johnny Clark. They continue to work freelance while pursuing their dream of opening a neighborhood restaurant with a Korean twist.

"GROWING UP WITH MORE OUT-THERE KIND OF FLAVORS IS SOMETHING I CRAVE, SO I BRING THAT INTO MY FOOD A LITTLE."

Nasi Goreng

Beverly says, "This recipe is representative of the complexity and range of spice, umami, sour, sweetness, and textures that are representative of my up-and-coming restaurant."

YIELDS 1 HEARTY ENTRÉE OR 4 SIDES

3 ounces grapeseed oil

3 whole dried Thai chilies

1 egg, whisked

2 tablespoons minced onions

½ teaspoon minced ginger

1 teaspoon minced garlic

½ teaspoon minced lemongrass

1 ounce chopped shrimp

2½ ounces chopped cooked chicken

¾ ounce barbecue pork (you can buy at a Chinese market)

¾ ounce lap cheong (Chinese sausage)

¼ cup shiitake mushrooms

¼ cup heirloom tomatoes

¼ cup edamame

¼ cup sugar snap peas

¼ cup bean sprouts

2 tablespoons peanuts

2 cups cooked brown rice

1 ounce Shaoxing wine

1½ tablespoons kecap manis

½ teaspoon salt

Pinch of sugar

Pinch of white pepper

Juice of 1 lime

1 teaspoon sambal

2 tablespoons chopped shallots

2 tablespoons chopped cilantro

2 tablespoons chopped scallions

1 Heat wok on high heat. Add oil. Add whole chilies and allow to darken, a few seconds. Add egg and cook for 10 to 15 seconds; the egg will quickly puff. Then add minced onions, ginger, garlic, and lemongrass, stirring constantly for 15 to 30 seconds. Then, add your proteins (shrimp, chicken, barbecue pork, lap cheong), stirring for 1 to 2 minutes. Add the rest of the ingredients, up to and including brown rice. Fry the rice and veggies in the oil for about 2 to 3 minutes.

2 Deglaze with Shaoxing; then season with kecap manis, salt, sugar, white pepper, lime juice, and sambal. Turn off the heat, garnish with crispy shallots and freshly chopped cilantro and scallions, and serve immediately.

SEAMUS MULLEN

> "Thanks to the beautiful irony of nature, it just so happens that many of the things that I love are in fact very good for me."
>
> —Seamus Mullen

SEAMUS MULLEN learned butchery and got his start in restaurants while growing up on an organic farm in Vermont. However, it wasn't until a trip he took his senior year in high school to Spain that he found his culinary calling. Enamored with the country's food and culture, he returned to enroll at Kalamazoo College in Michigan, where he concentrated on Spanish language and literature. He then returned to Spain to study at Universidad Autonoma de Extremadura in Cáceres and take in the ancient city's rich history before graduating in 1996. After returning home, he was encouraged by his grandmother Mutti to make cooking a career and eventually ended up in San Francisco working at Mecca, a modern American restaurant and lounge that focused on high-quality local produce; at the time the *San Francisco Chronicle* had given Mecca a three-star rating. Seeking the next challenge, Seamus moved to New York to work for Floyd Cardoz at *The New York Times* two-star contemporary Indian restaurant Tabla. There, Seamus says he learned more about spices from Floyd than anyone else. In 2003, he went on to open Crudo and crafted a Mediterranean-inspired menu based on raw fish.

Wanting to learn more about Spanish cuisines, Seamus moved back to Spain in 2003 and went on to work some of the best restaurants in the country, including Mugaritz (given two Michelin stars), in Errenteria, and both Abac

" [ARTICHOKES] ARE THE POET WARRIORS OF VEGETABLES. "

and Alkimia, in Barcelona. After two years, Seamus returned to New York to become a founding partner in Boqueria, a casual but authentic Spanish tapas restaurant that opened in 2006. After earning a strong local following with Boqueria's traditional tapas menu, Seamus gained national recognition in 2009 on Food Network's *Next Iron Chef*.

While still working at Boqueria, Seamus was diagnosed with rheumatoid arthritis, a particularly terrible disease for a chef who spends fourteen hours a day on his feet. While Seamus was able to manage the disease with medication, it also sent him down the path toward treating himself with what he already knew best: food. Seamus's experiments in the kitchen eventually led to the publication of his first cookbook: *Hero Food: How Cooking with Delicious Things Can Make Us Feel Better*. Unfortunately, unable to resolve a difference in the vision for Boqueria with his partner Yann de Rochefort, Seamus eventually struck out on his own. Today, Seamus is the chef and owner of Spanish restaurant Tertulia in Manhattan's West Village. Tertulia received three stars from New York magazine and two stars from *The New York Times* and was named one of the "Top 10 New Restaurants of 2011" by Sam Sifton of *The New York Times*.

Seamus got his Asian-inspired ¾ sleeves early in his career, not bringing them fully down so he could still

cover them with a chef's coat. However, he has one culinary tattoo that is particularly meaningful to him. Across his chest is an artichoke. Why an artichoke? Without missing a beat, Seamus says, "They are the poet warriors of vegetables." While you might get the thorns on the outside, artichokes have a soft heart in the center. In addition, in Seamus's view, artichokes are one of the hardest things to cook. When he has new chefs training at his restaurant, during a trial phase to see if they will make it, his favorite thing to give them is an artichoke. Like the tales of the final test at culinary school being to cook a perfect egg, he views the ability to properly cook an artichoke as a true test of a cook's skill.

Tosta Huevo Roto

YIELDS 4 SERVINGS

1 Spanish onion, julienned
2 whole cloves garlic
1 liter Arbequina olive oil
5 Yukon gold potatoes, peeled and
    sliced into $1/8$" thick slices
2 eggs
Salt, to taste
2 soft, olive oil rolls
4 slices jamón ibérico

1 Warm onion and garlic in a small pot with the olive oil over medium high heat. When onions soften, about 10 minutes, add sliced potatoes and reduce heat to medium. Cook potatoes until tender, about 30 minutes, stirring occasionally.

2 While potatoes are cooking, drop eggs into a pot of boiling water for 6 minutes. Remove from water and place immediately in an ice bath. Remove eggs from ice bath after 5 minutes, peel, and slice in half. Egg yolk should be slightly runny.

3 Remove potatoes from heat, strain oil, and season with salt to taste.

4 Cut rolls in half horizontally and toast. Top with a heaping spoonful of potatoes, half an egg, a pinch of salt, and a drizzle of Arbequina olive oil. Finish with 1 slice of jamón ibérico.

EXECUTIVE CHEF

CORNER HOUSE, DENVER, CO

MATT SELBY

> "I finally realized in doing what I love,
> I want to do it in a city that I love."
>
> —Matt Selby

BORN AND RAISED IN DENVER, Matt Selby has worked hard to help put Denver on the culinary map. He started his culinary adventures by serving up burgers and cheese sticks in Bennigan's kitchens and found his way into a lot of local Denver restaurants, most notably Rattlesnake Grill. Matt says, "Rattlesnake was my first real kitchen!" While there, he worked for Mel Master, a well-known Denver restaurateur, and worked at all of his restaurants at some point.

Matt soon made a move toward finer dining and earned local fame as the head of Vesta Dipping Grill in downtown Denver. He ran the kitchen as executive chef for fifteen years and received numerous write-ups in the local and national press.

In the fall of 2012, Matt finally left the restaurant to partner with James Iacino of the Seattle Fish Co. and real estate investor Scott Kinsey to create the bistro-style restaurant Corner House. Matt says, "Leaving the Vesta family was one of the most difficult decisions I've ever made! I made that decision though, simply based on the overwhelming feeling that it was time to take the lessons I learned from that family, and apply them to my own restaurant."

Food has inspired many of Matt's tattoos. He says, "[My tattoos] are really just predominantly things I'm interested in, which is food, cars, toys, and family." Matt drew his own first tattoo, a "little skateboarder dude." He also has full sleeves that feature images ranging from salt and pepper shakers to the atomic age red robot. He says, "I collect old vintage windup toys. Cars and things like that, so I got the Chevy bowtie. I'm pretty white trash that way." He also has chopstick instructions and his own take on the Catholic sacred heart, a "sacred peach." In 2006, he got the words "Foie Gras" across his knuckles, which is the tattoo he is best known for because it is the most visible of his tattoos. After his first culinary tattoo of fennel, he started thinking in terms of things he would want to get tattooed. He had the desire to tattoo his knuckles for a while and would often run ideas by his wife. He says "One day I was driving home after a long day of work and it hit me like a bolt of lighting. Two words eight letters, was what I was looking for and very much ties into what I enjoy and what I do for a living."

Truffle Salt–Cured Foie Gras

This recipe is included in honor of the "Foie Gras" tattoo on Matt's knuckles.

YIELDS 4 SERVINGS

FOR FOIE GRAS:
1 lobe Hudson Valley foie gras, Grade B
2 cups sweet Riesling
4 cups kosher salt
2 ounces truffle salt

FOR PICKLED CAULIFLOWER:
1 pound cauliflower, thinly sliced
1 quart white wine vinegar
1 cup water
1 cup sugar
½ cup kosher salt
1 ounce pickling spice, wrapped and tied in cheesecloth
Pinch of turmeric

1 **For Foie Gras:** Slice the foie gras lobe in half, lengthwise. By hand, pick the halves apart. Look for and discard veins, blood line, membrane, and any other impurities. Place the cleaned foie gras pieces into a container and chill. Meanwhile, in a small saucepan, pour the Riesling and place over medium heat. Bring the Riesling to a boil and allow it to simmer for about 2 to 3 minutes to cook out the alcohol. Remove from heat. Place in the fridge to chill for at least 30 minutes.

2 Pour the Riesling over the foie gras pieces, mix by hand, and allow foie gras to marinate for at least 1 hour in the refrigerator. Strain the foie gras and discard the wine. Then, in a mixing bowl, combine the kosher salt and truffle salt to homogenize. Set aside until after you've rolled the foie gras.

3 Roll out 2 lines of cheesecloth, about 1½ feet long, vertically onto a work surface. Place ½ of the foie gras onto 1 line of the cheesecloth, about 4" from the bottom and centered. At the end closest to you, where the foie gras has been placed, roll the bottom of the cheesecloth over the foie, so that the end touches cheesecloth to cheesecloth. Roll the cheesecloth with one hand firmly planted on the excess cheesecloth above the top of the roll and the other hand firmly pulling the foie to tighten. About halfway through rolling, pinch the sides of the foie to compact the foie roll. After you have finished rolling, twist the ends of the cheesecloth around the foie, to tighten the roll. Use a piece of butcher twine to tie one end, retighten, and then tie the other end. Repeat process with remaining foie.

4 In the bottom of a baking dish or terrine pan, spread enough of the salt mixture to be sure that the foie gras will not touch the bottom of the pan. Place the foie rolls over the salt and then cover completely with the remaining salt. Allow foie rolls to cure covered in the salt in the refrigerator for at least 16 hours. After they have cured, pull the foie rolls out of the salt, brush away excess salt, and unwrap from cheesecloth. Rewrap foie rolls with a clean linen until ready to serve.

5 **For Pickled Cauliflower:** Place the thinly sliced cauliflower in a mixing bowl. Combine the remaining ingredients in a saucepan and simmer uncovered on medium-low heat for about 10 minutes. Strain; then pour the mixture over the cauliflower. Allow the mixture to sit at room temperature uncovered for 1 hour and then chill for at least 1 hour (can hold cold for at least 1 month).

FOR PEAR GASTRIQUE:

1 Bosc pear, peeled, cored, and finely diced

½ cup red wine

2 cups water

1 cup sugar

1 teaspoon minced Fresno chili

½ teaspoon minced fresh rosemary

TO COMPLETE:

Finely snipped chives, for garnish

6 **For Pear Gastrique:** In a saucepan, combine the diced pears, red wine, water, sugar, and Fresno chili. Place mixture over high heat and allow mixture to reduce until thick and syrupy, about 10 minutes. Whisk in the minced rosemary, remove from heat, and place covered in fridge, until cold, at least 1 hour.

7 **To Complete:** To plate, slice Foie Gras into ¼" disks. Place the disks on a plate, and then place a small amount of Pickled Cauliflower over each piece. Finish by spooning about ½ teaspoon of the Pear Gastrique over each piece of Foie Gras. Garnish with finely snipped chives.

PART 4
ROOTED

JILL BARRON

"[Duck fat] is the best fat in the world, clean and pretty. It is like snow."

—Jill Barron

CHEF/PARTNER

MANA FOOD BAR, CHICAGO, IL

> ❝ If [tattoos] aren't personal . . .
> I don't know, [getting one] just
> doesn't make a lot of sense to me. ❞

JILL BARRON started her culinary career by interning for Michael Short at Star Top Cafe in Chicago before further developing her culinary skills in Los Angeles. The farmers' markets in L.A. are where she found her passion for fresh ingredients but also many ingredients she had never seen in Chicago. The city's Asian and Hispanic population brought many fruits and vegetables that were not commonly used in cooking at the time and this opened up new possibilities for cooking. But Jill got more than her love for farmers' markets in L.A. She also got an ear of corn tattoo on her right leg as a tribute to her Midwestern roots when she started to get homesick. She says, "I started missing Chicago. People in the Midwest are just solid."

Jill decided to return to Chicago and took a job with the restaurant group Big Time Productions opening restaurants such as Ooh-la-la and Vinyl, as well as consulting on Angelina, an Italian bistro. She would go on to work in myriad different cuisines, taking jobs with Mediterranean restaurant Tizi Melloul, Latin restaurant Watusi, and Japanese restaurant Sushi Wabi. Finally, in 2004, Jill opened De Cero, a taquería, with Susan Thompson and Angela Lee of Sushi Wabi. Their taquería concept at De Cero has had great reviews, winning the restaurant a spot in *Chicago* magazine's "20 Best New Restaurants" as well as "Dish of the Year."

In 2008, Jill, along with business partner Susan Thompson, opened MANA Food Bar, an all-vegetarian restaurant. Jill loves eating meat, and she has the tattoos to prove it, but she strongly believes we eat too much meat in America and hopes MANA can show people how to abstain at least one day a week. Yet, more than simply going without something, or imitating the main protein, Jill's goal is to get people to fall in love with vegetarian dishes. "When I go to vegetarian restaurants, it is a lot about fake food. Why would you want to eat a fake cheeseburger?"

Like her food, Jill's tattoos—similar to those of her husband and fellow chef, Chris Barron (see entry in Part 1)—are a collection of self-expression. She says, "If they aren't personal . . . I don't know, it just doesn't make a lot of sense to me." Her right arm is inked with her "Canadian monkey pope." Why? Because she was born the year of the monkey, her family is French Canadian, and she was raised Catholic. Below that, wrapped around her arm are the words "white sugar," one of her go-to ingredients for bringing balance to a dish. On her other arm, the tattoo of sparrows holding a ribbon reading "Duck Fat" is a tribute to another of her favorite ingredients. Above the ear of corn on her leg, she has a skull and crossbones breakfast in one of her favorite kitchen tools, a cast-iron pan. While there may be more tattoos in her future, her only rule is no neck or hand tattoos. "I like that I can cover up and no one is the wiser."

Ma Po Tofu

While Jill eats meat she owns and operates MANA, an all-vegetarian restaurant. This meat-free spicy dish is a regular item on her menu.

SERVES 4

1 medium eggplant, diced
½ cup olive oil
½ cup hoisin sauce
¾ cup sambal chili paste
2 tablespoons Chinese black beans, rinsed
1 teaspoon ground Sichuan peppercorns
12 ounces diced tofu
Kosher salt, to taste
2 cups cooked hot rice
Sliced green onions, to garnish

In a sauté pan over high heat, working in batches, brown the eggplant in olive oil, uncovered, about 3–5 minutes. Stir to keep moving, so it browns evenly and does not burn. Add oil as needed. When all eggplant is cooked, add it all back to pan, add hoisin, mix thoroughly, and then add sambal, black beans, and ground peppercorns. Add diced tofu and heat thoroughly. Taste for salt, sweetness, and heat; all flavors should stand out. Adjust seasoning if necessary. Serve over rice and garnish with green onions.

COOK

YUSHO, CHICAGO, IL

SCOTT MALLOY

"If I want something I will get it. I am ambitious, I am a fighter, I am going to be successful."

—Scott Malloy

YOU MIGHT SAY that Scott Malloy was born to cook. Not only was his mother a culinary school student at Johnson & Wales University; his dad had a history of working as a cook at one of the best country clubs in Columbus, Georgia; his grandmother went to culinary school in Germany; and his great grandfather owned a restaurant in Boston. However, despite his culinary lineage, Scott didn't plan on becoming a chef. He was enrolled in auto mechanics school, and it wasn't until after he graduated high school that he made the fateful decision to pick up a chef's knife over a socket wrench. He had the opportunity to go to Johnson & Wales like his mother, but after assessing the cost, he opted for Nashville State Community College. He had a grant that would cover his schooling if he stayed in Tennessee, and the decision hasn't hurt him in the least.

Scott seems to have aimed high from the beginning. He always aimed to work at the best restaurant his skills would allow him to, and he took on any and all challenges with the tenacity of his youth. When offered a chance to work a trial shift at Graham Elliot, a Chicago restaurant known for its contemporary cuisine, he jumped at it. Despite not living near Chicago, he says, "I drove up, worked a shift, and drove back, all in about twenty-four hours straight. It was a little crazy." But the next day, they called and offered him a job as chef de partie. Despite chef Graham Elliot's fame from television appearances and his well-known clientele, Scott wasn't satisfied working there. "[Elliot] would come in, put on a chef's coat, walk around the dining room and greet guests, then be the first to go home." Scott felt like he wanted to learn from a chef that was more hands on in the kitchen.

> ## "I GUESS [GETTING MY TATTOO RIGHT DOWN MY ARM] IS KIND OF PART OF MY 'GO BIG OR GO HOME' PERSONALITY."

It wasn't until Scott took a position at L20, a modern fine dining seafood restaurant in Chicago, that he started to find the mentor he was looking for in Laurent Gras, a French-born award-winning chef who worked in top Michelin-rated restaurants in France before coming the United States. Scott says, "Laurent was always the first one there and stayed to scrub down the stations with us." Soon after L20's three-Michelin-star review, it became known that Laurent was going to leave because of disagreements with the owner, so one night Scott, along with several of the other chefs, went out to get tattooed with three Michelin stars as a tribute to Laurent and their time together. Scott says, "A lot of the chefs got them smaller somewhere, but I put them right down my arm. I guess it is kind of part of my 'go big or go home' personality."

After he left L20 in 2011, Scott took a sous-chef position at a restaurant called Arami to pursue one of his true culinary passions, Japanese food. When he was younger, eating at a sushi restaurant in his hometown, he told the chef he was interested in learning to cook sushi. Scott says, "He asked to grab my hands and told me they were too warm and I could never be a sushi chef because I would cook the fish. I was hooked! How could this guy know just from grabbing my hands?" In late 2012 Scott left to take a cooking position at the more casual restaurant Yusho and explore another part of Japanese cuisine, street food.

Scott tattooed an octopus on his right shoulder as the start of a sleeve of all Japanese fish. But his first tattoo was the knife and toque, or chef's hat, on his left arm, which he got to celebrate his graduation from culinary school. He also has a line of veggies on his right leg. Scott says, "The veggies are on my leg because I feel like they are the base of cuisine. It started with the carrot, celery, and onion, or mirepoix as known by chefs."

When asked what's next, Scott admits he has plans to open his own restaurant. But when it comes to pursuing his own three Michelin stars, he doesn't think he is crazy enough to ever pursue that . . . but he does admit that one would be nice.

Nuka Pickle

Scott is a Japanese-trained chef, and this traditional Japanese pickling technique speaks to his passions.

YIELDS AROUND 8 CUPS OF PICKLING "BED," WHICH CAN BE USED MULTIPLE TIMES

FOR NUKA:
1000 grams nuka (rice bran)
12 ounces pilsner beer
20 grams konbu (kelp)
10 grams mustard powder
peels of 2 apples
15 grams dried shiitake mushrooms
10 grams salt

TO PICKLE:
Vegetables of your choice. Depending on the size of the container and the vegetables, you should be able to pickle 6 to 10 cups.
1 cup sea salt

1 For Nuka: Combine all ingredients in a large container. Mix thoroughly by hand. Let sit for 24 hours to allow lactobacteria to bring the mixture to life; then mix daily with a clean, dry, bare hand to aerate. (Note: You will need to bulk up your nuka about once a month. For this, you can just repeat the recipe and add it to your existing mix. If your mix begins to sour, then you can add mustard powder or egg shells to alkalize your mixture. For a better result with vegetables that tend to oxidize, such as eggplant, you can bury an iron nail in the mixture to retain color.)

2 To Pickle: Rub the outside of the vegetables that you wish to pickle with sea salt and bury in the mixture until desired level of pickling and flavor has developed. Some vegetables only take a few hours, while others may be left in longer if you like a sourer pickle.

3 To Complete: Eat the pickle!

NOTES FROM THE CHEF

You can pickle anything from radishes to cucumbers, eggplant, carrots, etc. Cucumbers may only take 2 to 4 hours to pickle once you have a live active nuka bed, while carrots and other heartier vegetables may take a day or two. Much of this depends on your flavor preference.

CAROLYNN SPENCE

"I had to dress up in a suit and work in an office, and after that I knew there was no way I was going to do that kind of work for a living."

—Carolynn Spence

ORIGINALLY FROM NEW JERSEY, Carolynn Spence attended Northeastern University for journalism and art history, but after completing her first internship, she dropped out of Northeastern and instead decided to go to culinary school at Newbury College in Brookline, Massachusetts. After graduating, Carolynn stayed in Boston and worked under chef Chris Schlesinger at East Coast Grill and the Blue Room. When the restaurants she was working for went through ownership changes, she decided it was a good time for her to make a change too, and she headed for New York City. Carolynn says, "I'm from New Jersey so the move brought me closer to family and friends, and the restaurant scene in NYC has always been booming and full of interesting chefs and restaurants."

Carolynn took a job as a line cook, eventually learning and transitioning to the sous-chef role, at Bobby Flay's Mesa Grill. Carolynn says, "It's a big challenge learning how to go from line cook to manager of line cooks." After Mesa Grill, she opened Danny Meyer's Blue Smoke as a sous-chef under Ken Callaghan before landing the sous-chef position at the Spotted Pig, which is now known for its pub-like atmosphere and use of natural and organic ingredients. Though she'd opened a few restaurants before, opening the much buzzed-about New York hot spot was an entirely new experience. Carolynn says, "It started out as executive chef April Bloomfield, me, and one other kid, sanding the floor, setting up the kitchen—literally putting the place together—and our

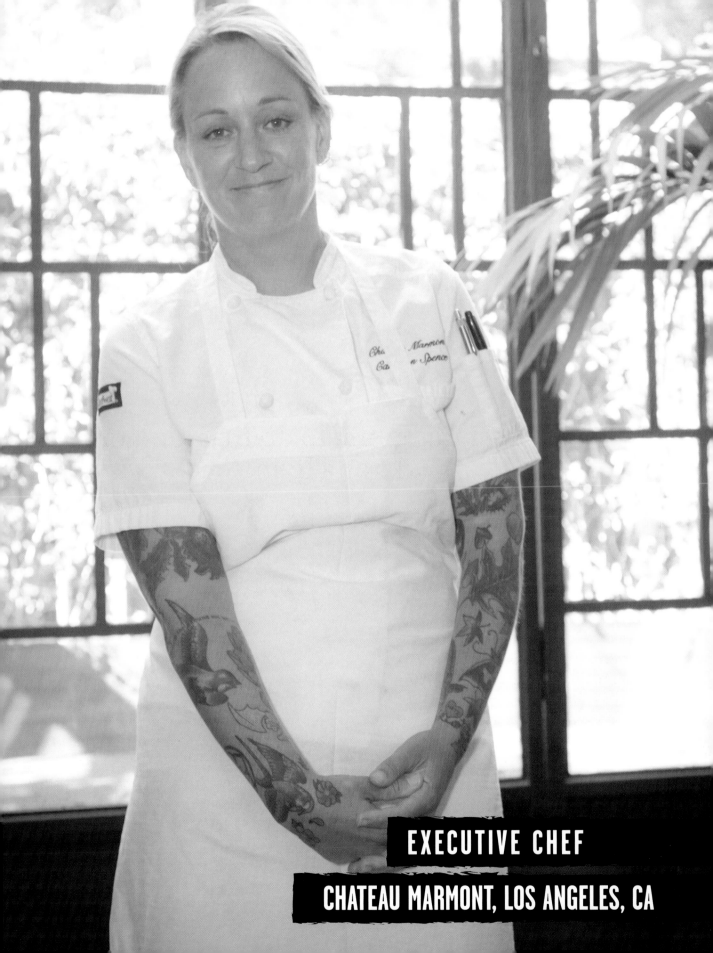

EXECUTIVE CHEF

CHATEAU MARMONT, LOS ANGELES, CA

first night was supposed to be dinner for twelve people, but it ended up being about thirty people. We had a lot of celebrity clientele right away. We didn't know what we were getting into. We took a chance on this tiny little joint in the West Village, and it just kicked in the first day and never stopped. It's still going crazy."

A chef headhunter who had friends in common with Carolynn contacted her about a chef position at Chateau Marmont. She says, "A random phone call, turned into a random interview, which a month later turned into a move to Los Angeles." Carolynn took over as executive chef of both the hotel and bar restaurants at Chateau Marmont in August 2006 and turned the restaurants into something special. Bar Marmont, along with most of Los Angeles, wasn't particularly known for its culinary prowess. But Carolynn, along with a handful of other chefs, have been on the leading edge of slowly changing Los Angeles's calorie-conscious menus into something with more flavor, shifting the menu from shrimp cocktail to heartier gastro pub fare. While the change seemed risky at the time, both Carolynn and Chateau Marmont gained and continue to enjoy great success.

Carolynn is inspired by many types of cuisines, and she brings her culinary interests to Chateau Marmont, which she says "is always changing, evolving, and interesting." She explains her culinary point of view by saying, "I go into food moods where I'm really into something for a while, then find something new to obsess on." She enjoys creating food that takes time and layering, such as braising and terrines. She says, "I find the process of all parts equaling a glorious sum to be very rewarding, not just to cook but also to eat."

Carolyn has incorporated the same edge that she brought to Chateau Marmont into her large and eclectic collection of tattoos, the majority of which are culinary in nature. She has the classic mirepoix mix of a carrot, onion, and celery, but with hers they are drawn to express "see no evil, speak no evil, hear no evil." Her "working class hand" includes a ruler on the side of her hand, along with tattoos of a teaspoon and a tablespoon. Down her left arm is a trio of fall leaves, the tattoo that started the whole collection off. Down her left arm, Carolyn has one of her favorite vegetables, an artichoke.

Lightly Toasted Brioche Roll

Carolyn says, "I use a brioche roll that's been baked with turmeric, which gives the roll a bright, yellow finish. [Bar Marmont] is a beautiful courtyard full of vegetation. It's important for the food to be bright, clean, and eye-catching. Richness in color, texture, and flavor adds to the full experience. A bit of theater, if you will."

YIELDS 1 SANDWICH, PLUS SOME LEFTOVER PICKLED ONIONS AND PESTO

FOR BASIL PESTO:

2 cloves garlic, peeled
¼ cup toasted pine nuts
2 cups clean, dry basil leaves
⅔ cup extra-virgin olive oil
Zest of 1 lemon
1 teaspoon lemon juice
½ cup Parmesan cheese
Salt and pepper, to taste

FOR PICKLED RED ONION:

1 pint sugar
1 cup salt
1 quart white distilled vinegar
1 medium red beet, peeled and roughly chopped
1 pound sliced red onions

TO COMPLETE:

1 brioche roll, cut in half and lightly toasted
½ cucumber (about 4 ounces), thinly sliced lengthwise
½ avocado, sliced
2 pieces thinly sliced Muenster cheese (about 2 ounces)
¼ cup assorted sprouts
5 leaves butter lettuce

1 For Basil Pesto: Add garlic and pine nuts to a mortar and pestle or food processor, and grind to make a fine paste. Quickly mix in basil to just purée (too much will make it turn dark and muddy). Stir in olive oil, lemon zest and juice, cheese, and salt and pepper. Season to taste.

2 For Pickled Red Onion: Add sugar, salt, vinegar, and beets to a saucepan. Bring to boil over high heat and simmer uncovered for about 5 minutes. Place sliced onions in a large bowl. Pour beet-vinegar mixture over red onions to cover. Add a layer of plastic wrap directly to top of onions while hot. Let sit and cool to room temperature. Refrigerate for at least 2 hours before using. Pickled onions will keep in the refrigerator for up to 2 weeks in covered container.

3 To Complete: Spread both sides of brioche roll with about 2 tablespoons of Basil Pesto. Layer sandwich with thin slices of cucumber, avocado, Pickled Red Onion, Muenster cheese, assorted sprouts, and butter lettuce. What you end up with is a highly satisfying vegetarian sandwich (that's fun to look at, too!).

NOTES FROM THE CHEF

Carolyn says, "I usually add a small arugula salad and French breakfast radish salad to my plate. Toss salad in a bit of olive oil and lemon juice and season with sea salt."

Garnish this sandwich with some French Breakfast Radishes and maybe serve with some extra Basil Pesto for dipping.

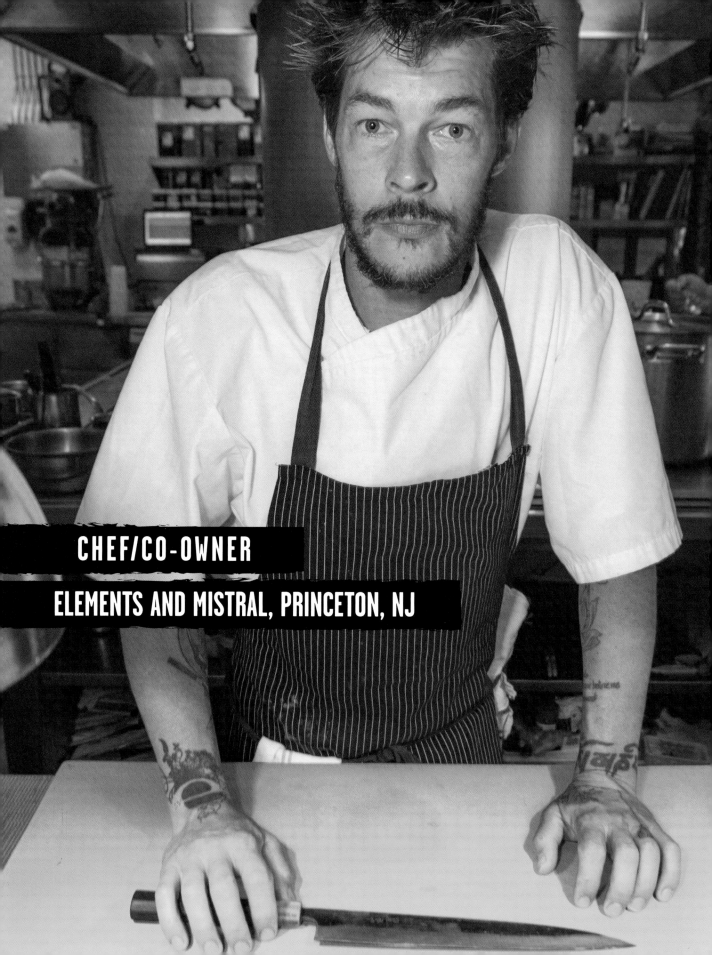

CHEF/CO-OWNER

ELEMENTS AND MISTRAL, PRINCETON, NJ

SCOTT ANDERSON

"I have so many more [tattoos] to get. It's going to be a lifetime's work."

—Scott Anderson

IF YOU HAVE EVER BEEN to Princeton, New Jersey—a charming, small college town with an excellent food scene and a pretty decent brewery—hopefully you stopped into one of the best things about the town: Scott Anderson's restaurant Elements. There, chef and co-owner Scott Anderson has been making dishes that go head-to-head with many of the top restaurants in the big cities across the country since October 2008.

Scott was born in New Jersey, but grew up in Florida and Japan as his father traveled working for IBM. Scott had, from a young age, worked as a busser or server for spending money but when he was eighteen and working in a small restaurant in Florida the dishwasher didn't show and Scott filled in. In addition to washing dishes he was soon helping with prep and raw ingredients. Scott says, "I was good at it and worked really fast so the chef asked if I would rather work in the kitchen and learn to cook, rather than just be a busser."

Scott enrolled at Rutgers University in 1991 to study psychology and sociology but says "Too many Phish shows and girls got in the way." He spent the next several years traveling and cooking until he landed in Princeton, New Jersey, cooking at Teresa's Café, a casual Italian restaurant that was part of the Terra Momo Restaurant group, a local restaurant group that owned several Italian-themed restaurants in the area. In 1997 he was able to take a head chef role at Mediterra Restaurant and Tavern the group's main higher end Italian Restaurant. From there the group had Scott move to Denver to be the head chef for their new Mediterra location. Scott lived in Denver for ten months but things didn't work out and he moved back to New Jersey. When he returned

Scott started to become uneasy at the Princeton Mediterra location as he started to feel stifled creatively. He says, "I was experimenting a lot with my pastas and dishes and they really just wanted me to cook the same food."

In 2001 Scott left to take a line cook position at the Ryland Inn, the modern American fine dining restaurant and New Jersey's only ever *New York Times* 4 star restaurant. There, working under head chef Craig Shelton, Scott began to learn and take his cooking to another level. He worked his way up through the ranks in the kitchen and eventually took over as sous-chef. He worked as sous for eight months before a water main burst, flooding the restaurant, and eventually forcing it to close in 2007.

While unfortunate, the Ryland's closure left Scott free to work on his own concept with his soon-to-be new partner, Stephen Distler, a semiretired private-equity executive turned restaurateur. In October of 2008 they opened Elements. Scott's success there led him to be named one of *Esquire* magazine's "Best New Chefs of 2011." The magazine states, "If Anderson had merely given Princeton its one great eatery, he'd be a hero, but he is in fact in the vanguard of modern global-American cuisine." Also, in 2012, Opinionated About Dining ranked Elements as number thirty-five on its list of "Top 100 U.S. Restaurants." Scott is constantly working to improve his cooking and that same attitude flows into his tattoos and, with quite a few already, he is not sure he will ever be finished. Scott got his first tattoo, a back piece that combines Japanese symbols with the Anderson tartan, when he was eighteen years old living in Florida. In fact,

you can see the Asian influences from his time growing up in Japan throughout Scott's ink. His right arm sports the Steal Your Face Skull of the band The Grateful Dead with the sitting Buddha. Below this are Scott's crossed Zakuri shashimi knives. The piece combined forms a Jolly Roger–style pirate symbol. Under that is the Chinese symbols for Wu Wei or "effortless action" placed purposely on his knife hand and on the other side of his wrist is the logo for Elements. His left arm sports a lotus blossom with a passage from the *Tao te Ching*, the fundamental text to both philosophy and religion of Taoism.

In addition to these tattoos, Scott has a symbol of his commitment to his wife inked on his left hand. In 2012 Scott finally got married to his girlfriend of seventeen years. He doesn't wear jewelry, not wanting anything to get caught in the kitchen, so didn't want to wear a wedding ring. Soon after they were married Scott went out one morning and got the tattoo on his left hand that combined his love of fishing and his love for her, fishing for the ring all those years. He didn't tell her about the tattoo in advance, but luckily, she loves it.

Scott continues to grow and improve his cooking and, in 2012, Scott and Stephen opened their second location, Mistral, a casual Mediterranean-inspired tapas restaurant. When not getting tattooed or fishing, Scott can usually be found outside of Elements, replacing yet another small patch of grass to plant herbs for the restaurant.

Tomato Soup with Ciabatta Toast and Grilled Cheese

SERVES 4

FOR BASIL PURÉE:
6 cups salted water
2 packed cups basil
½ cup olive oil

FOR CIABATTA TOAST:
1 loaf Ciabatta bread, ripped into chunks
2 tablespoons olive oil
3 cloves garlic
Salt and pepper, to taste
2 branches thyme leaves
Oil, for frying (enough to fill a pan 2" high)

FOR MARINATED FETA CHEESE:
4 ounces feta cheese
¼ cup of your preferred fresh herbs (basil, thyme, and sage all work well)
¼ cup extra-virgin olive oil
black pepper

FOR SOUP:
12 large Brandywine or other heirloom tomatoes (a variety of colors doesn't hurt)
3 tablespoons olive oil
4 cloves garlic

TO COMPLETE:
⅓ cup fresh basil and basil flowers

1 **For Basil Purée:** Bring salted water to a boil in a large pot. Blanch basil in salted water for 45 seconds. Remove basil and immediately shock in an ice bath until cold. Pat dry and purée in a blender with olive oil until smooth. Keep covered in cool place.

2 **For Ciabatta Toast:** Marinate bread chunks in olive oil, garlic, salt, pepper, and thyme leaves at room temperature until bread is soaked fully. Fill a large, deep pot with 2" of oil and bring to 350°F. Carefully add bread chunks and deep-fry until golden brown, 5 to 10 minutes. Remove from oil and lay on paper towels to drain.

3 **For Marinated Feta Cheese:** Break feta into small chunks. Marinate in herbs, extra-virgin olive oil, and black pepper for as long as you wish. The longer you wait the more the flavors will be absorbed. Store in refrigerator.

4 **For Soup:** Peel, coarsely chop, and deseed tomatoes. Wrap ⅓ of the tomatoes in cheesecloth and hang to drain overnight with a receptacle underneath to collect the tomato "water." Discard the tomatoes in the cheesecloth after water is collected. When making the soup, sauté in a sauce pan on high heat in olive oil a couple slices of garlic and remainder of the chopped tomatoes for 1 minute. Add the tomato "water" and bring just to a simmer then immediately remove from heat. (Do not simmer for a long time. Prolonged cooking destroys the freshness of flavor.)

5 **To Complete:** Arrange the dish as artfully as you care to. Add a few dots of basil purée out of a squeeze bottle, a few chunks of feta cheese and Cibatta, and garnish with basil and basil flowers. Add soup just before serving.

LISH STEILING

"You're making them smile through their stomachs. You can completely change a person's day by making them a good meal."

—Lish Steiling

AS MANY TEENAGERS DO, Lish Steiling earned extra money by bussing tables at the Chancery in Mequon, WI. The restaurant had an open kitchen, with a wood-burning oven in the middle of the restaurant where the guests could watch pizzas being made. After getting an opportunity to learn the station and how to make pizza, she soon found herself becoming the main chef for the job. She says, "I was this fifteen-year-old girl trying to train forty-year-old men who couldn't keep up with me. That was my first exposure to real restaurant cooking, and I loved it."

Her culinary fire stoked, Lish later enrolled in the Culinary Institute of America and worked at a variety of restaurants in Germany, Wisconsin, and New York for the following ten years. While in New York, she found a job working with BR Guest, a large and very successful restaurant group. Starting as a sous-chef at Blue Fin, their modern seafood concept, she soon went on to work at Hilo, the lounge in the Meatpacking District, and then Dos Caminos, the Mexican restaurant before ending at another fine dining seafood restaurant, Blue Water Grill.

ASSISTANT FOOD STYLIST

THE TODAY SHOW, NEW YORK CITY, NY

There, working in the largest restaurants she ever had before, she began learning all the logistics needed to run a kitchen from the computer systems to the scheduling to expediting. "It was a great experience in that I truly learned how to run a kitchen from an office perspective."

Again, restlessness overtook her, and she decided to pursue working in television food show production through a chance connection. She says, "The senior vice president of production at Food Network used to dine at Vento," another now-closed restaurant from BR Guest. "Sooo . . . I might have accidentally taken his name and number out of the reservation book before I left." The rest, as they say, is history. A few meetings later, Lish found herself freelancing for Food Network as an assistant food stylist.

Lish has since done food styling for such places as Food Network, *Gourmet* magazine, and *The Today Show*, where she currently works as one of the assistant food stylists. She says, "I get to work with some of the best chefs in the world, and they come to me and I get paid for it. It's like going on a stage every day." Lish continues to keep her cooking skill sharp—winning an episode of *Chopped* in 2009—and dreams of one day returning to a kitchen. "I'll end up back in restaurants. . . . When you are in that environment, it's a whole rush when you are doing it and you either love it or you hate it, and I love cooking on a line."

Lish's passion for cooking carries over onto her body. A radish and a carrot adorn her forearms, and she has a spoon and fork inked on the back of her arm. Lish got her first tattoo from her sister for her sixteenth birthday. The two each have matching tattoos of "sister" in Chinese. Lish says, "That was my first one, and from there you're addicted." Seems like there are more tattoos—and more great food—in Lish's future.

> **"I GET TO WORK WITH SOME OF THE BEST CHEFS IN THE WORLD, AND THEY COME TO ME AND I GET PAID FOR IT. IT'S LIKE GOING ON A STAGE EVERY DAY."**

Autumn in a Bowl: Roasted Parsnip and Kale Salad

Lish says, "[I] just love all of the flavors that happen in this recipe. It's comforting without being heavy."

SERVES 2 AS AN ENTRÉE OR 4 AS A SIDE DISH

2 good-size parsnips, about 1 pound or so, halved horizontally, each half cut in half lengthwise and then into equal-size wedges

3 sprigs of thyme

¼ teaspoon red chili flakes

1 teaspoon kosher salt, divided

4 tablespoons extra-virgin olive oil, divided

⅓ cup chopped bacon, about a ¼-inch dice

¾ cup sliced yellow onion

3 tablespoons red wine vinegar

8 cups chopped curly-leaf kale

1 tablespoon sesame oil

1 teaspoon chopped rosemary

½ an apple, such as Honeycrisp, cut into ¼-inch matchsticks

1 Preheat the oven to 425°F.

2 On a large baking sheet, toss together the parsnip wedges, thyme sprigs, chili flakes, ½ teaspoon salt, and 2 tablespoons olive oil. Place the tray in the oven and roast, stirring once, for 20 to 25 minutes or until golden brown and tender. Remove the thyme branches and set parsnips aside to cool slightly.

3 Meanwhile, sauté the bacon over medium heat until almost entirely crisp, about 4 minutes. Add the onions and sauté a few minutes more, until the onions are soft and just beginning to brown. The bacon should be completely crisp. Turn off the heat and deglaze with the red wine vinegar, scraping up the good bits from the bottom of the pan. Set aside to cool.

4 In a large bowl, toss together the kale with ½ teaspoon of salt. Massage the salt into the kale rather aggressively by hand for about 20 seconds. Now begin to build the salad. Add the cooled onions and bacon dressing along with 2 tablespoons olive oil and the sesame oil. Toss in the cooled parsnips, rosemary, and apple matchsticks. Mix gently with your hands. Taste it, think about it, and season as needed. Serve immediately.

MATT McCALLISTER

"If you really want to cook and really want to learn how to cook, just go get a job at a kitchen. Go get a job at a good kitchen. Not a bullshit kitchen, but a real one, and you'll get paid while you're learning."

—Matt McCallister

MATT McCALLISTER wasn't always sure that he wanted to be a chef. He had cooked since he was a kid, but was also drawn to the visual arts. In fact, he enrolled in the Metropolitan Arts Institute in Phoenix to study fine arts in 2000, but never ended up graduating. Matt ultimately found that he was more drawn to cooking, which offered a combination of visual and culinary arts. However, while there, Matt got his first tattoo of a graffiti cityscape across his back.

Though Matt had been cooking since he was fourteen it was always more of a way to make cash. He didn't really begin his culinary career until 2006. When he applied for a job at the famous Stephan Pyles restaurant in Dallas, TX, he hadn't had any formal training. "I could never get my shit together to get to culinary school." But he ate at the restaurant and says, "I was blown away. I asked [Stephan], what do I have to do to get a job here? He said, talk to my executive chef, so I did and that was it." Despite his lack of knowledge of classic cooking, Matt rapidly ascended the kitchen hierarchy, becoming sous-chef in just over a year and executive chef within three years. What he lacked in knowledge he made up for by staying up late and reading about and practicing

new techniques. He says of cooking, "I think it was always what I was meant to do." The hard work Matt did in the kitchen inspired him to finish the sleeve on his left arm that depicts fire, water, and a Taoist symbol for moving forward. The tattoo is a tribute to Matt's tumultuous path to becoming a chef—a dark five-year period he had prior to finding focus through cooking as well as his hard work to reach the success he enjoys today. He says, "It essentially tells my life story."

Matt took the lessons he inscribed in the tattoo to heart and continued to learn as much as he could about the culinary world. Wanting to further expand his knowledge and skills, Matt started to take short stages at the best restaurants he could find, including José Andrés's minibar in Washington, D.C.; Marc Vetri's eponymous restaurant in Philadelphia; Sean Brock's McCrady's in Charleston, SC; Grant Achatz's Alinea in Chicago; and Daniel Boulud's Daniel in New York. Upon returning to Dallas in 2011, Matt finally felt ready to take charge of his own project and opened FT33 on October 13, 2012, in Dallas.

FT33 serves seasonally inspired modern cuisine, and Matt won't even print a menu until the day of service. He prefers to let the best ingredients available dictate his cooking rather than creating recipes and trying to force the only ingredients available at the time into them. With this philosophy of respect for the ingredient and its grower, Matt and his wife founded Chefs for Farmers, a grassroots organization supporting local farmers by introducing their products to chefs, and vice versa. Today, Matt's restaurant FT33 continues to grow in popularity, and he continues to strive to bring culinary innovation to Texas.

> " [MY TATTOO] ESSENTIALLY TELLS MY LIFE STORY. "

Roasted Cauliflower Soup

YIELDS 12 SERVINGS

FOR ROASTED CAULIFLOWER SOUP:

3 heads white cauliflower
3 garlic cloves, minced
2 shallots, chopped
2 tablespoons olive oil
5 cups water
1 teaspoon finely chopped fresh thyme
    leaves
1 bay leaf
Salt and white pepper, to taste

FOR BROCCOLI PURÉE:

1 head broccoli
Salt, to taste
½ cup spinach purée
.04% xanthan gum

TO COMPLETE:

Wild cress, for garnish
Chickweed, for garnish

1 For Roasted Cauliflower Soup: Preheat oven to 425°F. Cut cauliflower into 1" florets. In a large baking pan, toss cauliflower, garlic, and shallots with oil to coat and roast in middle of oven about 30 minutes. In a medium-size pot, add water, roasted cauliflower mixture, and herbs. Simmer covered over medium heat for 30 minutes, or until cauliflower is very tender. Discard bay leaf. In a blender, purée soup in batches until smooth; season to taste with salt and white pepper. Use immediately, or refrigerate and then reheat when ready to use.

2 For Broccoli Purée: Cut broccoli into florets, place in pot of boiling water with a dash of salt, and blanch for 1 minute. Shock in an ice bath and purée broccoli in a blender with spinach purée and xanthan gum until a smooth velvety consistency. Season with salt to taste.

3 To Complete: In a wide soup bowl use a spoon to ladle a small amount of purée into the bottom of the bowl and paint a stripe to one corner of the bowl. Finish garnishing with wild cress, chickweed, and any fresh herbs and vegetables from the garden. Pour cauliflower soup in center filling bowl halfway.

NOTES FROM THE CHEF

".04% xanthan gum" refers to the percent total weight of the ingredient. So, for example, if the total weight of the vegetables was 100 grams you would want to add .04 grams xanthan gum.

CONSULTANT

LOCAL 360, SEATTLE, WA

ROBIN LEVENTHAL

"I had always been the good . . . well, not the good girl. I was the bad girl who didn't show her parents what she did."

—Robin Leventhal

CHANGE BEST DEFINES ROBIN LEVENTHAL'S creative career. When she started in the industry after receiving her MFA from the University of Michigan, cooking was a blue collar profession, and despite the industry's current media profile, Robin still insists, "not for a minute am I creating art with my food, even though it's a creative medium." Despite her background in art, Robin fell in love with the culinary world to connect with other people, to create something people will want to consume.

In 2008, Robin organized a charity auction and was put on the spot by its emcee to run the bidding. She's since become a licensed auctioneer and runs charity auctions regularly as a way to do good for mission-driven organizations. She opened Crave, a neighborhood bistro in Seattle, and worked there until 2009, when she

became a contestant on *Top Chef*, where she finished fifth. Even though her charity work has started to take more of her focus, in 2012 Robin took a head chef role at Local 360, a restaurant dedicated to local sourcing and sustainability located in Seattle, to contribute part-time menu development and "creative support" for chef de cuisine Gabe Skoda.

Robin has two tattoos, and she got both of them to mark times of illness and recovery in her life. Her first tattoo, a stylized version of a nautilus inked on the nape of her neck, was a mark of empowerment, an expression of taking back control of her body from cancer. The nautilus's spiral shell has become a symbol of Fibonacci's mathematical sequence that can be found in much of nature. Robin has always found

[To be a chef,] you have to love chaos, managed chaos. . . . Can you do ten things at once? Can you think about ten things at once?

Fibonacci's work to be fascinating, and she feels it speaks to the interconnectedness of the world. Robin says that the tattoo has a "new age-y and everything is connected" significance for her. She goes on to say, "It was the documentation of being diagnosed with two kinds of lymphoma, one of them deadly! After six months of toxic chemo, I was left with a bald head and a neck tattoo felt right. The placement is very much a power spot on the body. It is the fifth chakra and governs our expression, both verbally and in the ways we interact with the world. This diagnosis was incredibly scary, and chemo was hands down the biggest challenge of my life."

Robin has also had a fish and hummingbird done, one on the top of each foot, after rotator cuff surgery put her on bed rest for three months. The fish is a reference to her being a Pisces. The hummingbird symbolizes her energy. She started to relate to the animal when a former boyfriend told her, "Stop acting like a hummingbird and start acting like the robin bird that you are!" "I'm a hummingbird, damn it!" she laughs. She says that she

has to be doing ten things at once. It's a quality she thinks you have to have while being a chef. "You have to love chaos, managed chaos. . . . Can you do ten things at once? Can you think about ten things at once?" Robin can, and we'll likely see more—more great food and more tattoos—from her in the future.

Sunrise Lentil Cakes

Robin says, "Local 360 is all about locally sourced ingredients from 360 miles or less. Eastern Washington is the lentil and chickpea capital of the United States. We proudly use them in a few different places at Local 360, including these cakes, which make a hearty vegetarian dish or a great side for a fish, lamb, or pork dish."

FOR LENTIL CAKES:
1 cup minced thick-cut bacon (optional)
1 cup finely diced yellow onions
¼ cup minced shallots
1 tablespoon fresh thyme
1 tablespoon kosher salt
1 tablespoon minced fresh garlic
2 teaspoons cumin, whole seeds toasted
    and ground
1 tablespoon coriander, whole seeds
    toasted and ground
1 cup finely diced carrots
½ cup white wine (use whatever you have
    on hand that you enjoy drinking)
4 cups stock or water (use whatever you
    have on hand; any type of stock or even
    just water will do)
2 bay leaves
2 cups red lentils (any lentils will work)
Salt and pepper, to taste
1 large lemon, zested and juiced
1 whole egg
½ cup flour
Semolina or fine cornmeal
1–4 tablespoons vegetable or grapeseed
    oil (as needed)

1 **For Lentil Cakes:** In a heavy, deep saucepot, sauté diced bacon on medium until crisp and fat is rendered, about 5–10 minutes. Remove bacon bits from pan and reserve. Add onions and sauté in bacon fat on low until translucent, about 10 minutes. Add shallots to onions along with thyme and kosher salt. Turn heat to medium and cook for 3 minutes, stirring. Then add garlic, cumin, and coriander and cook a few minutes more. If pan is dry, add more oil or butter, or bacon fat if you have some extra on hand.

NOTES FROM THE CHEF

You can make these Lentil Cakes vegetarian if you so choose. Simply cut out the bacon fat and start the onions in vegetable oil, grapeseed oil, or butter instead.

2 Add carrots and sauté quickly to coat with seasoned onion mixture. Once brown bits form on the bottom of the pot, about 5 minutes, it's time to deglaze with the wine (you can use water if you don't have wine). Scrape bits off the bottom of the pot with a wooden spoon; then add stock, bay leaves, lentils, and a bit of salt and pepper. Cook on medium-high until lentils are tender but not mushy, about 30 minutes. Add lemon zest and juice, taste for seasoning, and adjust as needed. All the liquid should be absorbed before you purée. A loose mixture will require more egg and flour to bind the cakes. Remove pot from heat.

3 Remove ½ the lentils and pulse in a food processor; then add back to the pot. Add bacon and mix well to incorporate the lentil mixture. It's best to let this cool before forming patties. Either cook one day ahead, or spread on sheet pans and let cool for an hour before adding flour and egg to assist with binding.

4 Once cooled, add egg and enough flour to bind mixture, approximately ½ cup. When you squeeze the mixture in your hand, it should maintain that shape. Now form into 10 round balls, roll each one in semolina or fine cornmeal, and slightly flatten. (Bread crumbs will work but won't give the crunchy outside that semolina or cornmeal will.) In a sauté pan with vegetable or grapeseed oil over medium-high heat, pan-fry cakes until golden brown, about 5 minutes. Then flip and continue cooking until both sides are golden brown and crispy, about another 5 minutes. Remove from heat, place on a paper towel to drain, and put aside.

NOTES FROM THE CHEF

Freeze formed raw lentil cakes for a quick meal later. Lentil cakes make a great side dish, especially for lamb or fish, and also work on a bed of shaved carrots and greens for a light lunch or dinner. They're great in a sandwich as a burger replacement with the Coriander-Lemon Aioli below, or you can make small, bite-size cakes and serve them as an appetizer. You can also make the recipe with additional stock and serve as a soup.

FOR CORIANDER CARROT PURÉE:

2 tablespoons butter

1 tablespoon minced shallots

2 cups chopped carrots

1 teaspoon minced garlic

2 teaspoons coriander, whole seeds toasted and ground

2 cups stock or water (use whatever you have on hand; any type of stock or even just water will do)

1 teaspoon lemon zest

Pinch of cayenne

Kosher or sea salt, to taste

Lime juice, to taste

FOR CORIANDER-LEMON AIOLI:

1 teaspoon minced fresh garlic

1 large lemon or 2 small lemons (including all the juice and zest that the lemon yields)

1 tablespoon Dijon mustard

2 teaspoons coriander, whole seeds toasted and ground

½ teaspoon turmeric (optional)

1 egg, yolk only

Salt and pepper, to taste

1 cup olive or vegetable oil

TO COMPLETE:

1 cup chopped salad greens

1 cup julienned carrots

1 tomato, sliced

5 **For Coriander Carrot Purée:** Melt butter in a medium-size saucepan over medium heat. Sweat shallots in butter until they just begin to brown, about 10 minutes. Add carrots, minced garlic, and toasted coriander. Sauté until fragrant, about 5 minutes. Add water or stock and lemon zest and simmer until carrots are tender, about 10 minutes. Remove from heat and blend immediately. In a blender, purée carrots, cayenne, and enough liquid to reach a velvety consistency. Season with salt and lime juice to taste, adding more coriander or cumin if you desire. Will keep up to 4 days in the fridge, or freeze in small containers for easy sauce "on the fly."

6 **For Coriander-Lemon Aioli:** Add all ingredients except oil to a blender. On purée setting, slowly stream in oil. You can also do this with a hand mixer in a tall container or in a mixing bowl with a whisk. Cover and keep cool in refrigerator.

7 **To Complete:** Spread ⅓ cup Coriander Carrot Purée across the bottom of a plate. Place two lentil cakes on top and garnish with salad, carrots, and tomato. Feel free to substitute other local vegetables. Add 1–2 tablespoons Coriander-Lemon Aioli.

NOTES FROM THE CHEF

Robin says, "Lentil cakes make a great side for a fish, pork, duck, or lamb dish, or even make them larger and serve them as a lentil burger and enjoy as you would a beef burger. Creativity is your friend here. Caramelized or grilled onions, roasted peppers, or sautéed spinach would all be fantastic with these cakes. The Coriander-Lemon Aioli is a versatile sauce that adds great flavor and balance to these hearty patties. Use about a tablespoon per cake as garnish on the plate, or spread it on a bun if you are enjoying them as a lentil burger. Shaved fennel and picked herb salad is a nice way to dress up the plate, add some crunch, and add some complexity of flavors to this dish. I enjoy picked parsley leaves, tarragon, and chervil. Oranges would also be delicious in that herb mix with the shaved fennel. Simply toss with a little olive oil and season with salt and pepper. This should be dressed at the last minute. Another tip for storing shaved fennel is to crisp it in ice water. This step can be done up to one day ahead of time. Just squeeze a touch of lemon into the ice water to prevent the fennel from oxidizing."

She also says, "My favorite way to bring out the flavors of spices is to purchase them as whole seeds and toast them in a hot dry skillet until you start to smell them and they turn a nice dark golden brown. This can be done in a 400°F oven or over a medium-high heat on the stovetop. Once toasted, let them cool; then grind them in a coffee grinder that you use only for spices or simply with a mortar and pestle. They are best used within a week and will change the way you treat spices and season your food forever. Once you've had *fresh* toasted and ground [spices], there is no turning back!"

WILL ARTLEY

"Behind every great chef there is a greater team, and behind every great restaurant is a great neighborhood!"

—Will Artley

WHILE TRAVELLING THE WORLD with his military parents, Will developed a passion for cooking at a young age. He even spent time as a young boy working on a pig farm. Years later his passion drove him to work for free in several great restaurants just for the opportunity to learn. Later on, having staged at two of the best restaurants in New York City (Danube and Jean-Georges), Will Artley started at the prestigious Culinary Institute of America (CIA) in Hyde Park, New York, with a background of which many students would be jealous. Not one to rest on his laurels, while at the CIA, Will worked with Marcus Samuelsson at Aquavit and did an externship with chef Seth Bixby Daugherty at D'Amico Cucina in Minneapolis. Will earned a master's in artisan bread and later studied

under two of America's best pizzaiolos (respected, professional pizza-makers) and became certified by the Italian government as a Master Pizzaiolo himself.

After graduating from CIA in 2003, Will moved to Washington, D.C., to open Chef Bob Kinkead's Colvin Run Tavern in Tysons Corner, VA, while simultaneously working the line at Kinkead's eponymous D.C. restaurant, Kinkead's. He moved to Evening Star Café, a high-end diner in Alexandria, VA, in August of 2005, where he started as a sous-chef and moved up to executive chef. In October of 2011, after six years at Evening Star Cafe, Will decided it was time to move on. He left without knowing his next job.

EXECUTIVE CHEF
PIZZERIA ORSO, FALLS CHURCH, VA

> **❝ I don't think a lot of people want to eat fine dining. I think people want to eat fine food. ❞**

After four months off, except for a week-long gig with a pop-up restaurant, Will was hired at Pizzeria Orso in Falls Church, Virginia. Before taking over, his new bosses sent him to VPN Americas, an international nonprofit organization that cultivates the art and traditions of Neapolitan pizza. When faced with the question of why he transitioned from working for chefs of Kinkead's caliber to cooking "comfort pizza," Will says, "I don't think a lot of people want to eat fine dining. I think people want to eat fine food." The fine-dining training is hard to shake though, and Will still plates like he's working in a fine-dining establishment.

The success of Pizzeria Orso led Will to his first national TV appearance as a contestant on Food Network's show *Chopped* in 2012. Will describes his experience on Food Network's competition show *Chopped*, which aired in November of 2012, as "eye opening" and one of the hardest things he's ever done. Will says, "[The] biggest lesson I learned was to truly appreciate how great my team is . . . and that the reason for my success is because of them . . . it was the first time in my career I didn't have them to help me." He came back from *Chopped* with a new outlook and appreciation for his core team, which has been with him for seven years. As Will says, "That's a long time" for people in the food industry to stick around.

And as much as Will is passionate about food, he's also passionate about his ink. Will's first tattoo was his family crest on his left upper arm that he got when he was fifteen years old. He hoped the tribute to his family would mellow his father's anger at finding body art on his teenage son. Although it never resulted in any family drama, Will disliked the tattoo and eventually had it covered up with a huge bear claw, which he says is his animal totem. However, he liked the idea of the family crest and had a new one inked on by his regular tattoo artist, Duong Nguyen, who works at Way of Ink in Springfield, Virginia. The crest, now on his left leg, serves as a reminder of his parents' hard work. Will says, "It keeps you going a little bit more."

The tattoos on Will's arms tell two different stories. The left forearm is a blend of gods and symbols with wildly diverse origins (Aztec, Polynesian, Pacific Northwest, and his own family) that he and Duong designed into a cohesive sleeve. The tattoo on Will's right arm represents his cooking travels, " . . . starting in New York . . . different direction[s] . . . the stairs I had to take." The sleeve has traces of the art deco style to remind him of his time in New York, and vegetables from his garden (beets, carrots, peas, tomatoes, Swiss chard, squash blossoms, and artichokes) adorn his shoulder. Will says, "If I wasn't a chef, I'd be a farmer." Once the vegetable sleeve is done, Will plans to commission a back piece based on a large pig that will encompass all the products that can be made from the animal.

Sourdough Pizza Dough

The type of pizza made from this recipe is served at Pizzeria Orso.

YIELDS 4 DOUGH BALLS, ONE PIZZA EACH

FOR PIZZA DOUGH:
½ cup water, at 80°F
2 teaspoons sea salt
3 cups organic bread flour, divided
2 cups sour starter

TO COMPLETE:
Handful of cornmeal (to coat baking tray)
3 ounces handmade buffalo mozzarella, hand-torn (regular fresh mozzarella will work too)
1½ ounces hand-chopped San Marzano tomatoes
2 ounces fresh basil

1 For Pizza Dough: In a small mixer with a dough hook, or by hand with a strong spoon in a bowl, combine the water and salt and mix on low speed or stir for 1 minute. Then add half the flour and mix on low/stir for 2 minutes. Add the sour starter and mix on low/stir for 2 minutes; then add the rest of the flour and mix on low/stir for 13 minutes. If using mixer, scrape sides of bowl every 3 minutes. Place dough in a very large plastic container with lid for 6 hours at room temperature (dough will expand up to 9 times its original size, so make sure you have plenty of room). After 6 hours, portion the dough into 4 equal balls and allow to rest for another 2 hours covered at room temperature.

2 To Complete: Put your stone in the oven and set the temperature to 500°F. Allow stone to heat with oven for 40 minutes. While stone is heating up, using a basic rolling pin, roll one ball of dough out to ¹⁄₁₆ of an inch. Will says, " . . . the thinner the better in my opinion." After the dough is rolled out, place it on an upside-down cookie tray that has a touch of cornmeal spread on it. Top with buffalo mozzarella, San Marzano tomatoes, and basil. After you put the topping on evenly (remember, less is more), you will slide the pizza from the upside-down cookie tray onto the stone. Cook until pizza is golden brown, about 17 to 20 minutes. When your pizza is cooking, look for even browning because it might need to be rotated once. Remember that cornmeal makes an interesting change and adds crispness to the bottom of the pizza! Enjoy!

NOTES FROM THE CHEF

Will says, "My preference for tomato is San Marzano. These tomatoes are the best! No other tomato is this sweet and perfect. You can taste the *terroir* in the tomato."

SOUS-CHEF

POQUITOS, SEATTLE, WA

SEAN HAWES

"Without food, we would not live. Without good food, we would not live well."

—Sean Hawes

WHEN SEAN HAWES WAS FIFTEEN, he started taking cooking classes at Whole Foods. A chef from the Culinary Institute of America taught the courses and inspired Sean, who says, "I just saw what he could do with food and fell in love with it." The instructor helped Sean find a connection to well-known Seattle chef and restaurateur Ethan Stowell's restaurant Union, a fine-dining new American/Italian restaurant. Sean spent the next several years working his way through Seattle's kitchens, learning and advancing as he went. In 2011, Sean met Manny Arce (see entry in Part 1), who asked him to come on as sous-chef and help open Poquitos, an upscale Mexican restaurant in Seattle. Sean says, "My favorite thing to cook is anything I have not cooked before. I love to play with new ideas, new ingredients, and new flavors.

I practice this constantly at Poquitos. Most of my culinary background has been French and Italian food, so cooking high-end Mexican is all new for me. I am learning and growing each and every day."

Sean got his first tattoo, a VW logo on his ankle, when he was eighteen. Super Genius Tattoo is located across the street from Poquitos, and Sean has gotten the majority of his ink there. All of his tattoos are pieces he has drawn himself. The only modifications the artist made were done to allow the image to better fit the curve of the spot on his body where he got the tattoo. The tattoo on Sean's right forearm shows his hometown pride with the Seattle skyline and the caption "embrace the rain." Sean explains the tattoo by saying, "It's a dual meaning of

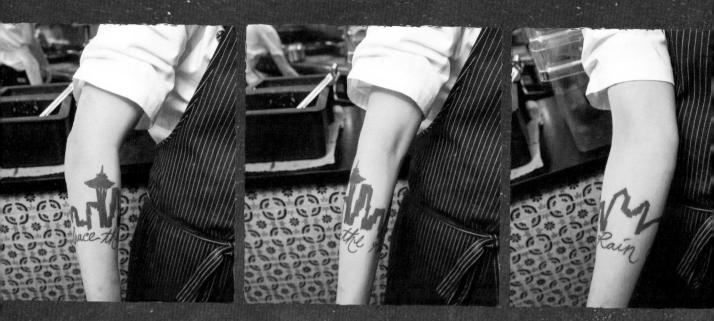

embracing the hardships. What doesn't kill you makes you stronger . . . as well as that it always fucking rains in Seattle." The stick figure on his right bicep is his "Kitchen Ninja" drawn to the same proportions as Leonardo da Vinci's Vitruvian Man. The tree on his right arm began as a tree, but Sean added crows that represent someone significant in his life who has passed away, making it "kinda like a 'tree of life.'" In addition to the tree, there is an eight-digit binary code for the word "salt," which Sean considers to be the most important thing in cooking. He says, "It's a tribute to both my love of food and my nerdy side." On his left shoulder are the letters "e v o l." "It's love backwards," Sean says. "Kinda twisted but attributes to my past experiences with 'love.' It can be backwards and 'evol' sometimes." Sean plans to continue to get tattooed. He hopes next to draw something inspired by the fixed-gear bicycle that he rides to work every day and the community of fixed-gear riders he has met. Whatever he ends up wanting, you know he'll be across the street from Poquitos getting inked.

Beet Salad

YIELDS 4 SERVINGS

FOR AVOCADO SAUCE:
1 avocado
Juice of 1 lime
1 clove garlic, minced
Salt, to taste

FOR SALAD:
1 pound red beets
1 pound golden beets
4 tablespoons olive oil, divided
Salt and pepper, to taste
1 serrano chili, thinly sliced
1 orange, segmented
1 handful arugula

1 For Avocado Sauce: Blend all ingredients in food processor until smooth, about 1 minute.

2 For Salad: Toss beets in a small mixing bowl with half the olive oil, salt, and pepper. Spread beets onto ovensafe pan; roast in the oven at 350°F until tender, about 40 minutes. Peel with a dry towel and cut into quarters. Refrigerate until cool. Once cooled, toss beets with remaining olive oil, and more salt, and pepper. Remove beets from mixing bowl and set aside in separate bowl. Using the same bowl with residual dressing, mix serrano chili, orange segments, and a handful of arugula.

3 To Complete: Spoon Avocado Sauce onto plate. Place beets on top of sauce. Top beets with arugula-orange-chili mixture.

BRANDON BALTZLEY

"I was looking for something that says 'important,' because that's exactly what crux means. It's the definition, the most important part, or a focal point or a puzzling problem."

—Brandon Baltzley

BRANDON is a self-described "Louisiana-born, low-country raised, nomadic chef, musician, writer, lover, fighter, and part-time schizo." He has lived everywhere from Jacksonville to Savannah to Minneapolis to Washington, D.C. Growing up working in the kitchens of small-town bistros as a way to pay the bills, he focused his youth on the Savannah sludge metal music scene. He even spent several years touring with his band Kylesa. After tiring of being on the road for ten months out of the year, Brandon left the band in 2005.

He spent two years working at Cha Bella, an American-style restaurant focused on organic ingredients, first as sous-chef and later at executive chef. Brandon then moved to New York and spent the next five years working in various kitchens, including Marc Forgione's (see entry in Part 1) Michelin-star Restaurant Marc Forgione and the brew pub 508 GastroBrewery. All of this experience culminated in Brandon taking the executive chef position at 6th Street Kitchen in East Village, known for its new American cuisine. In 2010, he moved to Chicago to work at the world-renowned restaurant Alinea, a three-Michelin-star restaurant regarded as one of the top restaurants in the world.

Chicago became Brandon's stage to both reach new culinary highs and yet also fall to his lowest. Struggling to keep his drug addiction under control, Brandon lost or left four jobs at top restaurants across Chicago in less than a year: at Alinea; Schwa, *GQ* magazine's 2009 "The Most Revolutionary Restaurant in America"; Mado, which he walked out of as executive chef along with his entire kitchen staff only a month after the opening; and lastly, after winning the executive chef job at Tribute, Brandon didn't even make it to the opening. Instead, he checked himself into rehab after a five-day-straight binge on cocaine. Once out of rehab, he returned to cooking with a fury and focus like never before. He knew he had a lot to prove to redeem himself, but wasn't sure how to start. "I wanted to do my own thing, but didn't have the money to open a restaurant."

Drawing inspiration from his own struggles with the structure and conformity of a professional kitchen, he formulated a project intended to give a solution to line cooks and sous-chefs who wanted to do their own food for people. In August of 2011, he created CRUX, a monthly pop-up, with a group of local Chicagoans. "I knew a lot of chefs who wanted to do their own dinners and menus but couldn't use the name of the restaurant or sometimes even their own name because of contractual obligations. CRUX was created to give them an umbrella to have an outlet." The dinners at first were once a month for around forty people, but soon expanded to weekly dinners for around ten people as well. Six months into starting the dinners in Chicago, Brandon took CRUX on the road and has now collaborated with dozens of chefs and served dinners in Maine, Pittsburgh, Miami, Atlanta, Calgary, New York, and many other locations in the United States. More dinners continue to be planned in more cities every month.

Although he doesn't intend to fully give up life on the road, Brandon will soon pass CRUX's reins to another chef, with the intention of it becoming an annual baton passing. CRUX is an outlet for chefs who don't have a space to express their creativity, and now Brandon is finally getting that outlet. He is currently developing a farm-to-table modern restaurant called TMIP, which is slated to open soon. Situated on a plot of land an hour and a half outside of Chicago, with only ten to fifteen seats, he hopes to have an ever-developing menu based on what can be grown and foraged from the area. He doesn't truly see his concept being fully farm-to-table, instead jokingly calling it "Hippy Molecular."

Brandon's eclectic, ever-changing tattoos echo the years he spent on the road. And there are a lot of tattoos to discuss. Brandon estimates he'll have spent nearly twenty-two hours in a tattoo parlor just in 2012. Given that he's been getting tattoos since before he was eighteen, many of them are in the process of being covered up or altered from the type of tattoos he got in his youth. He laughs, "I got a lot of old band logos and really shitily done stick and poke tattoos." A goat head pentagram is across his stomach, and song lyrics and many of the logos down his left arm are now being reworked into vegetables and cuts of meat. As his rock-and-roll ink is being replaced by his new passion, his skin is a visual metaphor for his own life changes. Still, playful pieces like the crudely scrawled "chomp" (a piece he did himself) across his arm will stay to serve as reminders of the wild journey he has taken to get to where he is today.

Others he will keep but hopes to touch up are his "I heart GA" tattoo from his time in Savannah and his "ragn cajn" across his knuckles. His knuckle tattoos he got as a gift from a friend on his nineteenth birthday in Orlando, Florida. A friend brought him there and told him that he would pay to have anything he wanted tattooed on his knuckles and that the next day they were going to Disney World. Prior to getting the tattoo, they drank a whole bottle of Wild Turkey, and the tattoo bled out at the theme park, ensuring its faded quality to this day.

Brandon continues to work on his culinary left sleeve of vegetables and says that he wants it to wrap up around his shoulder. All his work right now is done by John Biswell of Made-Rite Tattoo in Portland, Maine. He met him while doing a farming internship in Maine in preparation for the opening of TMIP. No longer living there, Brandon arranges times to go there and do eight-hour sessions at a time. He says, "It makes for expensive tattoos since I travel up there, but he is really good."

Butternut Squash with Goat's Yogurt, Spirulina, and Stevia

Taken from the CRUX pop-up dinner at a private home in Lincoln Park, IL, with chef Keith Fuller, on November 1, 2012.

YIELDS 35–40 AMUSE-BOUCHE PORTIONS OR 4–5 FULL SERVINGS

FOR SQUASH:
1 butternut squash
250 grams lard
Salt, to taste

FOR YOGURT:
1 quart of a local farm's goat yogurt
Spirulina powder, to taste (check your local health food store)

TO COMPLETE:
40–50 leaves, or about 1 cup, Stevia leaves (check your local health food store)

1 For Squash: Cut the squash into 1" × 1" cubes. Vacuum seal in a bag with lard and salt to taste. Cook sous-vide at 185°F for 15 minutes or until tender. Remove from bag hot and use a quarter-inch melon baller to remove a small sphere on top of each cube. Save balls.

2 For Yogurt: Blend yogurt with spirulina to taste. Store in a squeeze bottle.

3 To Complete: Squeeze spirulina-yogurt mix into empty hole on top of each piece of Squash. Place squash melon balls next to the green yogurt on top of each piece of Squash. Place a single stevia leaf in between each squash ball and dot of green yogurt. Serve at room temperature.

NOTES FROM THE CHEF

Sous-vide is a method of cooking food in a sealed plastic bags in a water bath.

When cutting the squash, I like to peel all twelve edges to give an almost cylindrical aesthetic.

BRANDON BIEDERMAN

"He has been tattooing me now for ten years. Through that, we became best friends. I was actually down [in Mexico] to be the best man at his wedding."

—Brandon Biederman

BRANDON BIEDERMAN, like many thirteen-year-olds, needed a job and found one working as a prep cook at a steak house on the south side of Chicago. The experience was his first introduction to the culinary world and later influenced him to attend Northern Arizona University, where he earned a degree in hotel and restaurant management. While in school, he spent his nights cooking in various kitchens in Flagstaff. After graduating in 1999, he moved to Denver, CO, with the girl he was dating at the time and continued to advance his culinary career.

In Denver, Brandon started working as a line cook at the now-closed Tommy Tsunami's, an Asian fusion restaurant. He quickly moved up the ranks to sous-chef and ultimately became the executive chef. In 2001, however, Brandon left Tommy Tsunami's to take a line cook position at Vesta Dipping Grill, one of Denver's most well-known and highly regarded restaurants. There, Brandon worked as fellow *Eat Ink* chef Matt Selby's (see entry in Part 3) sous-chef before taking the executive chef position at Steuben's, the newest addition to the Vesta restaurant family.

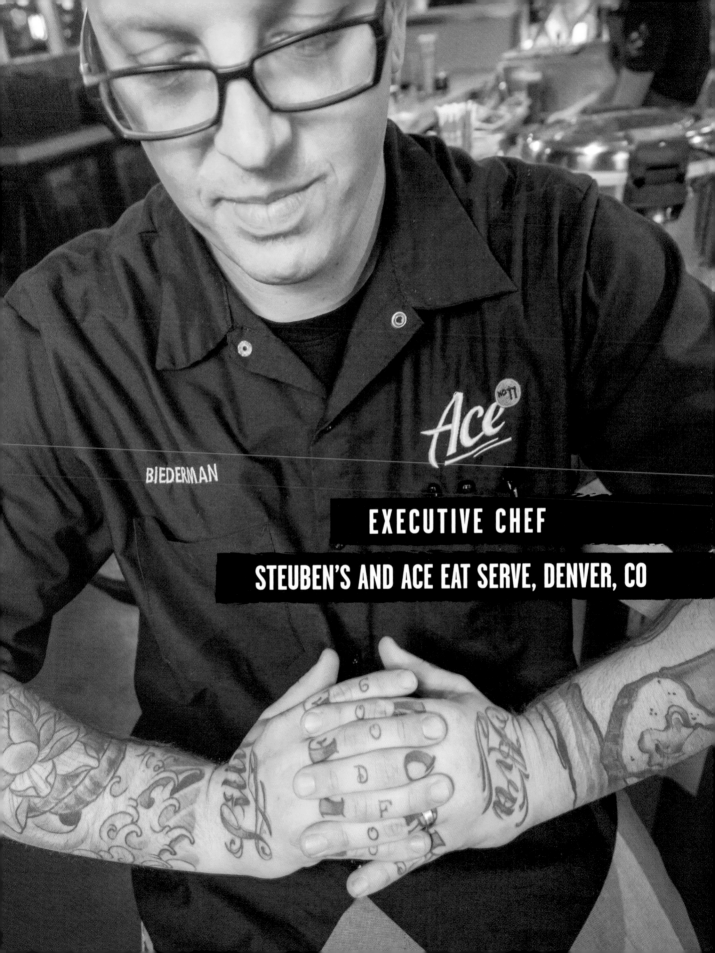

BIEDERMAN

EXECUTIVE CHEF

STEUBEN'S AND ACE EAT SERVE, DENVER, CO

Steuben's, which opened in 2006, has allowed Brandon's culinary point of view—classic Americana dishes with a creative twist—to shine. Most notably, in 2011, Brandon's "Maine Lobster Roll" attracted the attention of Guy Fieri and his show *Diners, Drive-Ins and Dives*, which featured both Brandon and his restaurant. In 2012 the group opened another restaurant directly next door to Steuben's called Ace, a large casual bar space that features ping pong tables, craft beer, and Asian inspired food. Brandon now manages both kitchens.

But Brandon has done more than advance his culinary career since moving to Denver. He's also got inked. Brandon got a "real crappy" tattoo when he was young, but considers his first real tattoo to be the Buddha and sun on the inside of his right arm that he had done soon after he moved to Denver in 1999. Since then he has added quite a bit of ink. His left arm sports a full breakfast motif, with fried eggs in a pan, bacon, buttered bread and coffee. The words "Clog Life," the style of shoes most chefs (Brandon included) live and work in, are tattooed on his ankles. In 2006 he got his first set of knuckles done with the words "WORK" and "LIFE." Later in 2010 on a whim, Brandon got the letters G, O, F, and O tattooed on his right hand, and the letters O, D, O, and O tattooed on his left hand. When he crosses his fingers together, the letters spell out "GOOD FOOD." Not long after his that he had the back of his hands inscribed with the names of his daughters, Lilly and Ava.

The majority of Brandon's ink has been done by Josh Ford at Lifetime Tattoo in Denver. Brandon says, "I've always liked tattoos, and when I met Josh Ford, I gave him freedom to do his art with my ideas. It just worked out really well. Most of my tattoos are food-related and/or family-related, so it's easy to say they are things close to my heart." Spending all that time together working on Brandon's tattoos, Josh and Brandon have become very close. Brandon says, "We met through mutual friends soon after he moved back to Denver. He is pretty much one of my only outside the [restaurant] industry friends."

In 2012, Brandon traveled to Mexico to be Josh's best man at his wedding, and the two talked about Brandon's desire to get a traditional Japanese-style full body suit, a tattoo that covers the entire torso, often representing a rite of passage. Josh agreed to do it as soon as the summer was over. Brandon says, "It was one of those; I opened my mouth up so now I had to back it up." So, in November 2012, Josh and Brandon started work on his biggest piece yet. We'll have to wait and see what other big things come to Brandon as time goes on.

Tiger Wings with Som Tum

Both the Tiger Wings and Som Tum are featured at Ace.

YIELDS 2–3 SERVINGS

FOR GREEN PAPAYA SALAD (SOM TUM):

¼ ounce cilantro, torn
¼ ounce Thai basil, torn
¼ ounce mint, torn
1 teaspoon dried baby shrimp
1 teaspoon minced Thai chilies (more if you like it hot)
Pinch of salt
Pinch of sugar
Juice of ½ a lime
1 tablespoon fish sauce
1 tablespoon rice wine vinegar
1 teaspoon chopped ginger
1 teaspoon minced garlic
⅛ ounce diced Thai basil or mint, for garnish
6 ounces shredded green papaya (available in most Asian markets)
2 ounces diced tomatoes
2 ounces julienned green beans
Crushed roasted peanuts, to garnish

FOR TIGER WINGS:

1 pound fresh chicken wings
½ cup cornstarch, to coat
Salt and pepper, to taste
1 teaspoon Thai chilies (more if you like it hot)
1 teaspoon minced ginger
1 teaspoon minced garlic
1 lime leaf
4 tablespoons sambal
1 cup brown sugar
1 ounce fish sauce

1 **For Green Papaya Salad (Som Tum):** With a mortar and pestle, muddle all ingredients except for shredded green papaya, diced tomatoes, julienned green beans, and crushed roasted peanuts. Muddle until soft and well combined. Adjust seasoning to taste. Toss the papaya, tomatoes, and green beans with the dressing and plate. Garnish with more herbs and crushed roasted peanuts.

2 **For Tiger Wings:** The use of a deep fryer is recommended for this recipe. If no deep fryer is available, use a deep frying pan with at least 2" of oil. Dredge chicken wings in cornstarch seasoned with salt and pepper to coat. Fry in 250°F oil for 8 minutes. Freeze wings until they are solid. Remove wings from freezer. Fry wings for another 6 minutes in 250°F oil. Freeze wings again until solid. Remove wings from freezer when ready to finish dish. In a wok, combine all other ingredients over medium-high heat and sauté until a thick sauce is achieved, about 5–10 minutes. Adjust seasoning if necessary and remove from heat. Fry wings for the third and final time at 350°F for 6 minutes. Toss wings in sauce.

3 **To Complete:** Plate to your preference. In the restaurant these dishes are served separate family style.

EXECUTIVE CHEF

WEST TOWN BAKERY, CHICAGO, IL

CHRIS CURREN

"You know each one [tattoo] is from a place and time in my life. They all have meaning at that point."

—Chris Curren

GROWING UP in Cleveland, Ohio, Chris Curren's parents allowed him to experiment in the kitchen from a young age, but cooking wasn't always his passion. Chris initially pursued a bachelor's degree in prelaw at the University of Dayton in Dayton, Ohio, but by his junior year, he realized that he just wasn't that interested in it anymore. While in college, Chris earned extra money working in the cafeteria, and after graduating in 2001, he applied to the Pittsburgh Culinary School (now called Le Cordon Bleu Institute of Culinary Arts in Pittsburgh).

After finishing culinary school, Chris returned to Cleveland, where he worked in many of the top restaurants in the area, including Three Birds in Lakewood, Ohio. He found a mentor in chef Bruce Kalman, who offered him the chef de cuisine position at Three Birds, where Kalman was executive chef. Chris says of Kalman, "I worked for Bruce when I was just getting into the field. He opened my eyes to the 'culinary scene' as opposed to just working in restaurants. He taught me techniques I still use today, and showed me how to effectively run a kitchen. He has always been a guide and a voice of reason when I have come to crossroads in my career and remains a close friend today. I would say he is one of three people who truly influenced my cooking style." Writing seasonal menus and weekly specials, Chris helped Three Birds gain national notoriety, being named *Esquire* magazine's "Best New Restaurant" in 2003, *Cleveland Magazine*'s "Best New Restaurant" in 2003, and one of *Bon Appétit*'s "Top 50 Restaurants in America" in 2005.

> **66** [My tattoo is] a reminder that no matter how tough it gets, you have to stay humble. **99**

In 2006, Chris, who was looking to grow professionally, decided he wanted to hone his skills in the larger market of Chicago, but once there, he realized that his abilities were more developed than he thought. He says, "I thought there would be something more, but I became disheartened by the fine-dining scene. I was further along than I knew." Wanting more, by 2008 Chris, along with business partner and fellow Clevelander Dan Marunowski, opened Blue 13, an American fine-dining restaurant that prided itself on its accessibility and ability to remove the pretense or self-importance of other fine-dining establishments. Before closing its doors in 2012, the restaurant earned a recommendation from Michelin as well as a mention in *Chicago* magazine's "Best Restaurants in Chicago: 30 under $30" in 2010. Today, Chris has joined the Fifty/50 Restaurant Group as executive chef in charge of the opening of Homestead, which according to the restaurant's website is "A literal farm-to-table restaurant."

Chris is very focused on his cooking, but when you start to talk to him about his tattoos, you see another side of him. Most of his ink isn't food related, but rather speaks to his spirituality and his love for his friends and family. He got his first tattoo on his back, an Aztec sun. Why? His roommate in college was a fine arts major and he

inspired Chris to take a greater interest in visual arts. Chris now sports full sleeves on both his arms: His left arm is modeled after a traditional Japanese screen, a decorative divider used in the home. His forearm features blossoms with a samurai warrior. His right arm is what he calls a "collage of old school and new school." His upper arm features the green devil from an old print ad for Maurin Quina, a French aperitif. On his forearm is the Catholic sacred heart. He says, "I grew up religious, but turned from organized religion in college. I'm still very spiritual and getting the sacred heart was a symbol of that." He also has two skulls across his arm, the first a sugar skull from the Mexican celebration, the Day of the Dead. Chris says, "This holiday, literally translated, is a day for the dead and the children. It's a celebration of loved ones who have passed and the continuity of life." The second skull is paired with a banner that says "True til death" and it serves as a reminder to Chris to not only be a truthful person, but to be true to himself.

Chris also has a chest piece that he got after a dear friend passed away. The piece has the inscription "There but for the grace of God go I." Chris says, "It's a reminder that no matter how tough it gets, you have to stay humble." It's a policy that Chris puts into practice both in the kitchen and in the tattoo shop.

Panzanella with Roasted Acorn Squash

YIELDS 4 SERVINGS

FOR HERBED GOAT CHEESE:
½ pound fresh goat cheese
¼ cup minced chives
¼ cup minced parsley
¼ cup minced tarragon
1 ounce lemon juice

FOR DRESSING:
1 cup peeled garlic cloves
Blended oil, as needed
1 tablespoon Dijon mustard
1 cup champagne vinegar
3 cups extra-virgin olive oil
Salt and pepper, to taste

FOR ACORN SQUASH:
1 large acorn squash
¼ cup brown sugar
½ shallot, sliced into ⅛" rings
1 tablespoon paprika
2 sprigs rosemary
2 sprigs thyme
Salt and black pepper, as needed
Extra-virgin olive oil, as needed

FOR SEEDS:
Seeds from 1 large acorn squash
Extra-virgin olive oil, enough to lightly coat the seeds
Salt and pepper, to taste
1 teaspoon cayenne pepper

FOR CROUTONS:
1 loaf artisan sourdough bread (cut off crust and cut into 1" × 1" cubes)
Salt and pepper, to taste

TO COMPLETE:
½ pound baby arugula
½ bulb fennel, shaved on a mandoline
½ red onion, julienned
½ cup toasted pecans
1 cup shaved three-month-old manchego cheese

1 **For Herbed Goat Cheese:** In a food processor, place goat cheese, herbs, and lemon juice. Blend until smooth and the goat cheese turns bright green.

2 **For Dressing:** In an ovensafe pan, put garlic and just enough oil to cover. Wrap with aluminum foil and roast at 350°F for about 45 minutes until the garlic is soft. Strain the oil and reserve for croutons. In a food processor, purée the garlic cloves until smooth. In a blender, place Dijon mustard, vinegar, and 2 tablespoons of roasted garlic purée. Turn blender on high speed and slowly drizzle in the olive oil to create an emulsification. Season with salt and pepper to taste.

3 **For Acorn Squash:** Cut the squash in half and remove the seeds. Reserve the seeds for garnish. Toss the squash in a bowl with the brown sugar, shallot rings, paprika, rosemary, thyme, salt, and pepper and drizzle with olive oil until coated. Bake the squash at 350°F until the squash is soft, but not mushy, about 30 to 45 minutes. Once done, let the squash cool to room temperature and then remove the skin with a knife. Cut the squash into large cubes, about ½" × ½".

4 **For Seeds:** Toast the squash seeds in the 350°F oven until they are dry and crunchy, about 25 minutes. Be careful not to burn them. Toss the dried seeds in olive oil and season with salt, pepper, and cayenne pepper.

5 **For Croutons:** Toss the sourdough in garlic oil (reserved from the garlic roasting process) and season with salt and pepper. Place in oven at 350°F until golden brown and crunchy on the outside but soft and warm on the inside, about 5 minutes. Remove from oven and use immediately.

6 **To Complete:** In a bowl, smear the Herbed Goat Cheese along the bottom and one edge of the bowl. Once the Croutons are done, place them in a mixing bowl with warmed up Acorn Squash, arugula, fennel, and onion. Toss with small amounts of Dressing, adding Dressing until the salad is dressed properly (enough to taste both the dressing and the elements of the salad). Place salad mixture in a line in the bowl. Top with toasted pecans, Seeds, and shaved manchego cheese. Serve while Croutons and Acorn Squash are still warm.

NOTES FROM THE CHEF
Shave the manchego cheese using a peeler for best results.

DIRECTOR OF CULINARY EDUCATION,
FOUNDER, FORMER BUTCHER/CHEF COOK

STREET SCHOOL OF CULINARY ARTS,
ROCKY MOUNTAIN INSTITUTE OF MEAT,
IL MONDO VECCHIO SALUMI, DENVER, CO

MARK DeNITTIS

"The USDA stamp, I got it kind of on a whim while in New York . . . We went to some shop on 42nd Street. I went up there, showed him the tat, and he said eighty-five bucks I think, so I got it right before my James Beard dinner."

—Mark DeNittis

AS A MASSACHUSETTS-BORN, first-generation Italian-American, DeNittis came by his rich food heritage through his family. With his grandparents' influence at an early age, he gained a deep understanding and appreciation for gardening, hunting, fishing, traditional cooking, meat curing, and winemaking. Inspired by his family heritage, after high school Mark went to Johnson & Wales University in Rhode Island to earn his culinary degree. In 1993, when Mark was nineteen years old, while working an externship at the Breakers hotel in Palm Beach, he got his first ink: a shark on his left shoulder. The tattoo is an homage to his grade school nickname, "Mark the Shark." Mark later got a second shark on his back, described as "a version of the Ron Jon Surf Shop shark with a chef's hat and holding a French knife," which he got at an all-night biker party at a campground in West Virginia.

Over the years, Mark spent time in Houston, Texas, where he worked as the chef de cuisine of the main dining room at the four-diamond Houstonian Hotel, Club & Spa. A year later, he was promoted to open a $45 million project, the Houstonian and Shadow Hawk golf courses about twenty miles southwest of the hotel. But in 2000, with the birth of his daughter, he and his wife decided to try and get to Colorado to be closer to her family. He noticed Johnson & Wales University was opening a campus in Denver, so he applied to teach culinary classes. As it turned out, the dean of the campus was a former instructor of his from 1991, when he was at Johnson & Wales in Rhode Island. Mark stayed in education for nearly ten years after that.

In 2006, in addition to teaching, Mark began creating artisanal charcuterie. Not having a facility of his own that was USDA-certified, he outsourced the commercial production of his products to licensed butchers using his techniques. He first gained notoriety for his duck breast prosciutto and was later recruited to help create a peppered veal bacon for the Canyon Ranch spa and resort in Tucson, AZ. By 2009, he had reunited with former business partners to open a USDA-certified facility called Il Mondo Vecchio Salumi. There, finally making the products with his own hands, Mark had the freedom to experiment and soon added nearly forty new products to his line of cured meat products. Eventually, he needed to leave Johnson & Wales to focus on the business full-time. After a successful first two years, he started to have conflicts with the USDA over the aging process of the charcuterie. While he feels they couldn't fully explain to him what he was doing that was against health code, they still suspended his license until he could explain his processes. After nearly six months without revenue, Mark was forced to close down operations in 2012.

Even through the tough time at Il Mondo, Mark continued to educate himself and others, and in 2011, Mark founded and taught part-time at his Rocky Mountain Institute of Meat (RMIM) in conjunction with Cook Street School of Culinary Arts. The butchery program he helped to create eventually became Colorado's only fully accredited butchery program and led Mark to the position of Director of Culinary Education at Cook Street.

Mark says it's comforting to see the increased use of whole animals in restaurants, regardless of whether it's a by-product of the point-of-origin to plate movement in dining or a return to old guard notions of cooking, that include more connection to the farmers and use of whole animals in house.

The tattoos that Mark got over the years are big parts of his story, culinary and otherwise. In 2010, he commissioned a half sleeve on his right arm. It started with the map of Italy with the inscription "patria paese familia," which he describes as signifying "for love of family, country, and native land." Below the map are his children's initials. On the same sleeve are images of Saint Mark (his namesake and the patron saint of law

and order) and Saint Matthew (the patron saint of banking and money). Eventually he wants to add Saint Michael (the archangel who defeated Satan). He clarifies that he's not overly religious but that these things have gotten him through challenging periods in his life.

Mark's most culinary-related tattoo is also his simplest, a USDA inspection stamp on his left shoulder. He got it in New York in 2011 on the eve of preparing dinner at the James Beard House. The number on the tattoo was the plant number of Il Mondo Vecchio, the butchery he opened in 2009.

Mark continues to be an advocate and educator when it comes to butchery. While he will probably always have projects in the works, the latest he is focused on is a book called *Pinkerton the Pigsmith*. Part fictional storytelling about the travels of a humble butcher and part cookbook, it is a book geared toward helping parents and children connect to food and its regionalism through the main character's adventures.

Warm Panzanella Salad with Porchetta di Testa, Pepperoni, Mustard Greens, Fennel, and Tomato

Mark says, "The recipe is a representation of simple food of a simple life and simple pleasures. My tattoos are a daily reminder of that to me."

YIELDS 8–12 SERVINGS, DEPENDING ON SERVING SIZE AND APPETITE

FOR PORCHETTA DI TESTA (SLOW ROASTED BONELESS HOG HEAD):

1 pig's head, from a scalded and scraped hog

1 tablespoon sea salt or kosher salt

2 teaspoons finely minced fresh garlic

1 teaspoon coarsely ground black pepper

½ teaspoon crushed red chili flakes

½ teaspoon orange zest

½ teaspoon fennel seed or fennel pollen

½ teaspoon finely chopped rosemary

TO COMPLETE:

2 tablespoons olive oil

4 tablespoons finely diced pepperoni

1 shallot, peeled and sliced

2 cloves garlic, sliced

1 cup sourdough (or other favorite) bread, diced into ½" cubes

1 small or medium fennel bulb, cored, thinly sliced

2 medium Roma tomatoes, skinned, seeded, cut into eighths

2 tablespoons white balsamic vinegar or white distilled vinegar

2 cups mustard greens, washed, trimmed, stems removed, leaves torn into bite-size pieces

Sea salt and cracked black pepper, to taste

Extra-virgin olive oil, to garnish (high-quality truffle oil can be used instead as an optional enhancement to this dish)

Shaved pecorino cheese, to garnish

1 **For Porchetta di Testa:** Preheat oven to 450°F. Combine spices in a small bowl. Season the inside of the pork "mask" liberally. For more even cooking and an easier-to-handle product, split the mask in half lengthwise down the center. Lay in the tongue and the ears. Roll and truss or tie tightly. Wrap in foil tightly twice, twisting ends to ensure the roll is tight. Place on a raised roasting rack in a pan and cook in oven for 15 minutes. Then turn the oven down to 250°F and slow cook for 3 hours. Remove from oven and place directly into refrigerator to cool below 40°F. Once completely cooled, unwrap from foil. Cut ½ pound into ¼" × 1½" lardons. Use or store the rest as you wish (see sidebar).

2 **To Complete:** In a sauté pan over medium-high heat, add the olive oil. Add in the ½ pound of ¼" × 1½" Porchetta pieces to render and sear for about 3 minutes. Turn the heat down to medium-low and add the pepperoni, shallots, and garlic to cook until tender and translucent, about 1 minute. Add in the bread to warm. Add in the fennel and tomato to cook until tender, about 1 to 2 minutes. Add the vinegar to deglaze for 30 seconds. Add the mustard greens to simply wilt, approximately 10 to 20 seconds. Remove mixture from heat and adjust final seasoning with sea salt and cracked black pepper. Arrange on plates. Finish with a light drizzle of extra-virgin olive oil, allowing for a few drops around the plate, and a sprinkle of shaved cheese.

NOTES FROM THE CHEF

If your hog is not scalded and scraped, blowtorch or shave any minute hairs from the face skin's outer layer. Remove the face from the skull. Trim and clean the ears really well; split in half. Clean the tongue of any membranes, split in half lengthwise, and set all aside under refrigeration.

The Porchetta di Testa can be used in a variety of applications. Furthermore, it can be portioned into smaller sizes and put into sealable bags or wrapped tightly. The Porchetta can be served chilled or warmed through; sliced thin like a cold cut and eaten as a salad or sandwich; or served with arugula, vine-ripened tomatoes, extra-virgin olive oil, and lemon juice, with your desired amount of fresh cracked black pepper and sea salt or kosher salt.

AARON BENNETT

> "There are three acceptable answers in my kitchen: 'Yes chef,' 'no Chef,' or 'I don't know Chef.'"
>
> —Aaron Bennett

AARON BENNETT'S first move into cooking came at the age of fifteen when, after waiting tables and washing dishes in restaurants, a cook at the omelet station he worked at in his hometown of Lafayette, Colorado, called in sick. Aaron hadn't really considered a long-term career in cooking until that first gig on the line. However, since that first job, he's forged a solid background focusing mainly on French and contemporary American styles. He also appreciates locally sourced sustainable ingredients and incorporates them into his dishes whenever possible. From the omelet station, Aaron moved up through a variety of restaurants, mostly in the hotel and luxury resort arena, all the while realizing he possessed a natural aptitude for cooking.

Deterred by the cost of culinary school, Aaron looked for alternatives and found one through an American Culinary Federation apprenticeship. He wasn't initially accepted into the program. Not taking no for an answer, he persuaded the powers that be at the ACF to invite him into a three-year apprenticeship at Denver's four-star, four-diamond Brown Palace Hotel. After completing the apprenticeship, the ambitious chef had bigger things in mind. Aaron says, "I'm working at the best hotel in Denver. I thought, I want to work at the best hotel in the state." That sentiment in mind, Aaron then took a job at the five-star, five-diamond Little Knell in Aspen, CO. After a few years at the Little Knell, Aaron wanted a new challenge and took a job at the Ritz-Carlton Club in

EXECUTIVE CHEF

BÁCARO VENETIAN TAVERNA, BOULDER, CO

Aspen, CO, eventually working his way up to executive chef. Returning to Denver in 2009, Aaron bounced around, working at a few different restaurants until 2012, when he found himself helping with the menu relaunch of Bácaro Venetian Taverna, a farm-to-table restaurant in Boulder, CO.

Aaron's one tattoo came about a bit by chance. He has one large black-and-white tattoo of a skull across his left forearm. The tattoo is an original piece done by a good friend, Jason Lombardi, who works at Easy Choppers and Tattoos in Bellevue, Washington, and is a one-of-a-kind piece. "He's one of those guys," Aaron explains, "that if it's original artwork, he'll only put it on one person and

it's done. He won't give it to anyone else." While going through Jason's sketchbook, Aaron found a design that he loved and that Jason had luckily never done before. As payment, Aaron offered to let Jason stay in his small apartment in Lafayette, Colorado, for a couple of weeks and feed him meals at the restaurant.

Aaron's love for the Aspen area keeps drawing him back. He's moved back up to the area and is working as sous-chef at Crêperie du Village, a French-style bistro. He says, "Aspen is my place. I love it here." Aaron is planning on working with a new tattoo artist in Aspen to expand his forearm tattoo into a full sleeve piece.

Hazel Dell Mushroom Bruschetta with Local Goat Cheese

Aaron says, "Hazel Dell Mushroom Bruschetta . . . is simply a recipe that shows my passion for using high-quality, local products, as well as being one of our bestselling menu items."

YIELDS 1 SERVING

5 tablespoons whole unsalted butter, divided

½ cup Hazel Dell (Boulder, Colorado) cinnamon cap mushrooms, cleaned and cut into 1" pieces

½ cup Hazel Dell (Boulder, Colorado) oyster mushrooms, cleaned and cut into 1" pieces

½ cup Hazel Dell (Boulder, Colorado) shiitake mushrooms, cleaned and cut into 1" pieces

Salt and freshly cracked black pepper, to taste

1 teaspoon minced shallot

1 teaspoon minced garlic

1 tablespoon minced herbs (equal parts thyme, rosemary, and parsley)

1 (1"-thick) slice of freshly baked ciabatta bread

1 ounce sofrito

¾ cup fresh organic baby arugula

½ ounce extra-virgin olive oil

1 teaspoon freshly squeezed lemon juice

2 tablespoons Haystack Mountain (Longmont, Colorado) goat cheese

½ ounce 18-year, cherry wood, aged balsamic vinegar

1 Place a 12" sauté pan over high heat and add 4 tablespoons of butter. Once butter is melted and just starting to brown, add mushrooms and let sear without mixing or tossing for approximately 1½ minutes. Once mushrooms have gained a nice golden sear on one side, season with salt and freshly cracked black pepper. Then make a spot in center of pan and add the remaining tablespoon of butter, shallots, and garlic. Cook briefly until shallots and garlic are nicely sweated (translucent), about 45 seconds to 1 minute. Then combine with mushrooms, mixing well. When mushrooms are cooked to desired doneness, about 3 minutes, making sure mushrooms are tender and cooked through, add minced herbs and remove from heat.

2 Brush both sides of the sliced ciabatta bread with sofrito and grill on charbroiler set at 600°F (if no charbroiler is available, use oven broiler or toaster oven and bake) until nicely golden brown, for charbroiler about 45 seconds per side. Bread should be golden brown and crisp, but not blackened or burned.

3 Place toasted bread on a plate of your choice. In a small mixing bowl, toss arugula with extra-virgin olive oil and lemon juice; season to taste with salt and cracked black pepper. Place arugula on grilled bread in an even layer, place sautéed mushrooms atop the bread and arugula, crumble goat cheese on top of mushrooms, and drizzle the aged balsamic over the top. Serve.

NOTES FROM THE CHEF

Aaron says, "I always try to use as much local, small batch produced ingredients as humanly possible. That being said, of course, if Hazel Dell Farms mushrooms or Haystack Mountain goat cheese are not available to you, I recommend using the softest and creamiest goat chèvre possible. You can really use whatever type of fresh, exotic variety of mushroom that you desire—without using your standard white button mushrooms. Almost any grocery store should at the very least have shiitake, cremini, and oyster mushrooms available in bulk. The main point is, look, use your hands, and feel what you're buying. Organic *does* make a difference, and roadside farm stands are our friends."

EXECUTIVE CHEF

THE RYLAND INN, WHITEHOUSE STATION, NJ

ANTHONY BUCCO

"I was at a point in my life where I was looking for something I really wanted to focus on. It was late teens early twenties and it was hard to find something I felt comfortable doing, and the one kind of unique line though the course of my life was my interest in food."

—Anthony Bucco

CHEF ANTHONY BUCCO is no stranger to New Jersey's culinary scene. He was proudly born and raised in the state, and is now showcasing the best of what Jersey has to offer both in product and in cooking talent. Anthony cooks with produce and meat from Garden State family farms and uses herbs and vegetables from the garden of the Ryland Inn, where he is now executive chef. Anthony credits much of his cooking philosophy and passion— "food from the heart"—to his family growing up. He feels forever indebted to his grandmother, Adrianna Bucco, who passed the heritage of great home-cooked meals on to him and inspired him to enroll at the New York Restaurant School. He graduated in 1999 with a degree in culinary skills.

Now, with over a decade in the kitchen, Anthony's resume includes some of the leading kitchens of New Jersey and New York, including Provence in NYC, Restaurant Latour in Hamburg, NJ, and

Stage Left in New Brunswick, NJ. Anthony also opened Catherine Lombardi, a fine-dining Italian concept from the same owners, while he was executive chef at Stage Left. In 2009, Anthony went on to be the opening executive chef of Uproot in Warren, NJ, which was named "Best New Restaurant" by *New Jersey Monthly* and received a "Don't Miss" from *The New York Times*.

Anthony now has big shoes to fill as the executive chef at the helm of the reopened Ryland Inn, which aims to serve classic American dishes but in an upscale yet friendly environment. The restaurant was formerly run by famed New Jersey chef Craig Shelton. Craig started running the restaurant in 1991 and in 2000 won the restaurant the James Beard Awards's top prize in the Mid-Atlantic region. The Ryland Inn closed in 2007 after a burst pipe weakened the structure of the building, and the building

sat vacant until Frank and Jeanne Cretella, owners of the Landmark Hospitality group, reopened it and recruited Anthony to help rebuild the renowned restaurant.

Along with several friends, Anthony got his first tattoo, a tribal band around his ankle, when he was seventeen. He says, "It's kind of lame. . . . I've since got it redone, but it does conjure fun memories!" In 2009, inspired by his strong Irish ancestry and the fact that his mother even owns land in Ireland, Anthony got a large, traditional Celtic knotwork cross on his back. He says, "I did it at a time in my life that I needed to be grounded a bit, so in essence it's become the cross that I bear." Today, Anthony often talks of maybe opening a place in Manhattan one day, but for the time being, he is deeply focused on restoring the Ryland Inn to its former glory.

Potato Gnocchi with Surry Farms Ham and Micro Arugula

This is a popular dish at Uproot restaurant, where the dish was photographed.

YIELDS 240 PIECES OF GNOCCHI

FOR GNOCCHI:
2–3 cups salt
3 large Idaho potatoes
1 quart all-purpose flour
2 large egg yolks
1 tablespoon olive oil
1 tablespoon milk

FOR BROTH:
¼ cup chicken stock
2 tablespoons butter
2 tablespoons grated pecorino cheese
Salt, to taste

TO COMPLETE:
6 (2-ounce) pieces per bowl Surry Farms ham or prosciutto
5–7 micro arugula leaves per bowl, for garnish

NOTES FROM THE CHEF

Anthony says, "Note that the yield on this recipe is for about 240 pieces. It's the best way to make it, in volume, so 24 orders of 10 pieces each. It can be scaled back, but the results aren't as desirable. It freezes extremely well."

1 **For Gnocchi:** Preheat the oven to 400°F. Spread 2 to 3 cups salt on bottom of baking pan. Place potatoes on top of salt and bake the potatoes until just done, about 1 hour. While still hot, pass through a tamis or a potato ricer onto a flat surface, such as a sheet tray. Salt the potatoes and let cool. Then transfer to a bowl and start adding the flour. Rub the flour and potatoes between your hands until the mixture reaches a sand-like consistency.

NOTES FROM THE CHEF

Salt baking is the perfect dry heat method for roasting potatoes. It allows for even distribution of heat to the entire potato.

2 Create a well in the center of the potato mixture and add the egg, oil, and milk. Fold the potato mixture into the egg mixture until just combined—do not overmix; this will create a dense gnocchi. Roll the dough on a floured surface and cut into 6 wedges. Roll each wedge into logs and cut into 1" nuggets. With a floured gnocchi board (or fork), press each nugget down and roll over the board (or fork) to create the ridges of the gnocchi. At this point, you can freeze them (if not using right away) or cook them in salted boiling water. They are done cooking once they float to the surface of the water, about 3 to 4 minutes. Remove from liquid and reserve.

3 **For Broth:** In a saucepan, gently bring the stock to a simmer over medium heat. Using a whisk, incorporate the butter and pecorino. Adjust seasoning to taste with salt.

4 **To Complete:** Gently reheat Gnocchi in Broth over medium heat. Once warm throughout, spoon Gnocchi into a bowl with Broth. Top with thinly sliced Surry Farms ham or prosciutto. Garnish with arugula leaves. Serve immediately.

NOTES FROM THE CHEF

This is a great way to enjoy homemade pasta at home without a pasta maker. Gnocchi are made easily in bulk and freeze well. Remember not to overwork gnocchi dough, and you'll be enjoying light, tasty gnocchi.

PART 5
SUGAR

CHEF/OWNER

CHARM CITY CAKES, BALTIMORE, MD

DUFF GOLDMAN

"We're all dorks, we're all the weird kids.
. . . Even though I was a dumb jock, I
was still the weird dumb jock . . . I think
that [Charm City Cakes] is a place we all
feel safe being weird."

—Duff Goldman

DUFF GOLDMAN was born Jeffrey Adam Goldman in Detroit, Michigan. He got his nickname Duff, by which he is better known, from his toddler brother, who was unable to pronounce the name and kept calling Goldman "Duffy." Duff's parents separated when he was ten, and growing up, he split his time between Northern Virginia and the town of Sandwich, Massachusetts, on Cape Cod. Duff graduated from high school in 1993 and attended the University of Maryland, where he earned degrees in both history and philosophy. While he never intended to be a chef, Duff got his first major professional cooking experience in Baltimore, MD, during his sophomore year in college. He ate at a restaurant called Charleston,

where the cuisine is rooted in French fundamentals and the lowcountry cooking of South Carolina, and the experience was life changing.

Duff was so impressed by Charleston that he applied there with no real experience to speak of. Determined, Duff met with executive chef Cindy Wolf, a 2006 and 2008 James Beard Award finalist for "Best Chef Mid-Atlantic." Cindy agreed to give him a job making cornbread and biscuits only, which doesn't sound all that exciting, but for Duff his time at Charleston was when he decided he truly wanted to be a chef. Duff learned a lot working at

Charleston but came to realize that if he truly wanted to understand baking, there was only so much he could learn while working in a kitchen. Wanting to understand the chemistry and the fundamentals of baking, he came to the conclusion he needed some formal schooling. After graduation from the University of Maryland, Duff attended the Culinary Institute of America in Napa Valley to earn his baking and pastry arts certificate in 1998. During this time, Duff continued his studies of the baking and pastry arts while working as a *stagiaire* (intern) on the pastry team at legendary chef Thomas Keller's (*Time* magazine's "Best Chef 2001") restaurant, the French Laundry.

After finishing his time at the CIA shortly before the turn of the millennium, Duff left California to become executive pastry chef at the Vail Cascade hotel and resort in Vail, CO. While visiting Boulder with some coworkers, Duff got his first tattoo, the Little Prince, from the classic French children's book *Le Petit Prince* (*The Little Prince*) by Antoine de Saint-Exupéry, on his ankle. Growing up, his mother used to read the book to him, and to this day, the book helps remind Duff about the things that are important in his life.

After his time in Colorado, Duff returned to the Washington, D.C., area to bake bread at Todd English's Olives, before finally opening his own bakery, Charm City Cakes, in Baltimore in 2000. There, fully embracing his creativity, Duff began creating made-to-order, special-occasion cakes, some of which took more than 200 hours to complete. Employing power tools next to mixing bowls, Duff took on more and more challenging jobs. As word about his unusual and daring cakes spread, *Baltimore City Paper* included him on its "Best of Baltimore" list in both 2002 and 2003. To keep up with demand, Duff hired a large staff, favoring artistic people like painters, architects, and sculptors rather than the typical pastry chef. The uniqueness of Duff's bakery was eye-catching, and in 2006, Food Network premiered *Ace of Cakes*, a reality show about the daily operations of Charm City Cakes. The show ran for ten seasons, with the last episode airing in February 2011.

In 2009, Duff got his latest tattoo, a whisk that runs down his left bicep. While Duff isn't just a pastry chef, this aesthetical design of a whisk is his largest tattoo and represents himself and his success. He says, "People use titles like pastry chef and pâtissier, but I like to think of myself as a baker. That's what I do most, so that's the title I use." Duff also sports an homage to all things chef with a pair of crossed knives tattooed very small on the inside of each wrist.

> **"People use titles like pastry chef and pâtissier, but I like to think of myself as a baker. That's what I do most, so that's the title I use."**

Duff isn't done getting inked, and he's not done baking either. Duff's work has been featured on *Food Network Challenge*, *Iron Chef America*, *Oprah*, *The Tonight Show with Jay Leno*, and many more. Charm City Cakes, where Duff is still heavily involved, continues to succeed, and most recently, he was tapped to create a cake for President Barack Obama's second inauguration in January 2013. Duff, who is now doing a lot more work in television, often as a guest judge, splits his time between Los Angeles and Baltimore.

In Los Angeles, Duff recently opened a West Coast outpost of Charm City Cakes, along with a new endeavor next door called Duff's Cakemix, a DIY bakery where customers can come in and decorate their own "yummy masterpiece" in the bakery with Duff.

Pineapple Hummingbird Cake

Duff's Pineapple Hummingbird Cake recipe was modeled into a signature truffle by Godiva Chocolatier and is a favorite at Charm City Cakes.

YIELDS 2 (9") ROUND CAKES

FOR CAKE:
3 cups all-purpose flour
1 teaspoon baking soda
1 teaspoon salt
2 teaspoons ground cinnamon
½ teaspoon ground nutmeg
¼ teaspoon ground ginger
1¼ cups sugar
¾ cup brown sugar
3 large eggs, room temperature, beaten
1 cup vegetable oil
1½ teaspoons vanilla extract
1 cup fresh diced pineapple, with juice
1 cup chopped, toasted pecans
3 ripe bananas

FOR CREAM CHEESE ICING:
1 cup cream cheese, at room temperature
½ cup unsalted butter, at room temperature
1 teaspoon vanilla extract
1¾ cups sifted confectioners' sugar

1 **For Cake:** Preheat oven to 350°F. Prepare the cake pans with baking spray and line with parchment paper rounds. Combine all of the dry ingredients in a large bowl by hand with a wooden spoon or a rubber spatula. Add eggs and oil, stirring by hand until the dry ingredients are moistened. Stir in vanilla, pineapple, pecans, and bananas.

2 Pour batter evenly into the two prepared cake pans, scraping bowl with a rubber spatula. Spread batter with an offset spatula so that it is evenly spread in pan. Bake at 350°F for 25 to 30 minutes, or until a wooden toothpick inserted in the center of the cake comes out clean and the cake springs back when pressed lightly in the center. The cake will slightly shrink away from the sides of the pans.

3 Let the cakes cool in the pans on a wire rack for 10 to 15 minutes. Run a small offset spatula around the outside of the cake to loosen from the pan; then carefully flip the cake out of the pan onto the wire rack. Place the cake right-side up on rack and let it cool completely.

4 **For Cream Cheese Icing:** Combine cream cheese and butter in mixer until light and well blended. Add vanilla, continuing to blend. Slowly add confectioners' sugar until icing is rich, smooth, and spreadable.

5 **To Complete:** Assemble cake by spreading a layer of Cream Cheese Icing using an offset spatula onto one Cake layer. Place the second Cake layer on top of the buttercream-covered first. Ice the entire assembled Cake with Cream Cheese Icing.

ALINA EISENHAUER

"I always thought I would never get one [a tattoo] . . . but I knew I would never regret that one."

—Alina Eisenhauer

ALINA EISENHAUER'S childhood love of cooking and baking led her to become a successful dessert bar owner and entrepreneur, a competitor on *Chopped* and *Cupcake Wars*, and the winner of *Sweet Genius*, but she didn't always take the most direct route to success.

Alina took her first restaurant job cooking in her neighbor's breakfast place when she was thirteen. When she was sixteen, New York's SoHo restaurant Whole Wheat and Wild Berries opened a location in the nearby Berkshires. Alina decided she wanted to get her foot in the door, so she showed up at the restaurant with a tray of no-bake cheesecake and a chocolate cake and left with a job that would last her through high school. When Alina started college, she left her love of all things culinary behind and began to pursue a career in television and film. However, she soon found herself getting very interested in fitness. She moved from Fitchburg State to Northeastern University in Boston to study physiology, and started to compete in fitness competitions. In 1996, she placed in the finals at the Ms. Fitness USA pageant, Miss Fitness America, and the Miss Galaxy pageant. Alina's love of physical activity soon led to a ten-year stint in the health and fitness industry, primarily as a personal trainer. But all of that changed when Alina became pregnant with her son in 2003.

While taking a break from her fitness career during her pregnancy, Alina began to dread the idea of commuting back to Boston every day and started to think about other options. Then, when her husband came home one day complaining he couldn't find any good bread in their

town, inspiration took hold and Alina began to think about opening a bakery. She says, "I never worked in a bakery before in my life, but then that's my MO. Figure it out." While pregnant, she read and did the research, and in 2003, by the time her son was six months old, she opened her first bakery, Sturbridge Baking Company, in Sturbridge, Massachusetts.

Alina operated the bakery for five years, earning a "Best Bread" award courtesy of *Worcester Mag* and then expanding to sell cookies, tarts, pies, and cakes. Craving more of a restaurant feel, Alina sold the bakery in 2008 to raise the capital for Sweet, her current dessert and cocktail bar located in Worcester, MA. Since opening Sweet, Alina has garnered many accolades, including a "Worcester's Most Creative Chef" award by *Pulse* magazine in 2009; *Worcester Mag*'s "Best Dessert" award in 2009, 2010, and 2011; *Worcester Living*'s "Best Dessert" award in 2009, 2010, and 2011; and *City Living*'s "Best Dessert" award in 2008, 2009, and 2011.

Alina got her first tattoo in 2006 after attending the women's chef and restaurateur national conference in Rhode Island as a guest chef. Alina mentioned that she'd always wanted a tattoo to a chef she was working the event with, and the next thing she knew, they were headed to a tattoo shop where she had "Born to Cook" inked across her arm.

But Alina didn't stop there. After appearing on the first season of Food Network's *Chopped*, she had the opportunity to cook at the James Beard House in New York City. After a perfect service, the event was so amazing that she and two other chefs got tattoos to commemorate the event, the logo of the James Beard organization with the date of the dinner. Alina got hers on her left arm. Her next tattoo? Either a sugar molecule, or a pinup girl chef modeled after herself with the phrase "A woman's place is in the kitchen." You'll have to wait and see what she chooses.

Bread Pudding with Almond Brittle and Beer Jelly

Bread pudding is a regular feature on the menu at Sweet, and beer pairings are often recommended with the dishes, but with the beer jelly this is a way to include it right in the dish.

YIELDS ½ HOTEL PAN

FOR BREAD PUDDING:
7–8 quarts day-old Italian or French bread, enough to fill ½ hotel pan, cut into 1½" cubes
12 ounces sugar
9 eggs
1 teaspoon vanilla
¼ whole nutmeg, grated
1 pound plus 12 ounces whole milk

FOR BEER JELLY:
2 tablespoons powdered gelatin
4 ounces cold water
8 ounces water
8 ounces granulated sugar
12 ounces Belgian Strong Dark Ale, Dogfish Head Raison D'Être is preferred

FOR ALMOND BRITTLE:
11 ounces sugar
4 ounces water
2 ounces honey
2½ tablespoons unsalted butter
¼ teaspoon plus ⅛ teaspoon baking soda
¼ teaspoon sea salt
1 cup blanched, sliced almonds, toasted

TO COMPLETE:
Butter
Caramel, to garnish
Whipped cream, to garnish

1 **For Bread Pudding:** Grease pan well and fill with cubed bread. Whisk sugar, eggs, vanilla, and nutmeg in a bowl until well mixed and add in milk. Pour custard base over bread, pressing bread down to make sure it is all covered. Cover with foil and let rest at room temperature for 15 minutes. Preheat oven to 350°F. Once mixture has rested, bake in oven for 45 minutes with foil on and an additional 15 minutes with foil removed, or until center is set. Remove from oven, allow to cool, and then slice into approximately 3" × 1" slices. Cover and store in refrigerator until ready to serve.

2 **For Beer Jelly:** In a small bowl, sprinkle the gelatin over the cold water and let it sit to soften. Meanwhile, simmer water and sugar in a small saucepan over medium heat until all of the sugar is dissolved, about 5 minutes. Remove the pan from the heat and add the gelatin to the simple syrup (sugar and water). Whisk until all of the gelatin is dissolved. Add the beer and pour the mixture into an ungreased sheet pan or brownie pan. Cover and chill in the refrigerator until set, about 4 hours. Slice into ½" cubes before plating.

3 **For Almond Brittle:** Cook sugar, water, honey, and butter in a sauce pan over medium-high heat until light caramel color. Remove from heat and whisk in soda, salt, and almonds. Quickly spread on Silpat-lined tray and pull pieces to stretch brittle into organic shapes. Allow to cool for several hours. Once hard can be stored covered at room temperature.

4 **To Complete:** Melt butter in sauté pan over medium heat. Add 2 pieces of Bread Pudding, drizzle with caramel, and heat until warmed through about 3 to 8 minutes depending on the temp of the butter and size of the Bread Pudding, turning to coat. Place on plate, drizzle with more caramel, and top with whipped cream and a piece of Almond Brittle. Place cubes of Beer Jelly in random fashion on the plate. Serve immediately, with Dogfish Head's Raison D'Être beer if you have it.

CHEF/OWNER

SWEETPEA BAKING CO., PORTLAND, OR

LISA HIGGINS

"I got my first tattoo when I was eighteen. My parents always said, no tattoos no tattoos. So of course . . . that's what I did."

—Lisa Higgins

LISA HIGGINS comes from a long line of bakers. Her great grandfather was a baker, and she is now the fourth generation. Lisa, however, didn't grow up wanting to be a baker. In fact, she has a degree in film and video from the University of Oklahoma and no professional training, but she was destined to follow her family's legacy. When she decided to eat a vegan diet, she started baking and just couldn't stop. She says, "When I went vegan, I started veganizing family recipes." Making more and more, she often just gave her food away. However, when she moved to Portland, Oregon, in 2004, she met the owners of Food Fight! Grocery, an all-vegan grocery store, and starting with her cheesecake, she soon found herself selling many of her pastries to them.

In January of 2008, she opened Sweetpea Baking Co., where she focused on making vegan baked goods using organic ingredients and locally grown flour, seasonal produce, and fruits, proving that you don't have to kill animals to make great baked goods. Since opening, she has convinced Food Fight!, Herbivore (a vegan clothing company), and Scapegoat Tattoo (a vegan tattoo parlor) to all move to the same building, creating a central location for likeminded business owners and patrons.

Since she started operating a bakery next to a tattoo parlor, she has gathered a lot more ink. "It's hard not to get tattooed all the time with a tattoo shop next door." Lisa got her first tattoo at eighteen, a little falling star on her back, but it has since been covered by beets

and kale that sit over a little banner announcing "Leap Before You Sour." Her left leg is fully covered in bright smiling pastries, a tattoo that came about after she mentioned that she wanted pastries for a tattoo to Brian Wilson, the owner of Scapegoat. Her right leg has the crush hazard safety icon that portrays a hand being crushed between two gear wheels. This tattoo is shared by many of the employees at Sweetpea, all with different sayings. Under the crush icon, Lisa's tattoo says "You're Fired," but everyone else's has something you'd say after an accident, like "Not Again" or "Oops." Around 2005, prior to opening Scapegoat, Brian also did her "sink" and "swim" tattoos across her knuckles. "I love them. They are probably my favorite tattoo."

Across Lisa's neck she sports a pair of winter mittens. On one arm she wears a sleeve of architectural elements designed around a Northwest theme. On the other arm is a depiction of Ferdinand the bull smelling the flowers. As long as Lisa has room on her body we will likely see more ink popping up. Her bakery continues to be very popular in Portland.

Vanilla Cinnamon Coffee Cake

Lisa says, "[This Vanilla Cinnamon Coffee Cake] is one of my oldest original recipes."

YIELDS 4 (4") COFFEE CAKES, RAMEKIN-SIZE, OR 1 (9") COFFEE CAKE

FOR BATTER:
2 cups all-purpose flour
¾ cup sugar
1 teaspoon flaxseed meal
2 teaspoons baking powder
½ teaspoon salt
¼ cup vegan margarine, slightly softened
2 teaspoons vanilla
1 cup soymilk
¼ cup water

FOR CINNAMON FILLING:
1 tablespoon vegan margarine, melted
¾ cup brown sugar
¼ cup sugar
2 teaspoons cinnamon

FOR STREUSEL TOPPING:
½ cup vegan margarine
1 cup all-purpose flour
½ cup sugar

FOR POWDERED SUGAR GLAZE:
½ cup powdered sugar
2 teaspoons water, plus more if needed

1 **For Batter:** Combine dry ingredients (including sugar) and margarine in a stand mixer with the paddle attachment and mix until margarine is in pea-size chunks. Add wet ingredients and mix until a batter is formed, about 30 seconds.

2 **For Cinnamon Filling:** In a small bowl, mix all ingredients until the mixture resembles wet sand.

3 **For Streusel Topping:** In a small bowl, combine all ingredients. With a pastry blender or fork, mash the margarine into the flour and sugar until small balls of dough begin to form.

4 **For Powdered Sugar Glaze:** In a small bowl, whisk powdered sugar with 2 teaspoons of water, adding more water by drops as needed until the mixture is a thick, pourable consistency.

5 **To Complete:** Preheat oven to 350°F. Grease a 9" round cake pan, or 8" square baking dish. Spread half of the Batter into the bottom of the pan with a spatula; then spread a layer of Cinnamon Filling (⅓ to ½ cup) on top. Place small dollops of the remaining Batter over the Cinnamon Filling and spread carefully with a spatula. Cover the top of the Batter with the Streusel Topping and add any extra Cinnamon Filling if desired. Bake uncovered for 30 to 35 minutes (25 minutes for the 4" ramekin size), until a toothpick inserted into the center comes out clean. Cool for 10 minutes, drizzle with Powdered Sugar Glaze, and serve warm. Store in a covered container up to 3 days; warm in oven if desired.

DOUGLAS RICHEY

"Hindsight is twenty-twenty, but you don't have foresight as a kid."

—Douglas Richey

DOUGLAS RICHEY started cooking at a young age. In fact, his first job was in a kitchen. Douglas says, "I just never left. It seemed like the environment most conducive to my success. I have strong ADD, and in a kitchen you are always micromanaging small tasks." Early on, Douglas wanted to attend culinary school, but a few chefs early in his career reminded him that they were paying him to learn in their kitchen, so he never went. After a career of learning everything he could, he took a job and spent several years cooking at Santi Restaurant in Santa Rosa, CA. The restaurant was known for its executive chefs branching out to open their own restaurants. Unfortunately for Douglas, when it was his turn at the helm, the restaurant soon had to close. He remembers, "It was very disappointing for me to finally have my at bat and then have the place close." There were some investors who initially wanted to reopen Santi, but they later decided to go with an original concept.

They sent Douglas on a trip across the South, where he traveled from Memphis, Tennessee, to Charleston, South Carolina, on a culinary fact-finding mission. Once he had reported his findings and was back in CA, they opened Sweet T's, a Southern-themed restaurant and bar in the old Santi location.

Pursuing a more Italian culinary experience, Douglas left to help open a pizzeria. He says, "The simplicity of Italian cuisine speaks volumes of how I like to eat personally." He then met Zazu Restaurant & Farm owner Duskie Estes (see entry in Part 1) in 2012 and says, "We had exchanged a few e-mails, but when I met Duskie, it just became belligerently clear that we have just kick-ass food chemistry." Douglas had worked at some great restaurants around California—including Bouchon for Thomas Keller, and the Farmhouse Inn for Steve Litke—and spent time in other Michelin-star kitchens, but

Zazu became what he calls his most satisfying culinary experience to date. He says, "For some reason, I am most drawn to game and odd cuts of meat, or offal. I love anything that requires finesse."

Douglas's most controversial tattoo, the words "Foie Gras" on his knuckles, has also been a culinary experience. He says, "Foie Gras on my knuckles is the closest tattoo that I have that means something to me." The tattoo has actually brought Douglas a bit of notoriety since California banned the product in 2012 due to animal cruelty. *Edible Marin & Wine Country*, a quarterly magazine celebrating the harvests of Marin County, put Douglas's knuckles on the cover of the magazine, and now people often recognize him from his hands. He says, "I don't get tattooed to talk about it. I'm not one of those guys. But, people talk to me about it constantly." Of people commenting on his tattoos, Douglas says, "It doesn't bother me when people give the work attention, but hey, how was the meal?"

Not all of Douglas's tattoos are so inflammatory though. He got his first tattoo when he was seventeen. His closest friend, Ben Cheese, who is now a successful artist working out of Everlasting Tattoo in San Francisco, was an aspiring tattoo artist, and Douglas let him practice on him. He says, "I was his guinea pig. I never thought along the way that I would get a lot of tattoos, but I wanted to support him, and he has probably put twenty or so really bad tattoos on me." Now that Ben is a successful artist, he doesn't charge Douglas for tattoos anymore, for which Douglas is grateful.

> **"** I don't get tattooed to talk about it. I'm not one of those guys. But, people talk to me about it constantly. **"**

Foieaffle with Peach Sauce and Farm Egg

Douglas prepares this waffle dish with foie gras in homage to his "Foie Gras" knuckle tattoo.

YIELDS 2 FOIEAFFLES

FOR PEACH SAUCE:

1 ripe yellow peach, cut into chunks
1 ounce butter
1 ounce maple syrup
Zest of ½ orange
Juice of 1 orange

FOR WAFFLE:

1½ cups flour
½ cup cornmeal
¼ teaspoon baking soda
1½ teaspoons baking powder
1 tablespoon sugar
½ teaspoon kosher salt
2 farm eggs, separated
1¾ cups buttermilk
2 tablespoons foie fat
4 tablespoons melted unsalted butter

FOR FARM EGG:

2 farm eggs

TO COMPLETE:

4 ounces pan-seared Hudson Valley foie gras
Pinch of Maldon salt, for garnish
4 Satsuma tangerine slices, for garnish

1 **For Peach Sauce:** Sauté peach chunks in a heavy-bottomed saucepan over medium heat uncovered until they begin to break down, about 5 minutes. Add butter, maple syrup, and orange zest. Add orange juice. Slowly reduce until sauce forms a syrup consistency. Set aside.

2 **For Waffle:** Preheat your waffle iron. Sift the flour, cornmeal, baking soda, baking powder, sugar, and salt and set aside. Beat the egg yolks until they are pale yellow; then add the buttermilk, foie fat, and butter. Combine with the dry ingredients. Beat the egg whites until stiff. Fold the whites into the batter. Cook in your waffle iron to desired doneness.

3 **For Farm Egg:** Gently sauté farm eggs over low heat until sunny-side up.

4 **To Complete:** Top each finished Waffle with Peach Sauce and foie gras. Add one Farm Egg to each plate. Garnish finished plate and seared foie gras with Maldon salt flakes and Satsuma tangerine slices. Serve immediately.

NOTES FROM THE CHEF

Foie gras can be seared immediately before serving for best flavor and texture. Sear foie gras over high heat in a nonstick pan for 1–2 minutes on each side.

JAKE GODBY

"I'm passionate about cheese and salty, crunchy things."

—Jake Godby

ORIGINALLY FROM A SMALL TOWN in Ohio, Jake Godby moved to San Francisco to attend the California Culinary Academy. He graduated in 1997, although he says, "I wouldn't recommend culinary school to anyone." His real education began when he was working as a pastry chef at Boulevard, Fifth Floor, and Coi and continues today. Jake says, "I am constantly learning."

One thing Jake has learned over the years is how to make ice cream. Although Jake only made ice cream in small amounts at all of the restaurants he's worked at, he decided to open his own ice cream parlor when he came into an inheritance in 2009. Soon after, he and his business partner, Sean Vahey, opened Humphry Slocombe, where ice cream flavors range from the traditional (Chocolate, Mint Chocolate Chip) to the exotic (Candied Ginger, Hibiscus Beet Sorbet) to the downright mysterious (Government Cheese, Elvis The Fat Years). But

serving unique flavors didn't always help the store, and in 2012, Jake and Sean courted mild controversy for serving a foie gras ice cream sandwich after California banned the use of foie gras. Jake and Sean were undaunted by criticism, and today Humphry Slocombe has been featured in *The New York Times* and *Bon Appétit* magazine and is considered the ice cream authority in the Bay Area.

Jake's most notable food-inspired tattoos, a parade of ice cream cones around his forearm, were based on designs he drew during the process of opening Humphry Slocombe. He got them done in two five-hour sittings. Jake says, "Opening my shop was an arduous process that took two years, and I figured that if I got the tattoo that there would be no turning back. It was a sign of commitment to myself." His other prominent tattoos, a "5¢" on his right bicep and a companion "10¢" on his left, represent his hobby of collecting old fixtures and signs from Woolworth's (some of which adorn the ice cream shop).

CO-OWNER/CHEF

HUMPHRY SLOCOMBE, SAN FRANCISCO, CA

Secret Breakfast Ice Cream

Jake is known for his ice creams, and they are represented in his tattoos.

FOR CORN FLAKE COOKIES:
YIELDS 24 COOKIES

2 cups all-purpose flour
1 teaspoon baking soda
1 teaspoon salt
1 cup butter, at room temperature
1 cup granulated sugar
1 cup brown sugar
2 eggs
2 cups corn flakes

FOR ICE CREAM:

2 cups heavy cream
1 cup whole milk
2 teaspoons salt
3 egg yolks
1 cup sugar
½ teaspoon vanilla extract
½ cup bourbon

TO COMPLETE:
½ cup chopped Corn Flake Cookies

1 **For Corn Flake Cookies:** Sift together the flour, baking soda, and salt in a medium bowl. In a large bowl, using an electric mixer or beating by hand with a wooden spoon, cream the butter with both sugars until smooth and well blended. Add the eggs one at a time, beating just until smooth after each addition. Add the flour mixture to the butter mixture a little at a time, beating just until incorporated. Fold in the corn flakes. Refrigerate the dough for at least 2 hours; will keep up to 2 weeks.

2 Preheat the oven to 350°F. Scoop golf ball–size portions of dough onto ungreased baking sheets, spacing them about 1" apart. Bake until very well done and dark brown, about 30 minutes for crisp cookies. Transfer to wire racks to cool. If they are still soft when cooled, flip them over and cook for 5 minutes more. (You want crisp cookies to use in the ice cream, but you can also make soft cookies to enjoy separately. For softer cookies, bake 12 to 15 minutes.) When the cookies are cooled and crisp, roughly chop for folding into the ice cream. Store whole cookies in airtight containers at room temperature. They are best enjoyed on the same day but are good for at least 3 days before they start getting stale. (It's easy to keep dough in the fridge and bake fresh as desired. You'd be kinda silly to make them and not eat them, you know.)

3 **For Ice Cream:** Fill a large bowl or pan with ice and water. Place a large, clean bowl in the ice bath and fit the bowl with a fine mesh strainer. In a large, heavy-bottomed, nonreactive saucepan over medium heat, combine the cream, milk, and salt and cook, stirring occasionally, until hot but not boiling. Meanwhile, in a medium bowl, whisk together the egg yolks and sugar until well blended; then whisk in the vanilla.

4 Remove the cream mixture from the heat. Slowly pour about half of the hot cream mixture into the yolk mixture, whisking constantly. Transfer the yolk mixture back to the saucepan with the remaining cream mixture and return it to the medium heat. Cook, stirring constantly with rubber spatula and being sure to scrape the bottom of the saucepan so it doesn't scorch, until the liquid begins to steam and you can feel the spatula scrape against the bottom of the pan, 2 to 3 minutes.

5 Remove the custard from the heat and immediately pour it through the strainer into the clean bowl you set up in the ice bath. Stir in the bourbon. Let cool, stirring occasionally. When the custard has totally cooled, cover the bowl tightly and chill in the refrigerator for at least 1 hour or preferably overnight. When you are ready to freeze the custard, transfer it to an ice cream maker and spin according to the manufacturer's instructions.

6 **To Complete:** Right after spinning the ice cream, fold in the chopped cookies. Eat immediately, or transfer to an airtight container, cover, and freeze for up to 1 week.

> **"** Opening my shop was an arduous process that took two years, and I figured that if I got the tattoo that there would be no turning back. It was a sign of commitment to myself. **"**

WING BEAN SALAD w/ PORK & PRAWNS, COOKED IN A ROASTED CHILI JAM, LIME & COCONUT MILK DRESSING

CPR KIT AVAILABLE @ BAR

OWNER/CHEF

POK POK NY, BROOKLYN, NY; POK POK, PORTLAND, OR

ANDY RICKER

"Older folks in polite Thai society frown on tattoos because it is common for criminals to be tattooed. As part of their penance after release from jail, they will sometimes go be a monk for a while to make merit for their family for bringing dishonor and bad luck to them for being an asshole. Therefore, tattoos were once associated with only monks and criminals. Now they are pretty common with young folk. . . ."

Andy Ricker

GROWING UP IN VERMONT, Andy Ricker started his career washing dishes, like so many people who find themselves in kitchens for their careers. However, he spent much of his youth traveling abroad, working in kitchens in New Zealand, Australia, Thailand, and Europe. That time away exposed him to many flavors and foods not available in the United States, including the cuisine of Northern Thailand, which would become his passion. Andy actually travels to Thailand every year to continue his research on the food and culture and to try and preserve what he feels is a dying art as more modern ways of cooking arrive in the country.

The rapid expansion of Andy's restaurants has been aided by the national press he has garnered for his authentic Thai cooking. In 2011, he won James Beard Awards's "Best Chef Northwest," and he has been featured on many shows, including Anthony Bourdain's *No Reservations*. But all this notoriety came as a bit of a surprise to Andy. He says, "I had no idea Pok Pok would become what it has. I figured I was just escaping from being a painting contractor. I had been studying this food, I always wanted my own restaurant, and I honestly did not know what else to do."

Andy has applied the same care and research he puts into his food to his Thai-inspired tattoos, most of which he got in Thailand. Down his right arm are images of phak chii, phak chii farang, and tom hom (coriander, sawtooth coriander, and scallions), staple herbs in many of the dishes he cooks. On the same forearm is a mortar and pestle with "Pok Pok" written in Thai. On the same arm above that is a sitting man reminiscent of the sitting Buddha. He is wearing a maw hawn, a denim shirt worn by Thai rice farmers, and is preparing Laap, an iconic dish of Northern Thailand. Surrounding him are the typical herbs eaten with the dish: bai makhok, the sour leaves of the Thai olive; phak phai, Vietnamese coriander; and khao tong, an herb native to southeast Asia.

Not all of Andy's ink is inspired by Thailand, however. He got his first tattoo around 1995, a Viking design found on a headstone from the Isle of Man, a small island between Great Britain and Ireland. From his research, much of his family's history comes from there.

With Andy's continued success, he is always trying to improve. He has started his own line of drinking vinegars and is working on his first cookbook, titled *Pok Pok: Food and Stories from the Streets, Homes*, and *Roadside Restaurants of Thailand*.

It's this attention to detail that has led to Andy being regarded as the foremost expert when it comes to truly authentic Thai cuisine in the United States. He opened his first location of Pok Pok, named for how the Thai describe the sound a mortar and pestle make, in Portland, Oregon, in 2005 and over the last eight years has built a small restaurant empire. In 2009, he opened Ping, a pub-like space with an Asian fusion menu that made many food critics' "must try" lists. However, he later sold his interest in that restaurant to his partners to focus exclusively on Thai cuisine. That same year, he also moved into the beverage realm with the Whiskey Soda Lounge, a lounge with Thai-inspired cocktails. In 2011, Andy opened Pok Pok Noi, a smaller, more limited version of the original restaurant. In 2012, Andy expanded to New York, opening Pok Pok Ny in Brooklyn. In 2013, he opened two more locations dedicated to Thai noodle dishes, Sen Yai in Portland and Pok Pok Phat Thai on the Lower East Side of Manhattan.

Gin Rummy

Andy has been serving Thai drinking vinegars in his restaurants since 2005. He now has his own line, called Som, packaged and available for sale to use in your home. These vinegars can be served diluted with soda water as a soft drink or at full strength as a mixer in several cocktails, like this one.

YIELDS 1 COCKTAIL

¾ ounce gin
¾ ounce light rum
¾ ounce Thai Basil Shrub (basil drinking vinegar)
¼ ounce Meyer lemon juice
1 sprig fresh basil, for garnish

1 Combine gin, light rum, Thai Basil Shrub, and lemon juice in a shaker with ice; shake until fully chilled.

2 Strain into a tall glass. Garnish with fresh basil.

NOTES FROM THE CHEF

We recommend buying Andy's Thai Basil Shrub, which can be found at *www.pokpoksom.com*. You can also make your own using vinegar, sugar, basil, and water. You'll find lots of recipes for shrub online!

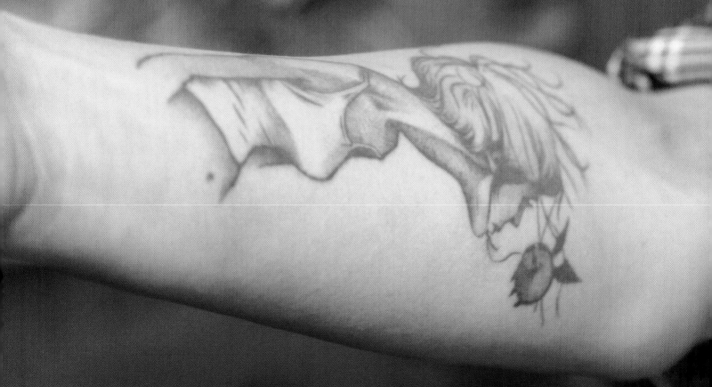

DOMINIQUE CRENN

"I always thought tattoos were part of history, a part of culture and ritual."

—Dominique Crenn

CHEF/OWNER

ATELIER CRENN, SAN FRANCISCO, CA

GROWING UP IN FRANCE, Dominique Crenn developed a keen interest in cuisine from her parents. While she grew up helping her mother in the kitchen, she also credits her father and his best friend, a well-respected French food critic, whom she went with on many of their dinners out to Europe's best restaurants. Dominique always wanted to be chef, but at the time in Europe, becoming a chef was something a woman just didn't do. Instead, she enrolled in the Academy of International Commerce of Paris and received her bachelor's degree in international business.

Dominique began her formal training as a chef when she moved to San Francisco in 1988 and fell in love with the Bay Area. During this time, she built an impressive resume, working under the tutelage of San Francisco luminaries Jeremiah Tower and Mark Franz for more than two years at the celebrated restaurant Stars, a landmark restaurant that was open from 1984 through 1999 and, along with Spago, Michael's, and Chez Panisse, is considered one of the birthplaces of California cuisine. Dominique moved on to work in the kitchens of Campton Place, 2223 Market, and the Park Hyatt Grill before becoming executive chef of Yoyo Bistro in the Miyako Hotel, where she earned a three-star review from *Access San Francisco* in 1996 and 1997.

In 1997, Dominique was offered a position to head the kitchen at the InterContinental hotel in Jakarta, but she wasn't sure it was the right move. Her reaction to the offer was, "At first I am like, Jakarta? Where is that?" But even though she was finally gaining notoriety at the time in San Francisco as a chef, the challenge proved too tempting, and Dominique decided to leave her comfort zone. Her acceptance made culinary history, and Dominique became the first female executive chef in Indonesia. When political unrest started to make the country dangerous, Dominique returned to the United States and spent the next eight years as executive chef of Manhattan Country Club in Manhattan Beach, California. During her time there, her skill in the kitchen was quickly recognized by the club's prestigious members, and she found herself catering to many of them, including numerous celebrities and dignitaries like Al Gore, L.A. Mayor Antonio Villaraigosa, Sidney Poitier, and Sharon Stone.

Returning to San Francisco in 2008, Dominique headed the kitchen at Luce in San Francisco's Intercontinental hotel, which focused on fine-dining, fresh cuisine that fit well with its extensive wine program. While there, she earned her first Michelin star in 2009 and again in 2010.

As with most chefs, the desire for Dominique to create a restaurant that was fully her vision was great, and in 2011, she finally got that chance and opened Atelier Crenn, where she was free to develop her take on modern French cooking. Creativity is a hallmark of her restaurant. She often borrows techniques and ingredients from many backgrounds, and the chef's tasting menu is written as a poem, conveying the feeling of the dishes rather than the ingredients. Less than a year after its opening, Atelier Crenn achieved its first Michelin star in October 2011. In 2012, Atelier earned two Michelin stars, making Dominique the first-ever female chef in the United States to receive the honor.

Dominique got her first tattoo in the early '90s when she first moved to San Francisco. She describes it by saying, "It was a sign of freedom. It's a little tattoo, a little heart with wings. . . . You have to understand, at the time I came from a country where my parents were very Catholic, and tattoos were understood as different and maybe bad." Her second and third tattoos wouldn't come until much later,

> ## " [MY TATTOO] HAS A MEANING THAT EVERYTHING IS POSSIBLE AND LIFE HAS MEANING AND THERE IS NO END TO IT. IT WAS KIND OF LIKE MY REBIRTH. "

in 2007. Showing respect for her roots, her second tattoo is of a British flag to represent her parents' homeland. Dominique's third tattoo is her name in Arabic. Her British parents had adopted her, so in 2000 she went looking for more information about her birth parents and found that her father was from Morocco. This tattoo represents her respect for her birth parents' culture and her heritage.

In 2009, Dominique almost lost her life to a freak accident in her bathroom, falling and tearing open her leg very close to the artery. The experience forced her to reflect on her life, and she found new beauty and resolve in what she was doing. She wanted to get a tattoo that reflected this, and around the same time, she discovered Brazilian artist João Ruas and fell in love with the dreamlike quality of his art. She had her tattoo artist do a design based on one of his sketches of a girl looking at a small flying creature and tattooed it on her forearm. Dominique says, "It has a meaning that everything is possible and life has meaning and there is no end to it. It was kind of like my rebirth."

Dominique continues to create and improve her vision at Atelier Crenn, but has also expanded outside the restaurant to do guest chef dinners in restaurants around the country. She is also very passionate about the farming community and hopes to find more ways to connect local farmers to chefs.

Birth

This is one of Dominique Crenn's signature dishes. This recipe, in various forms, is often used in her tasting menus and is a very difficult dish to complete in a home kitchen. The use of a food dehydrator as well as liquid nitrogen is required. It's included to give you a glimpse at what goes into a two-Michelin-star recipe. However, we recommend this only for the most adventurous of home cooks.

FOR CORN SILK NEST:

Silk from freshly shucked corn, about 4–5 cobs

Cooking oil, about 3–4 oz. for pan frying

FOR VANILLA GEL:

350 grams whole milk

35 grams sugar

4 grams agar

1 whole Tahitian vanilla bean, split and scraped

FOR APPLE PURÉE:

4 farm fresh apples

5 ounces olive oil

Salt, to taste

Sugar, to taste

50 grams simple syrup

FOR CHOCOLATE BRANCHES:

150 grams dark chocolate

FOR PUFFED WILD RICE:

100 grams wild rice

Cooking oil

1 gram dried porcini mushroom

FOR FOIE GRAS PEARLS:

50 grams foie gras fat

10 grams corn juice, reduced

1 egg yolk

1 cup liquid nitrogen

TO COMPLETE:

Micro chamomile, for garnish

Micro shiso, for garnish

1 **For Corn Silk Nest:** Fry the corn silk in a pan with cooking oil at 300°F until golden brown. Form a nest and leave it in dehydrator for 24 hours.

2 **For Vanilla Gel:** In a pot, whisk together all ingredients, including the vanilla bean shell. Bring to a boil, whisking occasionally. In order to activate the agar milk, mixture will need to boil for approximately 4 minutes. Strain and set liquid in a metal container in the cooler. Mixture will take a few hours to set, but should be firm to the touch. In a blender with a 2-ounce ladle, work the vanilla mix until it is fully blended and will spin without assistance in the blender. Season with a little bit of salt. Strain through a sieve.

3 **For Apple Purée:** Quarter and de-seed all four apples, leaving skin on. Toss in olive oil, salt, and sugar; roast them in a pan on the stove over medium heat until extremely soft and slightly brown on the skin. Peel will easily separate from the meat when ready. Remove the peel of the apple; purée the meat of the apple with simple syrup and season with salt and sugar to taste. Pass through a fine sieve.

4 **For Chocolate Branches:** Melt and temper the chocolate. Put it in piping bag and form branches by piping the chocolate in very cold water. Remove from water and set aside.

5 **For Puffed Wild Rice:** Fry rice in 375°F cooking oil until puffed. Remove rice from oil and allow to cool. In coffee grinder, grind the porcini to a fine powder. Mix with rice after it is cooled.

6 **For Foie Gras Pearls:** In a bowl, blend all ingredients (except nitrogen) and mix until the components emulsify. Put mixture in plastic squeeze bottle and, drop by drop, squeeze into bowl of nitrogen to form pearls. Remove pearls from nitrogen and place in corn silk nest on plate.

7 **To Complete:** Drizzle Vanilla Gel across plate; then lay Puffed Wild Rice, Chocolate Branches, and Apple Purée on top. Place Corn Silk Nest and spoon Foie Gras Pearls into the nest. Garnish with micro chamomile and micro shiso.

JOSHUA VALENTINE

"I just said what the hell and went for it."

—Joshua Valentine

BORN AND RAISED IN OKLAHOMA CITY, Joshua Valentine has made his mark working in great kitchens throughout the west. But this chef, now known for his obsession with bacon, first got interested in food when he was counting calories in order to make a certain weight to compete in wrestling competitions. Joshua's first exposure to professional cooking came at age nineteen when he started cooking in a Mexican restaurant, but then he joined the army and didn't think about a culinary career until after he got out. It wasn't until a friend saw an advertisement for Le Cordon Bleu College of Culinary Arts in Minneapolis that Joshua finally decided to make cooking a career.

After he graduated with an associate degree in applied science, Joshua says, "I'm constantly inspired by the traditions of food. Things people have been doing hundreds of years that we are still doing today." So, he went on to gain experience at a variety of restaurants, including Restaurant Alma in Minneapolis and Local in Dallas. Joshua continued his culinary career in Dallas, where he joined Stephan Pyles at Samar by Stephan Pyles as line cook and sous-chef. There, he met Matt McCallister (see entry in Part 4), which eventually led him to the job at Matt's restaurant, FT33. Joshua says, "I called him and told him, I would love to move back to Dallas and work with you, and he told me the only position he had open was pastry chef." Pastry is not actually Joshua's specialty, but he figured between Matt and himself, they could make it work.

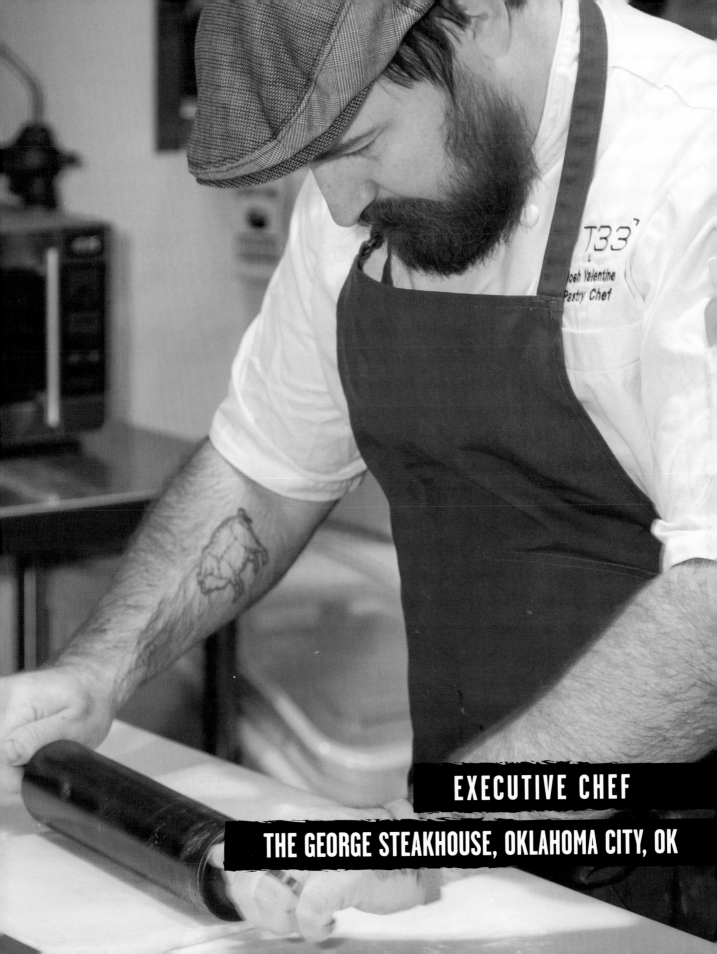

Joshua's first tattoo was a bulldog that says "U.S. Army." He got the ink right after he finished boot camp. Even though Joshua wasn't in the army for long, his father was in the army and his brother was a Marine who served for eleven years and did two tours of duty in Iraq, so he felt he was honoring the family tradition. Joshua also has the names of his three daughters tattooed on his right arm, along with one of his more prominent tattoos, a pig. "I've been tagged as this chef that loves pork. Obviously I love the animal, and to me it is just one of those chef tattoos." Joshua is not finished yet and has more culinary-inspired pieces planned. He has tons of ideas, and some of them may turn into reality. He says, "I think chefs are obsessed with food, and what better way to show it off than on your body?"

Joshua gained a lot of fame in 2012 as a contestant on Season Ten of *Top Chef*, where he made it to the final four contestants. He has recently left FT33 to return to his native Oklahoma, where he is opening the George Steakhouse as the executive chef. He wants to help the state gain national recognition for its food scene.

> "I think chefs are obsessed with food, and what better way to show it off than on your body?"

Lemongrass Panna Cotta with Mint Meringue, Lemon Curd, and White Chocolate Brown Butter Ganache

FOR LEMONGRASS PANNA COTTA:

15 lemongrass
2400 grams cream
240 grams white chocolate
400 grams sugar
6 grams kappa carrageenan

FOR MINT MERINGUE:

75 grams sugar
2½ grams Versawhip
½ gram xanthan gum
100 grams water
25 grams mint purée

FOR LEMON CURD:

4 eggs
340 grams sugar
175 grams lemon juice
Zest of 2 lemons
4 gelatin sheets, bloomed
100 grams butter

FOR WHITE CHOCOLATE BROWN BUTTER GANACHE:

280 grams white chocolate
76 grams butter
115 grams cream

FOR MEYER LEMON FOAM:

200 grams cream
Zest of 6 Meyer lemons
25 grams sugar
Liquid nitrogen

1 **For Lemongrass Panna Cotta:** Bruise lemongrass and combine with cream. Bring to simmer over low heat and steep 1 hour. Strain mixture into clean pot and bring to boil over high heat. Add white chocolate and mix with hand blender. Add sugar and kappa and mix with hand blender. Pour into desired molds and refrigerate. Work quickly because once the kappa is added, the mixture sets very fast.

2 **For Mint Meringue:** Mix all ingredients with hand blender. Transfer to a mixing bowl and whip on high until doubled in volume. Spread thin or pipe onto a dehydrator tray and dehydrate until crisp.

3 **For Lemon Curd:** Combine eggs, sugar, lemon juice, and zest in bowl set over pot of simmering water. Whisk until thick. Add bloomed gelatin sheets and mix until melted, then add the butter.

4 **White Chocolate Brown Butter Ganache:** Put chocolate in bowl. Brown butter in a saucepan over medium heat. Add cream to butter and bring to boil. Pour liquid over chocolate and stir to combine. Remove from heat.

5 **Meyer Lemon Foam:** Bring all ingredients to a boil and steep for 30 minutes. Strain into an iSi canister and charge twice. Dispense into a container of liquid nitrogen and crumble the frozen foam.

6 **To Complete:** Transfer Lemon Curd to squeeze bottle and White Chocolate Brown Butter Ganache to piping bag. Place Lemongrass Panna Cotta on plate. Dot Lemon Curd and Ganache all around plate randomly. Haphazardly sprinkle Meyer Lemon Foam around plate. Break Mint Meringue into pieces and decorate the plate with them.

Metric Conversion Chart

VOLUME CONVERSIONS

U.S. Volume Measure	Metric Equivalent
⅛ teaspoon	0.5 milliliter
¼ teaspoon	1 milliliter
½ teaspoon	2 milliliters
1 teaspoon	5 milliliters
½ tablespoon	7 milliliters
1 tablespoon (3 teaspoons)	15 milliliters
2 tablespoons (1 fluid ounce)	30 milliliters
¼ cup (4 tablespoons)	60 milliliters
⅓ cup	90 milliliters
½ cup (4 fluid ounces)	125 milliliters
⅔ cup	160 milliliters
¾ cup (6 fluid ounces)	180 milliliters
1 cup (16 tablespoons)	250 milliliters
1 pint (2 cups)	500 milliliters
1 quart (4 cups)	1 liter (about)

WEIGHT CONVERSIONS

U.S. Weight Measure	Metric Equivalent
½ ounce	15 grams
1 ounce	30 grams
2 ounces	60 grams
3 ounces	85 grams
¼ pound (4 ounces)	115 grams
½ pound (8 ounces)	225 grams
¾ pound (12 ounces)	340 grams
1 pound (16 ounces)	454 grams

OVEN TEMPERATURE CONVERSIONS

Degrees Fahrenheit	Degrees Celsius
200 degrees F	95 degrees C
250 degrees F	120 degrees C
275 degrees F	135 degrees C
300 degrees F	150 degrees C
325 degrees F	160 degrees C
350 degrees F	180 degrees C
375 degrees F	190 degrees C
400 degrees F	205 degrees C
425 degrees F	220 degrees C
450 degrees F	230 degrees C

BAKING PAN SIZES

U.S.	Metric
8 x 1½ inch round baking pan	20 x 4 cm cake tin
9 x 1½ inch round baking pan	23 x 3.5 cm cake tin
11 x 7 x 1½ inch baking pan	28 x 18 x 4 cm baking tin
13 x 9 x 2 inch baking pan	30 x 20 x 5 cm baking tin
2 quart rectangular baking dish	30 x 20 x 3 cm baking tin
15 x 10 x 2 inch baking pan	30 x 25 x 2 cm baking tin (Swiss roll tin)
9 inch pie plate	22 x 4 or 23 x 4 cm pie plate
7 or 8 inch springform pan	18 or 20 cm springform or loose bottom cake tin
9 x 5 x 3 inch loaf pan	23 x 13 x 7 cm or 2 lb narrow loaf or pâté tin
1½ quart casserole	1.5 liter casserole
2 quart casserole	2 liter casserole

General Index

Note: Page numbers in **bold** indicate recipes, and page numbers in *italics* indicate/include photographs of chefs and/or tattoos. For recipes by main ingredient or general category, see *Recipe Index*.

A

Ace Eat Serve (Denver, CO), 230
Adey, Kevin
    biographical sketch, 113–14
    photograph of, *112*
    Roasted Scallops with Sunchoke Purée, Wilted Spinach, and Walnut Salad, **115**
    tattoos of, *112*, 114
Anderson, Scott, 206–9
    biographical sketch, 207–8
    photograph of, *206*
    tattoos of, *206*, 207, 208
    Tomato Soup with Ciabatta Toast and Grilled Cheese, **209**
Andrés, José, 136, 216
Arce, Manny, 62–65
    biographical sketch, 63–64
    photograph of, *62*
    Tamarind Braised Short Ribs with Sweet Potato Purée, Arugula, Golden Raisins, and Spiced Pumpkin Seeds Hoofed: Manny, **65**
    tattoos of, 64
Artley, Will, 224–27
    biographical sketch, 224–26
    photograph of, *225*
    Sourdough Pizza Dough, **227**
    tattoos of, *225*, 226
Atelier Crenn (San Francisco, CA), 288, 289
Atwood Café (Chicago, IL), 116

B

Bácaro Venetian Taverna (Boulder, CO), 254
Baltzley, Brandon, 232–37
    biographical sketch, 232–35
    Butternut Squash with Goat's Yogurt, Spirulina, and Stevia, **236–37**
    photographs of, *233*, *235*, *237*
    tattoos of, *233*, 234–*35*
Bar Marmont (Los Angeles, CA), 204, **205**
Barnes, Derek, 113
Barron, Chris, 16–19, 196
    biographical sketch, 18
    Coppa and Egg, **19**
    photograph of, *16*
    tattoos of, *16*, 17, 18
Barron, Jill, 18, 194–97
    biographical sketch, 196
    Ma Po Tofu, **197**
    photograph of, *194–95*
    tattoos of, *194–95*, 196
Barwikowski, Jason, 50
Batali, Armandino, 72
Batali, Mario, 54, 72
Beast and the Hare (San Francisco, CA), 167
Bennett, Aaron, 252–55
    biographical sketch, 252–54
    Hazel Dell Mushroom Bruschetta with Local Goat Cheese, **255**
    photograph of, *253*
    tattoos of, *253*, 254
Berardino, Michael, 78–81
    biographical sketch, 79–80
    Malloreddus, **81**
    photographs of, *78*, *80*
    tattoos of, *78*, *80*
Beuchert's Saloon (Washington, D.C.), 146
Biederman, Brandon, 238–41
    biographical sketch, 238–40
    photograph of, *239*
    tattoos of, *239*, 240
    Tiger Wings with Som Tum, **241**
Black Pig Meat Co. (Sonoma County, CA), 69, 72
Blanc, Raymond, 158
Bloomfield, April, 202–4
Blumlo, Christopher, 38
Bollinger, Patrick, 90
Bonny, Jill, 168
Book overview, 7

Boulud, Daniel, 95, 142, 216
Bratalian (Las Vegas, NV), 28
Brownlow, Morgan, 84
Bucco, Anthony, 256–59
    biographical sketch, 257–58
    photograph of, *256*
    Potato Gnocchi with Surry Farms Ham and Micro Arugula, **259**
    tattoos of, *256*, 258

C

California
    Los Angeles: Bar Marmont, 204, **205**; Chateau Marmont, 204; Salt's Cure, 21
    Rancho Palos Verdes: Terranea Resort, 122
    San Francisco: Atelier Crenn, 288, 289; Beast and the Hare, 167; Humphry Slocombe, 278; Luella, 56–58; 20 Spot, 172
    Sonoma County: Black Pig Meat Co., 69, 72; Zazu Restaurant and Farm, 68, 69, 72, 275–76
Callaghan, Ken, 202
Campanale, Joe, 79
Cardoz, Floyd, 185
Chapel, Alain, 158
Charm City Cakes (Baltimore, MD), 264, **265**
Chateau Marmont (Los Angeles, CA), 204
Chef Tony's (Bethesda, MD), 104
Chicago, IL
    Atwood Café, 116
    CRUX, 234, **236–37**
    Francesca's Forno, 18
    MANA Food Bar, 18, 196
    Osteria di Tramonto, 158
    RT Lounge, 158
    Tramonto Steak and Seafood, 158
    Yusho, 200

Chittum, Tony, 145
Clark, Johnny, and Beverly Kim, 176–83
    biographical sketches, 176–78, 180
    meeting and marrying, *178*, 180
    Nasi Goreng, **182–83**
    photographs of, *177*, *178*, *181*
    tattoo of Beverly, *178*, *181*
Colorado
    Boulder: Bácaro Venetian Taverna, 254
    Denver: Ace Eat Serve, 230; Corner House, 189; The Populist, 76; Steuben's, 228–30
Corner House (Denver, CO), 189
Corsino (New York City, NY), 46
Crenn, Dominique, 286–91
    biographical sketch, 288–89
    Birth, **290–91**
    photographs of, *286–87*
    tattoos of, *286*, 288–*89*
Cretella, Frank and Jeanne, 258
CRUX (Chicago, IL), 234, **236–37**
Cucci, Justin, 74
Curi, Tomas, 44–47
    biographical sketch, 45–46
    Crispy Braised Mangalista Belly with Bitter Greens and Citrus, **47**
    photographs of, *44–45*, 46
    tattoos of, *44–45*, 46
Curren, Chris, 242–45
    biographical sketch, 243–44
    Panzanella with Roasted Acorn Squash, **245**
    photograph of, *242*
    tattoos of, *242*, 244

D

Dallas, TX, FT33, 216, 292, 294
Daugherty, Seth Bixby, 224
De Cuisine Departure (Portland, OR), **165**

Delouvrier, Christian, 95
DeNittis, Mark, 246–51
    biographical sketch, 248–50
    photographs of, *246–47, 249*
    tattoos of, *246–47,* 248–50, *249*
    Warm Panzanella Salad with
        Porchetta di Testa, Pepperoni,
        Mustard Greens, Fennel, and
        Tomato, **251**
Deshaies, David, 145
Devlin, Ciaran, 96
de Vries, Ben, 56–61
    biographical sketch, 56–58
    Luella's Coca-Cola Braised Pork
        Shoulder, **60–61**
    photographs of, *57, 58, 59*
    tattoos of, *57, 58, 59*
Dilullo, Vito, 84
Distler, Stephen, 208
Do or Dine (Brooklyn, NY), 108–10
Douglas, Tom, 66, 68, 71

E

Ed's Lobster Bar (New York City, NY),
    127–29
8407 Kitchen Bar (Silver Spring,
    MD), 142
Eisenhart, John, 52–55
    Batsoa, **55**
    biographical sketch, 53–54
    photograph of, *52*
    tattoos of, *52,* 53–54
Eisenhauer, Alina, 266–69
    biographical sketch, 266–68
    Bread Pudding with Almond
        Brittle and Beer Jelly, **269**
    photographs of, *267, 268*
    tattoos of, *267, 268*
Elements (Princeton, NJ), 207, 208
Elliot, Graham, 199
English, Todd, 264
Estes, Duskie, 66–69, 275
    biographical sketch, 66–68
    Brussels Sprouts, Gravenstein
        Apple, and Black Pig Bacon
        Salad, **69**
    John Stewart and, 68, 71, 72
    photographs of, *67, 68*
    tattoo of, *67, 68*

F

Fabbrica (Brooklyn, NY), 80
Favacchia, Michael, 32
Fiorelli, Michael, 120–25
    biographical sketch, 121–22
    Grilled Spanish Octopus with
        Salsa Verde, Fried Potatoes,
        Piquillo Peppers, Green
        Onion, Preserved Lemon, and
        Chorizo, **123–25**

photographs of, *120, 122*
    tattoos of, *120, 122*
Flay, Bobby, 28, 202
Foo, Susanna, 121
Ford, Josh, 240
Forgione, Larry, 36, 38
Forgione, Marc, 36–43, 232
    biographical sketch, 36–38
    photographs of, *37, 39*
    tattoos of, 36, *37,* 38, *39*
    Veal Tenderloin, Boudin Noir,
        Fingerling Potatoes, Grilled
        Green Garlic, Pearl Onions,
        and Porcini Mushrooms, with
        a Mustard Reduction, **40–43**
Francesca's Forno (Chicago, IL), 18
Franz, Mark, 288
French, Jason, 82–87
    biographical sketch, 84–85
    Pastured Pork, Sauerkraut, and
        Whey Sauce, **86–87**
    photographs of, *82–83, 85*
    tattoos of, *82–83,* 84–85
FT33 (Dallas, TX), 216, 292, 294
Fuller, Keith, 88–93
    biographical sketch, 90–91
    photograph of, *88*
    Pork Belly, Scallops, and
        Reindeer Lichen, with an
        Elderberry Gastrique, **92–93**
    tattoos of, *88,* 90, 91

G

G (Washington, D.C.), 136
Gagnaire, Pierre, 158
Gand, Gale, 158
Garces, Jose, 136
Ghaw, Brian, 130
Godby, Jake, 278–81
    biographical sketch, 278
    photograph of, *279*
    Secret Breakfast Ice Cream (and
        Corn Flake Cookies), **280–81**
    tattoos of, 278, *279*
Goldman, Duff, 262–65
    biographical sketch, 263–64
    photograph of, *262*
    Pineapple Hummingbird Cake,
        265
    tattoos of, *262,* 264
Gordon Ramsay, Paris Casino (Las
    Vegas, NV), 32
Gourdet, Gregory, 162–65
    biographical sketch, 164
    Curry Noodles, Slow Chicken,
        Pickled Mustard Greens, and
        Toasted Chili, **165**
    photograph of, *162*
    tattoo of, *162,* 164
Graffiato (Washington, D.C.), 136

Gras, Laurent, 200
Guérard, Michel, 36–38, 158

H

Hart, Chris, 13
Hawes, Sean, 228–31
    Beet Salad, **231**
    biographical sketch, 229–30
    photograph of, *228*
    tattoos of, *228,* 229–30
Higgins, Lisa, 270–73
    biographical sketch, 271–72
    photograph of, *270*
    tattoos of, *270,* 271–72
    Vanilla Cinnamon Coffee Cake,
        273
Hopfinger, Erik, 171
Humphry Slocombe (San Francisco,
    CA), 278
Husbands, Andy, 12–15
    biographical sketch, 13–14
    photograph of, *12*
    Smoked Ham Hock Croquettes
        with Dijon Aioli, **15**
    tattoos of, *12,* 13, 14

I

Illinois. *See* Chicago, IL
Il Mundo Vecchio, 250
Isabella, Mike, 134–39
    biographical sketch, 135–36
    Kapnos Octopus, **138–39**
    photographs of, *134, 137*
    tattoos of, *134,* 136, *137*

J

Jackson, Luke, 108

K

Kalman, Bruce, 243
Kapnos (Washington, D.C.), 136,
    138–39
Keller, Thomas, 68, 121, 264, 275
Kim, Beverly. *See* Clark, Johnny, and
    Beverly Kim
Kinkead, Robert, 66, 224, 226
Krikorian, Haig and Cindy, 171

L

Las Vegas, NV
    Bratalian, 28
    Gordon Ramsay, Paris Casino, 32
    Meatball Spot, 28
Lee, Angela, 196
Lee, Christina, 130
Le Pigeon (Portland, OR), 50, 64
Leventhal, Robin, 218–23

biographical sketch, 219–20
    photographs of, *218, 220*
    Sunrise Lentil Cakes, Coriander
        Carrot Purée, Coriander-
        Lemon Aioli, **221–23**
    tattoos of, *218,* 219–*20*
Litke, Steve, 275
Little Bird (Portland, OR), 50
Local 360 (Seattle, WA), 219, **221–22**
Luella (San Francisco, CA), 56–58
Luongo, Pino, 149

M

Maclise, Deming, 63–64
Malloy, Scott, 198–201
    biographical sketch, 199–200
    Nuka Pickle, **201**
    photograph of, *198*
    tattoos of, *198,* 200
MANA Food Bar (Chicago, IL), 18,
    196
Marciante, Tony, 102–7
    biographical sketch, 104
    Pan-Seared Diver Scallops with
        Seasonal Vegetables and
        Crispy Sweet Potatoes, **106–7**
    photographs of, *102–3, 105*
    tattoos of, *102–3,* 104
Markert, Andrew, 144–47
    biographical sketch, 145–46
    Drew's Mama's Crab Cakes with
        Mustard Cider Reduction and
        Walnut Brown Butter, **147**
    photograph of, *144*
    tattoos of, *144,* 145–46
Marks, Ian, 166–69
    biographical sketch, 167–68
    Duck Frites, **169**
    photograph of, *166*
    tattoos of, *166,* 168
Marunowski, Dan, 244
Maryland
    Baltimore: Charm City Cakes,
        264, **265**
    Bethesda: Chef Tony's, 104
    Silver Springs: 8407 Kitchen
        Bar, 142
Massachusetts
    Boston: Sister Sorel, 13, 14;
        Tremont 647, 13
    Worcester: Sweet, 268
McCallister, Matt, 214–17
    biographical sketch, 215–16
    Joshua Valentine and, 292
    photograph of, *214, 216*
    Roasted Cauliflower Soup, **217**
    tattoo of, *214, 216*
McFarland, Ed, 126–29
    biographical sketch, 127–28
    Lobster Rolls, **129**

photographs of, *126*, *128*
tattoos of, *126*, 128
McNeese, George, 108
Meatball Spot (Las Vegas, NV), 28
Metric conversion chart, 296
Meyer, Danny, 108
Militello, Mark, 122
Mina, Michael, 96
Mistral (Princeton, NJ), 208
Morris, Will, 94–99
    biographical sketch, 95–97
    Crispy Pork Belly with Littleneck
        Clams and Trumpet Royale
        Mushrooms, **98–99**
    photographs of, *94*, *97*
    tattoos of, *94*, 95, *96–97*
Mosimann, Anton, 158
Mullen, Seamus, 184–87
    biographical sketch, 185–86
    photograph of, *184*
    tattoos of, *184*, 186
    Tosta Huevo Roto, **187**

N

Ned Ludd (Portland, OR), 84
Nevada. *See* Las Vegas, NV
New Jersey
    Bloomfield: Orange Squirrel
        Restaurant, 150
    Princeton: Elements, 207, 208;
        Mistral, 208
    Whitehouse Station: Ryland Inn,
        208, 257–58
New York
    Brooklyn: Do or Dine, 108–10;
        Fabbrica, 80; Northeast
        Kingdom, 113–14; Pok Pok
        NY, 284
    New York City: Corsino, 46; Ed's
        Lobster Bar, 127–29; Recette,
        130–32; Restaurant Marc
        Forgione, 38; Tertulia, 186
Northeast Kingdom (Brooklyn, NY),
    113–14

O

Orange Squirrel Restaurant
    (Bloomfield, NJ), 150
Oregon. *See* Portland, OR
Osteria di Tramonto (Chicago, IL),
    158

P

Palladin, Jean-Louise, 95
Palmieri, Francesco, 148–53
    biographical sketch, 149–50
    Lobster Cobb Salad, **151–52**
    photographs of, *148*, *153*

tattoos of, *148*, 150
Paone, Anthony, 170–75
    biographical sketch, 171–72
    Chef's Day-After Breakfast,
        174–75
    photographs of, *170*, *173*
    tattoos of, *170*, *172–73*
Pazzo Ristorante (Portland, OR), 54
Pellegrino, Carla, 24–29
    biographical sketch, 26–28
    photographs of, *24*, *27*
    tattoos of, *24*, *27*, 28
    Vitello alla Milanese, **29**
Pellegrino, Frank, Jr., 26, 28
Pellegrino, Frank, Sr., 26
Pennsylvania. *See* Pittsburgh, PA
Phelps, Chris, 21
Pittsburgh, PA, Root 174, 91
Pizzeria Orso (Falls Church, VA),
    226, **227**
Pok Pok (Portland, OR), 284
Pok Pok NY (Brooklyn, NY), 284
The Populist (Denver, CO), 76
Poquitos (Seattle, WA), 64, 229
Portland, OR
    De Cuisine Departure, **165**
    Le Pigeon, 50, 64
    Little Bird, 50
    Ned Ludd, 84
    Pazzo Ristorante, 54
    Pok Pok, 284
    Sweetpea Baking Co., 271
Power, Jonathan, 74–77
    Bacon and Egg, **77**
    biographical sketch, 74–76
    photographs of, *75*, *76*
    tattoos of, *75*, *76*
Price, Noah, 76
Pyle, J.J., 108
Pyles, Stephan, 215, 292

R

Ramsay, Gordon, 32
Recette (New York City, NY), 130–32
Recipes. *See also Recipe Index*;
    specific chef names
Recipes, about, 9
Restaurant Marc Forgione (New
    York City, NY), 38
Restaurants of featured chefs. *See
    biographical sketch subentries of
    specific chefs; specific restaurant
    names; states where restaurants
    are located*
Richey, Douglas, 274–77
    biographical sketch, 275–76
    Foieaffle with Peach Sauce and
        Farm Egg, **277**
    photograph of, *274*
    tattoos of, *274*, 276

Ricker, Andy, 282–85
    biographical sketch, 283–84
    Gin Rummy, **285**
    photographs of, *282*, *284*
    tattoos of, *282*, 283, *284*
Ripert, Eric, 95, 113
Rocky Mountain Institute of Meat
    (RMIM), 248
Rodriguez, Douglas, 136
Rojas, Greg, 58
Root 174 (Pittsburgh, PA), 91
RT Lounge (Chicago, IL), 158
Rucker, Gabriel, 48–51
    Beef Carpaccio, Broccoli,
        Oysters, and Wasabi
        Vinaigrette, **51**
    biographical sketch, 49–50
    photograph of, *48*
    tattoos of, *48*, 50
Ryland Inn (Whitehouse Station,
    NJ), 208, 257–58

S

Sabatino, George, 32
Salt's Cure (Los Angeles, CA), 21
Samuelsson, Marcus, 136, 224
Schenker, Jesse, 130–33
    biographical sketch, 130–32
    photograph of, *131*
    Roasted Red Snapper, Corn
        Purée, Fresh Corn, Rock
        Shrimp, and Lobster Butter,
        133
    tattoos of, 130, *131*, 132
Schenker, Lindsay, 130, 132
Schlesinger, Chris, 13, 202
Seattle, WA
    Local 360, 219, **221–22**
    Poquitos, 64, 229
Selby, Matt, 188–91, 238
    biographical sketch, 189
    photograph of, *188*
    tattoos of, *188*, 189
    Truffle Salt–Cured Foie Gras,
        190–91
Shelton, Craig, 208, 258
Silvestri, Renee, 58
Simcik, Derek, 116–19
    biographical sketch, 116–18
    photograph of, *117*
    Sautéed Red Snapper with
        Purple Cauliflower Medley and
        Cauliflower Purée, **119**
    tattoos of, 116–18, *117*
Simon, Kelly, 122
Sister Sorel (Boston, MA), 13, 14
Spence, Carolyn, 202–5
    biographical sketch, 202–4
    Lightly Toasted Brioche Roll, **205**
    photograph of, *203*

tattoos of, *203*, 204
Steiling, Lish, 210–13
    Autumn in a Bowl: Roasted
        Parsnip and Kale Salad, **213**
    biographical sketch, 210–12
    photographs of, *211*, *212*
    tattoos of, *211*, *212*
Steuben's (Denver, CO), 228–30
Stewart, John, 70–73
    biographical sketch, 71–72
    Black Pig Bacon and Duck Egg
        Carbonara, **73**
    Duskie Estes and, 68, 71, 72
    photograph of, *70*
    raising livestock, 72
    tattoos of, *70*, 72
Stowell, Ethan, 229
Sweet (Worchester, MA), 268
Sweetpea Baking Co. (Portland,
    OR), 271

T

Tattoos (of)
    Adey, Kevin, *112*, 114
    Anderson, Scott, *206*, *207*, 208
    Arce, Manny, *62*, 64
    Artley, Will, *225*, 226
    Baltzley, Brandon, *233*, 234–*35*
    Barron, Chris, *16*, 17, 18
    Barron, Jill, *194–95*, 196
    Bennett, Aaron, *253*, 254
    Berardino, Michael, *78*, *80*
    Biederman, Brandon, *239*, 240
    Bucco, Anthony, *256*, 258
    Crenn, Dominique, *286*, 288–*89*
    Curi, Tomas, *44–45*, 46
    Curren, Chris, *242*, 244
    DeNittis, Mark, *246–47*, 248–50,
        249
    de Vries, Ben, *57*, 58, *59*
    Eisenhart, John, *52*, 53–54
    Eisenhauer, Alina, *267*, 268
    Estes, Duskie, *67*, 68
    Fiorelli, Michael, *120*, 122
    Forgione, Marc, 36, *37*, 38, *39*
    French, Jason, *82–83*, 84–*85*
    Fuller, Keith, *88*, 90, 91
    Godby, Jake, 278, *279*
    Goldman, Duff, *262*, 264
    Gourdet, Gregory, *162*, 164
    Hawes, Sean, *228*, 229–*30*
    Higgins, Lisa, *270*, 271–*72*
    Husbands, Andy, *12*, 13, 14
    Isabella, Mike, *134*, 136, *137*
    Kim, Beverly, *178*, *181*
    Leventhal, Robin, *218*, 219–*20*
    Malloy, Scott, *198*, 200
    Marciante, Tony, *102–3*, 104
    Markert, Andrew, *144*, 145–46
    Marks, Ian, *166*, 168

McCallister, Matt, *214*
McFarland, Ed, *126*, 128
Morris, Will, *94*, 96–*97*
Mullen, Seamus, *184*, 186
Palmieri, Francesco, *148*, 150
Paone, Anthony, *170*, 172–*73*
Pellegrino, Carla, *24*, *27*, 28
Power, Jonathan, *75*, *76*
Richey, Douglas, *274*, 276
Ricker, Andy, *282*, 283, *284*
Rucker, Gabriel, *48*, 50
Schenker, Jesse, 130, *131*, 132
Selby, Matt, *188*, 189
Simcik, Derek, 116–18, *117*
Spence, Carolyn, *203*, 204
Steiling, Lish, *211*, *212*
Stewart, John, *70*, 72
Tramonto, Rick, *156–57*, 158, *159*
Valentine, Joshua, *292*, 293
Walters, Zak, *20*, 21–22
Warner, Justin, *109*, 110
Wilson, Christina, *30*, 32, 33
Witt, Ed, *140*, 142
Terranea Resort (Rancho Palos
    Verdes, CA), 122
Tertulia (New York City, NY), 186
Texas. *See* Dallas, TX
Thompson, Susan, 196
Timmins, Peter, 121–22
The Today Show food stylist. *See*
    Steiling, Lish
Tourondel, Laurent, 36–38
Tower, Jeremiah, 288

Tramonto, Rick, 156–61
    biographical sketch, 156–58
    Gemelli con la Salsa dell Erba e
        Pollo (Gemelli with Chicken
        and Spring Herb Sauce),
        160–61
    photographs of, *156–57*, *159*
    tattoos of, *156–57*, 158, *159*
Tramonto Steak and Seafood
    (Chicago, IL), 158
Tremont 647 (Boston, MA), 13
20 Spot (San Francisco, CA), 172

V

Valentine, Joshua, 292–95
    biographical sketch, 292–94
    Lemongrass Panna Cotta with
        Mint Meringue, Lemon Curd,
        and White Chocolate Brown
        Butter Ganache, **295**
    Matt McCallister and, 292
    photograph of, *292*
    tattoos of, *292*, 293
Vermilion (Alexandria, VA), 97
Vetri, Marc, 216
Virginia
    Alexandria: Vermilion, 97
    Falls Church: Pizzeria Orso, 226,
        227
Vongerichten, Jean-Georges, 164

W

Walters, Zak, 20–23
    Beer Braised Chili Pork over
        Grits, **23**
    biographical sketch, 21–22
    photograph of, *20*
    tattoos of, *20*, 21–22
Warner, Justin, 108–11
    biographical sketch, 108–10
    Frog Legs with Spicy Dr. Pepper
        Glaze, **111**
    photographs of, *109*, *110*
    tattoo of, *109*, 110
Washington, D.C.
    Beuchert's Saloon, 146
    G, 136
    Graffiato, 136
    Kapnos, 136, **138–39**
Washington state. *See* Seattle, WA
Weimann, James, 63–64
Wilson, Christina, 30–35
    biographical sketch, 32
    Pan Roasted Fillet, Glazed
        Heirloom Carrots, and
        Gorgonzola Potato Purée, with
        Red Wine Bone Marrow Sauce,
        34–35
    photographs of, *30*, *33*
    tattoos of, *30*, 32, 33

Witt, Ed, 140–43
    biographical sketch, 142
    Duck Fat Poached Salmon,
        Forbidden Rice, Plum Wine
        BBQ Sauce, and Snap Peas,
        143
    Mike Isabella and, 135
    photograph of, *140*
    tattoos of, *140*, 142
Wolf Cindy, 263

Y

Yim Gi Ho, 176–78
Yusho (Chicago, IL), 200

Z

Zakarian, Geoffrey, 132, 149, 176
Zazu Restaurant and Farm (Sonoma
    County, CA), 68, 69, 72, 275–76

Recipe Index

A

Almond Brittle, **269**
Apples
    Apple Purée, **291**
    Brussels Sprout, Gravenstein Apple, and Black Pig Bacon Salad, **69**
Arugula Salad, **29, 65**
Autumn in a Bowl: Roasted Parsnip and Kale Salad, **213**
Avocado
    Avocado Mousse, **152**
    Avocado Sauce, **231**

B

Bacon
    Bacon and Egg, **77**
    Black Pig Bacon and Duck Egg Carbonara, **73**
    Brussels Sprouts, Gravenstein Apple, and Black Pig Bacon Salad, **69**
Basil Oil, **107**
Basil Pesto, **205**
Batsoa, **55**
Beans and other legumes
    Sunrise Lentil Cakes, **221–23**
    White Bean Purée, **60–61**
Beef
    Beef Carpaccio, Broccoli, Oysters, and Wasabi Vinaigrette, **51**
    Pan Roasted Fillet, Glazed Heirloom Carrots, and Gorgonzola Potato Purée, with Red Wine Bone Marrow Sauce, **34–35**
    Tamarind Braised Short Ribs with Sweet Potato Purée, Arugula, Golden Raisins, and Spiced Pumpkin Seeds Hoofed: Manny, **65**
Beer Braised Chili Pork over Grits, **23**
Beer Jelly, **269**
Beet Salad, **231**
Birth, **290–91**
Black Pig Bacon and Duck Egg Carbonara, **73**
Bread Pudding with Almond Brittle and Beer Jelly, **269**
Breakfast Ice Cream, **280–81**
Brioche roll, lightly toasted, **205**
Broccoli
    Beef Carpaccio, Broccoli, Oysters, and Wasabi Vinaigrette, **51**
    Broccoli Purée, **217**
Bruschetta, **255**
Brussels Sprouts, Gravenstein Apple, and Black Pig Bacon Salad, **69**
Buttered Corn Kernels, **152**
Butternut Squash with Goat's Yogurt, Spirulina, and Stevia, **236–37**
Butters
    Lobster Butter, **133**
    Walnut Brown Butter, **147**

C

Cakes. See Desserts
Carrots
    Coriander Carrot Purée, **223**
    Glazed Heirloom Carrots, **34–35**
Cauliflower
    Pickled Cauliflower, **190**
    Roasted Cauliflower Soup, **217**
    Sautéed Red Snapper with Purple Cauliflower Medley and Cauliflower Purée, **119**
Celeriac Purée, **98**
Champagne Grain Mustard Vinaigrette, **152**
Cheese
    Cream Cheese Icing, **265**
    Gorgonzola Potato Purée, **34–35**
    Hazel Dell Mushroom Bruschetta with Local Goat Cheese, **255**
    Herbed Goat Cheese, **245**
    Marinated Feta Cheese, **209**
    Tomato Soup with Ciabatta Toast and Grilled Cheese, **209**
Chef's Day-After Breakfast, **174–75**
Chicken. See Poultry
Chili Rub, **23**
Chocolate
    Chocolate Branches, **291**
    White Chocolate Brown Butter Ganache, **295**
Citrus
    Coriander-Lemon Aioli, **223**
    Crispy Braised Mangalista Belly with Bitter Greens and Citrus, **47**
    Lemon Curd, **295**
    Lemongrass Panna Cotta with Mint Meringue, Lemon Curd, and White Chocolate Brown Butter Ganache, **295**
    Meyer Lemon Foam, **295**
Coffee cake, vanilla cinnamon, **273**
Coppa and Egg, **15**
Coriander Carrot Purée, **223**
Coriander-Lemon Aioli, **223**
Corn
    Buttered Corn Kernels, **152**
    Corn Flake Cookies, **280**
    Corn Silk Nest, **291**
    Roasted Red Snapper, Corn Purée, Fresh Corn, Rock Shrimp, and Lobster Butter, **133**
Court Bouillon, **151**
Cream Cheese Icing, **265**
Crispy Braised Mangalista Belly with Bitter Greens and Citrus, **47**
Crispy Pork Belly with Littleneck Clams and Trumpet Royale Mushrooms, **98–99**
Croutons, **245**

D

Desserts
    Birth, **290–91**
    Bread Pudding with Almond Brittle and Beer Jelly, **269**
    Corn Flake Cookies, **280**
    Cream Cheese Icing, **265**
    Foieaffle with Peach Sauce and Farm Egg, **277**
    Lemongrass Panna Cotta with Mint Meringue, Lemon Curd, and White Chocolate Brown Butter Ganache, **295**
    Pineapple Hummingbird Cake, **265**
    Secret Breakfast Ice Cream, **280–81**
    Vanilla Cinnamon Coffee Cake, **273**
Deviled Quail Eggs, **151**
Dijon Aioli, **15**
Drew's Mama's Crab Cakes with Mustard Cider Reduction and Walnut Brown Butter, **147**
Drink, Gin Rummy, **285**
Dr. Pepper glaze, spicy, **111**
Duck Fat Poached Salmon, Forbidden Rice, Plum Wine BBQ Sauce, and Snap Peas, **143**
Duck Frites, **169**

E

Eggplant, in Ma Po Tofu, **197**
Eggs
    Bacon and Egg, **77**
    Chef's Day-After Breakfast, **174–75**
    Deviled Quail Eggs, **151**
    Foieaffle with Peach Sauce and Farm Egg, **277**
    Poached Egg, **175**
    Tosta Huevo Roto, **187**
Elderberry Gastrique, **92–93**

F

Fingerling Potatoes, **42, 124**
Fish and seafood
    Beef Carpaccio, Broccoli, Oysters, and Wasabi Vinaigrette, **51**
    Crispy Pork Belly with Littleneck Clams and Trumpet Royale Mushrooms, **98–99**
    Drew's Mama's Crab Cakes with Mustard Cider Reduction and Walnut Brown Butter, **147**
    Duck Fat Poached Salmon, Forbidden Rice, Plum Wine BBQ Sauce, and Snap Peas, **143**
    Grilled Spanish Octopus with Salsa Verde, Fried Potatoes,

Piquillo Peppers, Green
Onion, Preserved Lemon, and
Chorizo, **123–25**
Kapnos Octopus, **138–39**
Lobster Cobb Salad, **151–52**
Lobster Rolls, **129**
Lobster Salad, **129**
Pan-Seared Diver Scallops with
Seasonal Vegetables and
Crispy Sweet Potatoes, **106–7**
Pork Belly, Scallops, and
Reindeer Lichen, with an
Elderberry Gastrique, **92–93**
Roasted Red Snapper, Corn
Purée, Fresh Corn, Rock
Shrimp, and Lobster Butter,
133
Roasted Scallops with Sunchoke
Purée, Wilted Spinach, and
Walnut Salad, **115**
Sautéed Red Snapper with
Purple Cauliflower Medley
and Cauliflower Purée, **119**
Foieaffle with Peach Sauce and
Farm Egg, **277**
Foie gras, cured, **190–91**
Foie Gras Pearls, **291**
Frog Legs with Spicy Dr. Pepper
Glaze, **111**

G

Ganache, white chocolate brown
butter, **295**
Garlic
Grilled Green Garlic, **43**
Roasted Garlic Purée, **151**
Gastriques. *See* Sauces, marinades,
and rubs
Gemelli con la Salsa dell Erba e
Pollo (Gemelli with Chicken and
Spring Herb Sauce), **160–61**
Gin Rummy, **285**
Glazed Heirloom Carrots, **34–35**
Goat
Goat's Yogurt, **236**
Herbed Goat Cheese, **245**
Malloreddus, **81**
Gorgonzola Potato Purée, **34–35**
Green Papaya Salad (Som Tum), **241**
Greens, **47, 165, 251**
Grilled Green Garlic, **43**
Grilled Spanish Octopus with Salsa
Verde, Fried Potatoes, Piquillo
Peppers, Green Onion, Preserved
Lemon, and Chorizo, **123–25**
Grits
Beer Braised Chili Pork over
Grits, **23**
Chef's Day-After Breakfast,
174–75

H

Ham
Coppa and Egg, **15**
Potato Gnocchi with Surry
Farms Ham and Micro
Arugula, **259**
Smoked Ham Hock Croquettes
with Dijon Aioli, **15**
Hazel Dell Mushroom Bruschetta
with Local Goat Cheese, **255**
Herbed Goat Cheese, **245**

I

Ice cream, breakfast, **280–81**

K

Kale and parsnip salad, roasted, **213**
Kapnos Octopus, **138–39**

L

Lemon. *See* Citrus
Lentil cakes, **221–23**
Lichen, reindeer, **92–93**
Lightly Toasted Brioche Roll, **205**
Lobster. *See* Fish and seafood
Luella's Coca-Cola Braised Pork
Shoulder, **60–61**

M

Malloreddus, **81**
Ma Po Tofu, **197**
Marinated Feta Cheese, **209**
Metric conversion chart, 296
Meyer Lemon Foam, **295**
Mint Meringue, **295**
Mirepoix, **81**
Mushrooms
Crispy Pork Belly with Littleneck
Clams and Trumpet Royale
Mushrooms, **98–99**
Hazel Dell Mushroom
Bruschetta with Local Goat
Cheese, **255**
Porcini Mushrooms, **43**
Mustard
Champagne Grain Mustard
Vinaigrette, **152**
Mustard Cider Reduction, **147**
Mustard Reduction, **40–43**
Pumpkin Mustard, **55**

N

Nasi Goreng, **182–83**
Nuka Pickle, **201**

O

Octopus. *See* Fish and seafood
Onions
Pearl Onions, **42**
Pickled Onions, **174**
Pickled Red Onions, **61, 205**

P

Panna cotta, **295**
Pan Roasted Fillet, Glazed Heirloom
Carrots, and Gorgonzola Potato
Purée, with Red Wine Bone
Marrow Sauce, **34–35**
Pan-Seared Diver Scallops with
Seasonal Vegetables and Crispy
Sweet Potatoes, **106–7**
Panzanella with Roasted Acorn
Squash, **245**
Papaya salad, green, **241**
Parsnip and kale salad, roasted, **213**
Pasta
Black Pig Bacon and Duck Egg
Carbonara, **73**
Coppa and Egg, **15**
Curry Noodles, Slow Chicken,
Pickled Mustard Greens, and
Toasted Chili, **165**
Gemelli con la Salsa dell Erba e
Pollo (Gemelli with Chicken
and Spring Herb Sauce),
160–61
Potato Gnocchi with Surry
Farms Ham and Micro
Arugula, **259**
Peach Sauce, **277**
Pear Gastrique, **191**
Pearl Onions, **42**
Pickle, nuka, **201**
Pickled Cauliflower, **190**
Pickled Mustard Greens, **165**
Pickled Onions, **174**
Pickled Red Onions, **61, 205**
Pineapple Hummingbird Cake, **265**
Pizza dough, sourdough, **227**
Plum Wine BBQ Sauce, **143**
Poached Egg, **175**
Porchetta di Testa (Slow Roasted
Boneless Hog Head), **251**
Porcini Mushrooms, **43**
Pork. *See also* Bacon; Ham
Batsoa, **55**
Beer Braised Chili Pork over
Grits, **23**
Crispy Braised Mangalista Belly
with Bitter Greens and Citrus,
47
Crispy Pork Belly with Littleneck
Clams and Trumpet Royale
Mushrooms, **98–99**
Luella's Coca-Cola Braised Pork
Shoulder, **60–61**
Pastured Pork, Sauerkraut, and
Whey Sauce, **86–87**
Pork Belly, Scallops, and
Reindeer Lichen, with an
Elderberry Gastrique, **92–93**
Pork Belly Braising Liquid, **98**
Pork Brine, **98**
Pork Jus, **98–99**
Spiced Pork Sausage, **86–87**
Warm Panzanella Salad with
Porchetta di Testa, Pepperoni,
Mustard Greens, Fennel, and
Tomato, **251**
Potatoes
Fingerling Potatoes, **42, 124**
Gorgonzola Potato Purée,
34–35
Potato Gnocchi with Surry
Farms Ham and Micro
Arugula, **259**
Simple Garlic Mashed Potatoes,
107
Tosta Huevo Roto, **187**
Poultry. *See also* Eggs
Chef's Day-After Breakfast,
174–75
Curry Noodles, Slow Chicken,
Pickled Mustard Greens, and
Toasted Chili, **165**
Duck Frites, **169**
Gemelli con la Salsa dell Erba e
Pollo (Gemelli with Chicken
and Spring Herb Sauce),
160–61
Nasi Goreng, **182–83**
Tiger Wings with Som Tum, **241**
Truffle Salt–Cured Foie Gras,
190–91
Puffed Wild Rice, **291**
Pumpkin
Pumpkin Mustard, **55**
Spiced Pumpkin Seeds, **65**

R

Raisins, golden, **65**
Raita, **169**
Red Wine Bone Marrow Sauce,
34–35
Reindeer Lichen, **92–93**
Roasted Cauliflower Soup, **217**
Roasted Parsnip and Kale Salad, **213**
Roasted Red Snapper, Corn Purée,
Fresh Corn, Rock Shrimp, and
Lobster Butter, **133**
Roasted Scallops with Sunchoke
Purée, Wilted Spinach, and Walnut
Salad, **115**

S

Salads
- Arugula Salad, **29**, **65**
- Autumn in a Bowl: Roasted Parsnip and Kale Salad, **213**
- Beet Salad, **231**
- Brussels Sprouts, Gravenstein Apple, and Black Pig Bacon Salad, **69**
- Green Papaya Salad (Som Tum), **241**
- Lobster Cobb Salad, **151–52**
- Lobster Salad, **129**
- Panzanella with Roasted Acorn Squash, **245**
- Walnut Salad, **115**
- Warm Panzanella Salad with Porchetta di Testa, Pepperoni, Mustard Greens, Fennel, and Tomato, **251**

Sauces, marinades, and rubs
- Avocado Sauce, **231**
- Basil Pesto, **205**
- Black Pig Bacon and Duck Egg Carbonara, **73**
- Champagne Grain Mustard Vinaigrette, **152**
- Chili Rub, **23**
- Coriander-Lemon Aioli, **223**
- Dijon Aioli, **15**
- Elderberry Gastrique, **92–93**
- Lobster Butter, **133**
- Meat Marinade, **42**
- Mustard Cider Reduction, **147**
- Mustard Reduction, **40–43**
- Peach Sauce, **277**
- Pear Gastrique, **191**
- Plum Wine BBQ Sauce, **143**
- Pumpkin Mustard, **55**
- Raita, **169**
- Red Wine Bone Marrow Sauce, **34–35**
- Salsa Verde, **124**, **169**, **174**
- Spicy Dr. Pepper Glaze, **111**
- Spring Herb Sauce (Salsa dell Erba), **161**
- Wasabi Vinaigrette, **51**
- Whey Sauce, **87**

Sauerkraut, **86**
Sautéed Red Snapper with Purple Cauliflower Medley and Cauliflower Purée, **119**
Seafood. *See* Fish and seafood
Secret Breakfast Ice Cream, **280–81**
Simple Garlic Mashed Potatoes, **107**
Smoked Ham Hock Croquettes with Dijon Aioli, **15**
Sofrito, **124**
Som Tum (Green Papaya Salad), **241**
Soups

Roasted Cauliflower Soup, **217**
Tomato Soup with Ciabatta Toast and Grilled Cheese, **209**
Sourdough Pizza Dough, **227**
Spiced Pork Sausage, **86–87**
Spiced Pumpkin Seeds, **65**
Spicy Dr. Pepper Glaze, **111**
Spinach, wilted, **115**
Spring Herb Sauce (Salsa dell Erba), **161**
Squash
- Butternut Squash with Goat's Yogurt, Spirulina, and Stevia, **236–37**
- Panzanella with Roasted Acorn Squash, **245**

Sunchoke Purée, **115**
Sunrise Lentil Cakes, **221–23**
Sweet potatoes
- Pan-Seared Diver Scallops with Seasonal Vegetables and Crispy Sweet Potatoes, **106–7**
- Sweet Potato Purée, **65**

T

Tamarind Braised Short Ribs with Sweet Potato Purée, Arugula, Golden Raisins, and Spiced Pumpkin Seeds Hoofed: Manny, **65**
Tiger Wings with Som Tum, **241**
Tofu, in Ma Po Tofu, **197**
Tomatoes
- Oven-Dried Cherry Tomatoes, **161**
- pasta with. *See* Pasta
- Tomato Soup with Ciabatta Toast and Grilled Cheese, **209**

Tosta Huevo Roto, **187**
Truffle Salt–Cured Foie Gras, **190–91**

V

Vanilla Cinnamon Coffee Cake, **273**
Vanilla Gel, **291**
Veal
- Veal Tenderloin, Boudin Noir, Fingerling Potatoes, Grilled Green Garlic, Pearl Onions, and Porcini Mushrooms, with a Mustard Reduction, **40–43**
- Vitello alla Milanese, **29**

Vegetables. *See also* Salads; *specific vegetables*
- Butternut Squash with Goat's Yogurt, Spirulina, and Stevia, **236–37**
- Kapnos Octopus with, **138–39**
- Lightly Toasted Brioche Roll, **205**

Ma Po Tofu, **197**
Nuka Pickle, **201**
Pan-Seared Diver Scallops with Seasonal Vegetables and Crispy Sweet Potatoes, **106–7**
Vinegar (drinking), in Gin Rummy, **285**
Vitello alla Milanese, **29**

W

Walnut Salad, **115**
Warm Panzanella Salad with Porchetta di Testa, Pepperoni, Mustard Greens, Fennel, and Tomato, **251**
Wasabi Vinaigrette, **51**
Whey Sauce, **87**
White Bean Purée, **60–61**
White Chocolate Brown Butter Ganache, **295**
Wild rice, puffed, **291**
Wilted Spinach, **115**

Y

Yogurt
- Goat's Yogurt, **236**
- Raita, **169**

ABOUT THE AUTHORS

Birk O'Halloran began by studying for a career in hotel and restaurant management at Cornell University, but quickly decided that drinking was the best part of the job. After graduating college, he continued his training at the International Wine Guild to receive his sommelier certification. He then went on to open and operate three wine stores in three years, the last being recognized as "Best Wine Shop in New Jersey" by *New Jersey Monthly* and one of eight "Best Wine Shops in America" by *Imbibe* magazine. Presently he works as the head of sales and marketing for a rising star wine importer, A.I. Selections. A.I. Selections supplies wines to top-end restaurants throughout New York, Colorado, California, and several major cities, including nearly every Michelin-starred restaurant in Manhattan. His position at A.I. has provided him the opportunity to work with the top chefs and sommeliers in the country and given him a unique network from which to pull talent for *Eat Ink*. In 2010, Birk ventured into another area of wine by cofounding Iconic Wine, a Napa-based boutique wine company that has recently celebrated the release of its third vintage.

Having received his first tattoo at the age of seventeen while living in San Francisco, California, **Daniel Luke Holton** has developed a passion for the creativity and the art of ink. After graduating from The Colorado Institute of Art with a degree in photography and then pursuing more study at Brooks Institute of Photography, Daniel has worked tirelessly for more than ten years to refine his photographic style. He's also built on his background in creative arts to include graphic and web design. Daniel has operated his photography and design business since 2000. Working to create imagery and design for a wide range of clients and audiences, Daniel succeeds because of the drive he brings to the creation of outstanding and impactful imagery and design.